AN
INCLUSIVE-LANGUAGE
LECTIONARY

AN INCLUSIVE-LANGUAGE LECTIONARY

Readings for Year A

Revised Edition

*Prepared for voluntary use in churches by
the Inclusive-Language Lectionary Committee
appointed by the Division of Education and
Ministry, National Council of the Churches of
Christ in the U.S.A.*

Published for
The Cooperative Publication Association
by
John Knox Press, *Atlanta*
The Pilgrim Press, *New York*
The Westminster Press, *Philadelphia*

BOOK DESIGN BY ALICE DERR

PRINTED IN THE UNITED STATES OF AMERICA
9 8 7 6 5 4 3 2 1

Library of Congress Cataloging-in-Publication Data

An Inclusive-language lectionary. Readings for year A.

   Includes index.
   1. Bible—Liturgical lessons, English.   2. Lectionaries
—Texts.   I. National Council of the Churches of Christ
in the United States of America.   Inclusive Language
Lectionary Committee.
BS391.2.I52   1986   220.5′2   86-16930
ISBN 0-8298-0746-2 (Pilgrim Press)

Preface

All persons are equally loved, judged, and accepted by God. This belief has been promoted by the church and has its roots in the origins of the Judeo-Christian tradition. Young and old, male and female, and persons of every racial, cultural, and national background are included in the faith community. Basic to a sense of equality and inclusiveness is the recognition that God by nature transcends all human categories. God is more than male or female, and is more than can be described in historically and culturally limiting terms. Words and language, though inadequate and limited, are means by which we convey God's holiness and mystery. Seeking faithful expression about God and about God's inclusive love for all people, the Division of Education and Ministry of the National Council of the Churches of Christ authorized the preparation of *An Inclusive-Language Lectionary.*

A Task Force on Biblical Translation was appointed by the Division of Education and Ministry to investigate the way in which the language of the Bible presents the characteristics of God and of human beings. In 1980, after almost three years of study and discussion, the Task Force recommended to the Division the creation of an Inclusive-Language Lectionary Committee, which was then appointed. Members bring not only their personal commitment to the Christian faith and involvement in particular congregations but also their experience as pastors, teachers, and leaders who have relied on the Bible as their source of inspiration and basis for understanding God's word for the church today. They bring expertise in Hebrew, Greek, linguistics, English, worship, Old and New Testaments, theology, and education. In addition, the members come from a variety of denominations and liturgical traditions. The Inclusive-Language Lectionary Committee consists of Robert A. Bennett, Dianne Bergant, Victor Roland Gold (Chair), Thomas Hoyt, Jr., Kellie C. Jones, Patrick D. Miller, Jr., Virginia Ramey Mollenkott, Sharon H. Ringe

(Vice-Chair), Susan Thistlethwaite, Burton H. Throckmorton, Jr., and Barbara A. Withers (Editor). David Ng is the National Council of the Churches of Christ liaison to the Committee.

The Inclusive-Language Lectionary Committee followed the general guidelines provided by the Division of Education and Ministry to prepare lectionary readings for use in services of worship. These readings are based on the Revised Standard Version of the Bible, with the text revised primarily in those places where gender-specific or other exclusive language could be modified to reflect in English an inclusiveness of all persons. All modifications are supportable by the original Greek and Hebrew texts. The Committee worked on lectionary passages first in subcommittees, each committee consulting not only the original texts but also various translations and commentaries. All subcommittee work was submitted to an Editorial Committee which reviewed the texts for consistency of changes and agreement with guiding principles. The Editorial Committee consists of Barbara A. Withers (Editor), Burton H. Throckmorton, Jr. (Associate Editor), Patrick D. Miller, Jr., and Sharon H. Ringe. As the last step, the full Committee reviewed all work and made all final decisions.

Like most other lectionaries in use today, this lectionary follows the pattern of a three-year cycle beginning with the first Sunday in Advent. The readings for Year A were originally published in October of 1983 and followed the table of readings prepared by the Consultation on Church Union. The second and third volumes contained the readings from the Table of Readings and Psalms prepared for trial use by the North American Committee on Calendar and Lectionary. This revised edition of Year A follows the latter table of readings. A few additions and substitutions were made, consistent with the Committee's mandate (see Appendix, p. 277).

The Introduction which follows offers an explanation of what a lectionary is and discusses the need for inclusive language and how the Committee approached the gender-specific language of the Revised Standard Version. The lectionary passages, along with explanatory footnotes, form the major portion of this volume. An appendix stating a rationale for the major alternative words and phrases and an index of the biblical passages that appear in this lectionary complete this volume.

An Inclusive-Language Lectionary is offered to the church as a responsible attempt to represent the biblical writings in an inclusive manner. Respecting its commitment to be responsive to the interests and needs of the church for which the lectionary has been prepared, the Committee has put both the term "Lord" and its formal equivalent, "Sovereign," in the text. This change was first made in Year C (1985) in an attempt to meet a concern of many persons throughout the church who had used Years A and B. So if one prefers, one may always read "Lord." For example, "Give thanks to the SOVEREIGN [[*or* LORD]], call upon God's name" (Isa. 12:3). "Lord" is printed in this manner as an *alternate* or *substitute* for the word immediately preceding it. "Lord" is *not* to be read aloud *with* the word that precedes it.

While the use of the lectionary is voluntary, the hope is that no one will find that she or he has been excluded from hearing the words of promise and fulfillment. God loves all persons and seeks to bring them into God's community. This lectionary attempts to express that message.

Introduction

A lectionary is a fixed selection of readings, taken from both the Old and the New Testament, to be read and heard in the churches' services of worship. Most lectionaries are simply tables or lists of readings to be used in weekly worship; some include daily readings. They cite the biblical book from which the reading is taken, as well as the chapter and verses: for example, Christmas Day: *Luke 2:1-20*. By contrast, this lectionary contains the full text of each reading.

Recent History of Lectionary Development. The International Commission on English in the Liturgy created an ecumenical group known as the Consultation on Common Texts. One of the tasks of this Consultation was to explore the possibilities of creating a lectionary that would be acceptable to most English-speaking Christians: Anglican, Protestant, and Roman Catholic. To that end, a small working group known as the North American Committee on Calendar and Lectionary was formed. Over a period of five years a revised table of lections, or readings, was developed that took into account critiques of the Vatican II lectionary (early 1960s) and its subsequent adaptations by the major Protestant denominations. The report of the North American Committee was approved by the Consultation on Common Texts in 1982, and this "common texts" lectionary was recommended for trial use in the churches beginning with Advent 1983. It is this Table of Readings and Psalms which this lectionary follows, using the Revised Standard Version as its text.

Function of the Lectionary in Congregational Worship. In churches that use the lectionary every Sunday, congregations hear the same scriptures read. Thus the wider church, within denominations and across denominational lines, is united in its hearing, thinking, and praying. A lectionary provides a way for Christians to live out the church year, which begins on the first Sunday of Advent and proceeds through Christmas, Epiphany, Ash Wednesday, Lent, Passion (Palm) Sunday, Maundy Thursday, Good Friday, Easter, Ascension, and Pentecost. At least four readings are prescribed for each Sunday as well as for special days such as Christmas, Easter, All Saints, and Thanksgiving. The lectionary attempts to provide comprehensive and balanced coverage of the entire Bible. Over a three-year period about 95 percent of the New Testament is heard, as well as about 60 percent of the Old Testament.

It is apparent that any selection of scripture read in a service of worship has been lifted from its biblical context. In the study of the Bible, the context in which a biblical passage occurs is crucial to its interpretation. When passages are read in a service of worship, however, they are read in a new context, in relation to one another and to the church year. This radical change in the context of selections is a major fact that differentiates a lectionary from the Bible.

A lectionary thus has a special function in the worship of the church. It does not supplant the Bible. The Bible is the church's book—created by and for the church. A lectionary is also the church's book, being a prescribed set of readings selected by the church from its scripture for its own special use in worship. The unique feature of *An Inclusive-Language Lectionary* is that it recasts some of the wording of the Revised Standard Version in order to provide both to reader and to hearer a sense of belonging to a Christian faith community in which truly all are one in Christ.

Why Inclusive Language? The lectionary readings are based on the Revised Standard Version and original Greek and Hebrew texts, with the intent of reflecting the full humanity of women and men in the light of the gospel. A growing number of people feel they have been denied full humanity by a pattern of exclusion in English usage. Consider, for example, the traditional English use of the word "man." A man is a male human being, as opposed to a female human being. But in common usage "man" has also meant "human being," as opposed to "animal." On the other hand, "woman" means female, but never *human being*. No word that refers to a female person identifies her with humanity. So, in common English idiom, "man" has been defined by his humanity, but "woman" by her sex, by her relationship to man. "Woman" becomes a subgroup under "human." "Man" is the human race; "woman" is man's sexual partner, in traditional English usage.

This is but one example of how language *reflects* the way in which we think but also *informs* the way in which we think. The mandate to the Lectionary Committee is to seek "language which expresses inclusiveness with regard to human beings and which attempts to expand the range of images beyond the masculine to assist the church in understanding the full nature of God." In the Appendix the reader will find specific examples of how these kinds of excluding language and imagery have been dealt with in this lectionary.

10

The RSV is highly respected by biblical scholars and is widely used in this country. However, in this lectionary the wording of the RSV has been recast to minimize the gender-specific language and other excluding imagery reflected in its language in reference to human beings, Christ, and God. Except for these changes the text of the RSV, for the most part, has been retained.

Gender-specific language, however, is not unique to English translations of the Bible; it is characteristic of the languages in which the Bible was written. Both the Old Testament and the New Testament were written in languages and in cultures that were basically patriarchal; and as the English language is also patriarchal, the patriarchal character of both Testaments has slipped easily into the great English versions of the Bible.

Language About Human Beings. In a few instances the RSV Bible committee has already avoided male-specific language in reference to human beings. For example, in Rom. 7:1 the RSV has used "person" ("the law is binding on a *person*") as a translation of the Greek word *anthropos* (meaning "man" or "person"). But most of the time *anthropos* is translated "man," or, in the plural, "men." For example, Matt. 5:16 in the RSV reads, "Let your light so shine before *men*" where the meaning of "men" is obviously "people," but not male people exclusively. This verse can be rendered: "Let your light so shine before *others*"—that is, men and women, which represents the clear intention of the words.

Excluding language also appears when masculine pronoun subjects are supplied with third person singular verbs when the context does not require them. Compare, for example, the RSV of John 6:35-37: "Jesus said to them, 'I am the bread of life; *he* who comes to me shall not hunger, and *he* who believes in me shall never thirst . . . ; and *him* who comes to me I will not cast out." What is the intention of this passage? It surely is not that only *men* come to Jesus and believe in Jesus. Why, then, does the RSV read "he" and "him"? It is because of the assumption that "he" also means "she," though we know that it does not.

In this lectionary all readings have been recast so that no masculine word pretends to include a woman. For example, the word "brethren" has been rendered in a variety of ways, including "sisters and brothers." Formal equivalents have been adopted for other male-specific words and phrases. For example, "kingdom" is usually rendered "realm" but also by other terms such as "reign" or "dominion"; "king" in reference to God or a messianic figure is rendered "ruler" and "monarch."

In a few instances, references to women have been added—for example, "Abraham [*and Sarah*]." Where the name of a person or details in the narrative make the gender clear, no change has been made. Thus, David is referred to as a "king," the wounded traveler in the parable of the

Samaritan is a "man," and Jesus meets a "woman" by the well in Samaria. Where the gender of the person is not specified, the character is referred to as a "person" (e.g., John 9). Also, contemporary English usage suggests that we refer to a person as having a disabling condition, such as polio, rather than to a "cripple" or a "crippled person." So the biblical reference to "the blind and the lame" is rendered "those who are blind and those who are lame" (see Jer. 31:8). Where "darkness" is set in contrast with "light" and has a moral connotation, a substitute word for darkness is supplied—for example, "The light shines in the *deepest night*" (John 1:5).

Language About Jesus Christ. Jesus was a male human being. But when the Gospel of John says, "The Word became flesh" (John 1:14), it does not say or imply that the Word became *male* flesh, but simply *flesh.* Of course, to "become flesh," the one from God had to become male or female, but the language used in this lectionary tries to overcome the implication that in the incarnation Jesus' *maleness* is decisive—or even relevant—for the salvation of women and men who believe or for matters in which the imitation or model of Christ is a concern.

In this lectionary the fact of Jesus' maleness is taken for granted. The historical Jesus is referred to as a man, and the pronouns "he," "his," and "him" are used when the reference is to that historical person. These male-specific pronouns are not used to refer to the preexistent or post-crucifixion Jesus. They are replaced by proper names such as "Jesus," "Christ," and other words demanded by the context, so that in hearing the gospel the church may recognize the inclusiveness of all humankind in the incarnation.

Formal equivalents adopted in this lectionary for "the Son of man," "Son," and "Son of God" are, respectively, "the Human One," "Child," and "Child of God." (For a discussion of these terms, see the Appendix.)

Language About God. The God worshiped by the biblical authors and worshiped in the church today cannot be regarded as having gender, race, or color. Such attributes are used metaphorically or analogically. Father is only one metaphor for God in the Bible; other personal metaphors include mother, midwife, and breadmaker. Less familiar, but equally appropriate, are such impersonal images for God as love, rock, and light. Images for God in this lectionary are expressed in inclusive language so that when the church hears its scripture read, it is not overwhelmed by the male metaphors but is also enabled to hear female metaphors for God.

In the RSV Old Testament, the major names for God are "God" (*Elohim*), "LORD" (*Yahweh*), and "Lord" (*Adonai*), and several variations of these nouns—for example, "the LORD God" and "the Lord GOD." In this lectionary, "LORD" (*Yahweh*) is rendered "GOD" or "SOVEREIGN," using an initial capital letter and small capitals, and "Lord" (*Adonai*) is rendered "God" or "Sovereign," using an initial capital letter and lower-case letters. (For a discussion of these terms, see the Appendix.)

In the New Testament lections, the formal equivalent adopted in this lectionary for "God the Father" or "the Father" is "God the Father [*and Mother*]" or "God the [*Mother and*] Father." The words that have been added to the text are italicized and in brackets. If the reader chooses to omit the bracketed words, the sentence will read exactly as rendered in the RSV. Where God is called "Father" several times in a single passage, as is often the case in the Gospel of John, the word "Father" is frequently rendered "God." (For an explanation of metaphor, and of specific ways in which this lectionary has recast scriptural language about God and images for God, see the Appendix.)

TOWARD THE FUTURE

An Inclusive-Language Lectionary is a major attempt to recast the language of scripture so that it addresses women and men equally. The church has never believed that God is male or that God speaks to the church in male-oriented language more relevant to men than to women. So the Committee submits this lectionary to the church, remembering the words of the apostle Paul: "There is neither Jew nor Greek, there is neither slave nor free, there is neither male nor female; for you are all one in Christ Jesus" (Gal. 3:28).

The terms "Sovereign" and "God" are used in this lectionary in place of the term "Lord"; but "Lord" appears in brackets as an *alternate* or *substitute* reading. So if one prefers, one may always read "Lord." "Lord" is not to be read aloud with the word that precedes it. See Appendix, pages 271–272.

ADVENT 1

Isaiah speaks a prophecy concerning Judah and Jerusalem.

¹ The word which Isaiah the son of Amoz saw concerning Judah and Jerusalem.

² It shall come to pass in the latter days
     that the mountain of the house of GOD ⟦*or* the LORD⟧
   shall be established as the highest of the mountains,
     and shall be raised above the hills;
   and all the nations shall flow to it,
³   and many peoples shall come, and say:
   "Come, let us go up to the mountain of GOD ⟦*or* the LORD⟧,
     to the house of the God of Jacob, [*Rachel, and Leah**];
   that we may be taught the ways of God
     and may walk in God's paths."
   For out of Zion shall go forth instruction,
     and the word of GOD ⟦*or* the LORD⟧ from Jerusalem.
⁴ God shall judge between the nations,
     and shall decide for many people;
   and they shall beat their swords into plowshares,
     and their spears into pruning hooks;
   nation shall not lift up sword against nation,
     neither shall they learn war anymore.
⁵ O house of Jacob, [*Rachel, and Leah**],
     come, let us walk
     in the light of GOD ⟦*or* the LORD⟧.

---

*Addition to the text. See "Addition of Women's Names to the Text" in the Appendix.

¹ I was glad when they said to me,
  "Let us go to the house of GOD ⟦*or* the LORD⟧!"
² Our feet have been standing
  within your gates, O Jerusalem!
³ Jerusalem, built as a city
  which is bound firmly together,
⁴ to which the tribes go up,
  the tribes of GOD ⟦*or* the LORD⟧,
 as was decreed for Israel,
  to give thanks to the name of GOD ⟦*or* the LORD⟧.
⁵ There thrones for judgment were set,
  the thrones of the house of David.
⁶ Pray for the peace of Jerusalem!
  "May they prosper who love you!
⁷ Peace be within your walls,
  and security within your towers!"
⁸ For the sake of my kin and companions
  I will say, "Peace be within you!"
⁹ For the sake of the house of the SOVEREIGN ⟦*or* LORD⟧ our God,
  I will seek your good.

Lesson 2 ~ Romans 13:11-14

Paul writes to the Romans concerning the conduct of their daily lives.

¹¹ Besides this you know what hour it is, how it is full time now for you to wake from sleep. For salvation is nearer to us now than when we first believed; ¹² the night is far gone, the day is at hand. Let us then cast off the works of the night and put on the armor of the day; ¹³ let us conduct ourselves becomingly as in the day, not in reveling and drunkenness, not in debauchery and licentiousness, not in quarreling and jealousy. ¹⁴ But put on the Sovereign ⟦*or* Lord⟧ Jesus Christ, and make no provision for the flesh, to gratify its desires.

Gospel — Matthew 24:36-44

Jesus speaks to the disciples about the end times, especially the day on which the Human One will come.

36 But of that day and hour no one knows, not even the angels of heaven, nor God's Child,◇ but God⊗ only. 37 As were the days of Noah, so will be the coming of the Human One.○ 38 For as in those days before the flood they were eating and drinking, marrying and giving in marriage, until the day when Noah entered the ark, 39 and they did not know until the flood came and swept them all away, so will be the coming of the Human One.○ 40 Then two men are in the field; one is taken and one is left. 41 Two women are grinding at the mill; one is taken and one is left. 42 Watch therefore, for you do not know on what day your Sovereign [[*or* Lord]] is coming. 43 But know this, that if the householder had known in what part of the night the thief was coming, that householder would have watched and would not have let the house be broken into. 44 Therefore you also must be ready; for the Human One○ is coming at an hour you do not expect.

◇RSV *the Son*. See Appendix.
⊗RSV *the Father*. See Appendix.
○RSV *Son of man*. See Appendix.

ADVENT 2

Lesson 1 ~ Isaiah 11:1-10

Isaiah brings a promise to Israel.

¹ There shall come forth a shoot from the stump of Jesse,
   and a branch shall grow out of its roots.
² And the Spirit of GOD [*or* the LORD] shall rest upon this branch,
   the spirit of wisdom and understanding,
   the spirit of counsel and might,
   the spirit of knowledge and the fear of GOD [*or* the LORD].
³ And the delight of the one who comes shall be in the fear of GOD [*or*
   the LORD].
That one shall not judge by what the eyes see
   or decide by what the ears hear,
⁴ but shall judge the poor with righteousness
   and decide with equity for the meek of the earth,
 and with words of judgment shall smite the earth
   and slay the wicked with sentences.
⁵ The coming one shall be girded with righteousness,
   and girded also with faithfulness.
⁶ The wolf shall dwell with the lamb,
   and the leopard shall lie down with the kid,
 and the calf and the lion and the fatling together,
   and a little child shall lead them.
⁷ The cow and the bear shall feed;
   their young shall lie down together;
   and the lion shall eat straw like the ox.
⁸ The sucking child shall play over the hole of the asp,
   and the weaned child shall put its hand on the adder's den.
⁹ They shall not hurt or destroy
   in all my holy mountain;
 for the earth shall be full of knowledge of GOD [*or* the LORD]
   as the waters cover the sea.

¹⁰ In that day the root of Jesse shall stand as a sign to the nations that
this is the one whom they shall seek, whose dwellings shall be glorious.

Psalm 72:1-8

1 Give the ruler◫ your justice, O God,
   and your righteousness to the royal heir!
2 May the ruler judge your people with righteousness,
   and your poor with justice!
3 Let the mountains bear prosperity for the people,
   and the hills, in righteousness!
4 May the ruler defend the cause of the poor of the people,
   give deliverance to the needy,
   and crush the oppressor!
5 May the ruler live while the sun endures,
   and as long as the moon, throughout all generations!
6 May the ruler be like rain that falls on the mown grass,
   like showers that water the earth!
7 In the ruler's days may righteousness flourish,
   and peace abound, till the moon be no more!
8 May the ruler have dominion from sea to sea,
   and from the River to the ends of the earth!

Lesson 2 ~ Romans 15:4-13

Paul sends a message of praise and encouragement to the Christians at Rome.

4 Whatever was written in former days was written for our instruction, that by steadfastness and by the encouragement of the scriptures we might have hope. 5 May the God of steadfastness and encouragement grant you to live in such harmony with one another, in accord with Christ Jesus, 6 that together you may with one voice glorify God the Father [*and Mother**] of our Sovereign [[*or* Lord]] Jesus Christ.

7 Welcome one another, therefore, as Christ has welcomed you, for the glory of God. 8 For I tell you that Christ became a servant to the Jews to show God's truthfulness, in order to confirm the promises given to our ancestors in faith, 9 and in order that the Gentiles might glorify God for showing mercy. As it is written,

"Therefore I will praise you among the Gentiles,
and sing to your name";

◫RSV *king*. See Appendix.
*Addition to the text. See "Metaphor" and "God the Father and Mother" in the Appendix.

19

[10] and again it is said,

> "Rejoice, O Gentiles, with the people of God";

[11] and again,

> "Praise the Sovereign [[or Lord]], all Gentiles,
> and let all the people praise God";

[12] and further Isaiah says,

> "The root of Jesse shall come,
> the one who rises to rule the Gentiles,
> in whom the Gentiles shall hope."

[13] May the God of hope fill you with all joy and peace in believing, so that by the power of the Holy Spirit you may abound in hope.

Gospel ~ Matthew 3:1-12

Matthew recounts the preaching of John the Baptist.

[1] In those days came John the Baptist, preaching in the wilderness of Judea, [2] "Repent, for the realm☆ of heaven is at hand." [3] For this is the one spoken of by the prophet Isaiah,

> "The voice of one crying in the wilderness:
> Prepare the way of the Sovereign [[or Lord]],
> make the paths of the Sovereign [[or Lord]] straight."

[4] Now John wore a garment of camel's hair, and a leather girdle around his waist; and his food was locusts and wild honey. [5] Then Jerusalem and all Judea and all the region about the Jordan went out to him, [6] and they were baptized by him in the river Jordan, confessing their sins.

[7] But seeing many of the Pharisees and Sadducees coming for baptism, John said to them, "You brood of vipers! Who warned you to flee from the wrath to come? [8] Bear fruit that befits repentance, [9] and do not presume to say to yourselves, 'We have Abraham as our father'; for I tell you, God is able from these stones to raise up children to Abraham. [10] Even now the axe is laid to the root of the trees; every tree therefore that does not bear good fruit is cut down and thrown into the fire.

[11] "I baptize you with water for repentance, but the one who is coming after me is mightier than I, whose sandals I am not worthy to carry; that one will baptize you with the Holy Spirit and with fire. [12] With winnowing fork in hand, that one will clear the threshing floor and gather the wheat into the granary, but will burn the chaff with unquenchable fire."

☆RSV *kingdom*. See Appendix.

ADVENT 3

Lesson 1 ~ Isaiah 35:1-10

Isaiah speaks words of promise to Israel.

1 The wilderness and the dry land shall be glad,
   the desert shall rejoice and blossom;
like the crocus 2 it shall blossom abundantly,
   and rejoice with joy and singing.
The glory of Lebanon shall be given to it,
   the majesty of Carmel and Sharon.
They shall see the glory of the SOVEREIGN [[or LORD]],
   the majesty of our God.
3 Strengthen the weak hands,
   and make firm the feeble knees.
4 Say to those who are of a fearful heart,
   "Be strong, fear not!
Behold, your God
   will come with vengeance,
with the recompense of God.
   Your God will come and save you."
5 Then shall blind eyes be opened
   and deaf ears unstopped;
6 then shall those who are lame leap like a hart
   and mute tongues sing for joy.
For waters shall break forth in the wilderness,
   and streams in the desert;
7 the burning sand shall become a pool,
   and the parched ground shall become springs of water;
the haunt of jackals shall become a swamp,
   and the grass shall become reeds and rushes.
8 A highway shall be there,
   and it shall be called the Holy Way;
one who is unclean shall not pass over it,
   and fools shall not err therein.
9 No lion shall be there,
   nor shall any ravenous beast come up on it;
they shall not be found there,
   but the redeemed shall walk there.

¹⁰ The ransomed of GOD [[*or* the LORD]] shall return,
    and come to Zion with singing;
  everlasting joy shall be upon their heads;
    joy and gladness shall encompass them,
    and sorrow and sighing shall flee away.

Psalm 146:5-10

⁵ Happy is the one whose help is the God of Jacob,
    whose hope is in God, the SOVEREIGN [[*or* LORD]],
⁶ who made heaven and earth,
    the sea, and all that is in them;
  who keeps faith forever;
⁷   who executes justice for the oppressed;
    who gives food to the hungry.
  GOD [[*or* The LORD]] sets the prisoners free;
⁸   GOD [[*or* the LORD]] opens the eyes of those who are blind.
  GOD [[*or* The LORD]] lifts up those who are bowed down;
    GOD [[*or* the LORD]] loves the righteous.
⁹ GOD [[*or* The LORD]] watches over the sojourners,
    and upholds the widow and the orphan,
    but brings the way of the wicked to ruin.
¹⁰ GOD [[*or* The LORD]] will reign forever,
    your God, O Zion, to all generations.
  Praise GOD [[*or* the LORD]]!

Lesson 2 ~ James 5:7-10

James advises Christians about their daily living.

⁷ Be patient, therefore, my friends, until the coming of the Sovereign [[*or* Lord]]. Just as the farmer waits for the precious fruit of the earth, being patient over it until it receives the early and the late rain, ⁸ so you also be patient. Establish your hearts, for the coming of the Sovereign [[*or* Lord]] is at hand. ⁹ Do not grumble, sisters and brothers, against one another, that you may not be judged; behold, the Judge is standing at the gates. ¹⁰ As an example of suffering and patience, friends, take the prophets who spoke in the name of the Sovereign [[*or* Lord]].

Gospel ~ Matthew 11:2-11

Jesus is teaching and preaching in the cities of the disciples.

² Now John, having heard in prison about the deeds of the Christ, sent word by his disciples and ³ said to Jesus, "Are you the one who is to come, or shall we look for another?" ⁴ And Jesus answered them, "Go and tell John what you hear and see: ⁵ those who are blind receive their sight and those who are lame walk; people with leprosy are cleansed and those who are deaf hear; the dead are raised up; and to those who are poor good news is preached. ⁶ And blessed is the one who takes no offense at me."

⁷ As they went away, Jesus began to speak to the crowds concerning John: "What did you go out into the wilderness to observe? A reed shaken by the wind? ⁸ Why then did you go out? To see someone clothed in soft raiment? Those who wear soft raiment are in royal palaces. ⁹ Why then did you go out? To see a prophet? Yes, I tell you, and more than a prophet. ¹⁰ This is the one of whom it is written,

'I am sending my messenger before your face,
who shall prepare your way before you.'

¹¹ Truly, I say to you, among those born of women, there has risen no one greater than John the Baptist; yet one who is least in the realm☆ of heaven is greater than John."

☆RSV *kingdom*. See Appendix.

ADVENT 4

Lesson 1 ~ Isaiah 7:10-16

Isaiah brings a word of assurance from God to Ahaz, ruler of Judah, in the face of a threat from the rulers of Syria.

10 Again GOD [*or* the LORD] spoke to Ahaz, 11 "Ask a sign of the SOVEREIGN [*or* LORD] your God; let it be deep as Sheol or high as heaven." 12 But Ahaz said, "I will not ask, and I will not put GOD [*or* the LORD] to the test." 13 And Isaiah said, "Hear then, O house of David! Is it too little for you to weary human beings, that you weary my God also? 14 Therefore God [*or* the Lord] will give you a sign: a young woman shall conceive and bear a child, whom she shall call Immanuel. 15 When old enough to know how to refuse the evil and choose the good, the child shall eat curds and honey. 16 Before the child knows how to refuse the evil and choose the good, the land whose two kings you dread will be deserted."

Psalm 24

1 The earth is GOD's [*or* the LORD's] and the fullness thereof,
   the world and those who dwell therein;
2 for God has founded it upon the seas,
   and established it upon the rivers.
3 Who shall ascend the hill of GOD [*or* the LORD]?
   And who shall stand in God's holy place?
4 Those who have clean hands and a pure heart,
   who do not lift up their soul to what is false,
   and do not swear deceitfully.
5 They will receive blessing from GOD [*or* the LORD],
   and vindication from the God of their salvation.
6 Such is the generation of those who seek God,
   who seek the face of the God of Jacob.
7 Lift up your heads, O gates!
   and be lifted up, O ancient doors!
   that the Ruler□ of glory may come in.
8 Who is the Ruler□ of glory?
   GOD [*or* The LORD], strong and mighty,
   GOD [*or* the LORD], mighty in battle!

□RSV *King*. See Appendix.

⁹ Lift up your heads, O gates!
   and be lifted up, O ancient doors!
   that the Ruler▢ of glory may come in.
¹⁰ Who is this Ruler▢ of glory?
   The GOD [or LORD] of hosts,
   that one is the Ruler▢ of glory!

Lesson 2 ~ Romans 1:1-7

Paul greets the church in Rome.

¹ Paul, a servant of Jesus Christ, called to be an apostle, set apart for the gospel of God ²promised by God beforehand through the prophets in the holy scriptures, ³the gospel concerning the Child of God,◇ descended from David according to the flesh ⁴and designated Child◇ of God in power according to the Spirit of holiness by Christ's resurrection from the dead, Jesus Christ our Sovereign [or Lord], ⁵through whom we have received grace and apostleship to bring about the obedience of faith for the sake of the Sovereign's [or Lord's], name among all the nations, ⁶including yourselves who are called to belong to Jesus Christ;

⁷ To all God's beloved in Rome, who are called to be saints:

Grace to you and peace from God our Father [*and Mother**] and from the Sovereign [or Lord] Jesus Christ.

▢RSV *King*. See Appendix.
◇RSV v. 3 *concerning his Son;* v. 4 *Son*. See Appendix.
*Addition to the text. See "Metaphor" and "God the Father and Mother" in the Appendix.

Matthew describes the birth of Jesus Christ.

[18] Now the birth of Jesus Christ took place in this way. When Jesus' mother Mary had been betrothed to Joseph, before they came together she was found to be with child of the Holy Spirit; [19] and her husband Joseph, being a just man and unwilling to put her to shame, resolved to divorce her quietly. [20] But as Joseph considered this, behold, an angel of God [[or the Lord]] appeared to him in a dream, saying, "Joseph, son of David, do not fear to take Mary your wife, for that which is conceived in her is of the Holy Spirit; [21] she will bear a child, whose name you shall call Jesus, for this child will save the people from their sins." [22] All this took place to fulfill what the Sovereign [[or Lord]] had spoken by the prophet:

[23] "A virgin shall conceive and bear a child,
   whose name shall be called Emmanuel"

(which means, God with us). [24] When Joseph woke from sleep, he did as the angel of God [[or the Lord]] had commanded, and married Mary, [25] but knew her not until she had borne a child; and Joseph named the child Jesus.

CHRISTMAS EVE/DAY

Lesson 1 ~ Isaiah 9:2-7

An oracle points to the coming of one who brings a new age of peace and justice.

    ² The people who walked without light
        have seen a great light;
    those who dwelt in a land of deep shadows,
        on them has light shined.
    ³ You have multiplied the nation,
        you have increased its joy;
    they rejoice before you
        as with joy at the harvest,
        as victors rejoice when they divide the spoil.
    ⁴ For the yoke of Israel's burden,
        and the staff for its shoulder,
        the rod of its oppressor,
        you have broken as on the day of Midian.
    ⁵ For every boot of the tramping warrior in battle tumult
        and every garment rolled in blood
        will be burned as fuel for the fire.
    ⁶ For to us a child is born,
        to us an heir is given;
    and the government will be upon the shoulder
        of that one whose name will be called
    "Wonderful Counselor, Mighty God,
        Everlasting Father [*and Mother**], Prince of Peace."
    ⁷ Of the increase of that government and of peace
        there will be no end,
    upon the throne of David, and over David's kingdom,
        to establish it, and to uphold it
    with justice and with righteousness
        from this time forth and forevermore.
    The zeal of the GOD [[*or* LORD]] of hosts will do this.

---

*Addition to the text. See "Metaphor" and "God the Father and Mother" in the Appendix.

¹ O sing to GOD [[*or* the LORD]] a new song;
    sing to GOD [[*or* the LORD]], all the earth!
² Sing to GOD [[*or* the LORD]]; bless God's name.
    Tell of God's salvation from day to day.
³ Declare God's glory among the nations,
    God's marvelous works among all people!
⁴ For great is GOD [[*or* the LORD]], and greatly to be praised,
    indeed, to be feared above all gods.
⁵ For all the gods of the nations are idols;
    but the SOVEREIGN [[*or* LORD]] made the heavens.
⁶ Honor and majesty are before God;
    strength and beauty are in God's sanctuary.
⁷ Ascribe to GOD [[*or* the LORD]], O families of nations,
    ascribe to GOD [[*or* the LORD]] glory and strength!
⁸ Ascribe to GOD [[*or* the LORD]] the glory due God's name;
    bring an offering, and come into God's courts!
⁹ Worship GOD [[*or* the LORD]] in holy array;
    tremble before God, all the earth!
¹⁰ Say among the nations, "GOD [[*or* The LORD]] reigns!
    The world is established; it shall never be moved.
    God will judge the nations with equity."
¹¹ Let the heavens be glad, and let the earth rejoice;
    let the sea roar, and all that fills it;
¹²   let the field exult, and everything in it!
  Then shall all the trees of the wood sing for joy
¹³   before GOD [[*or* the LORD]], who comes,
    who comes to judge the earth,
  and will judge the world with righteousness,
    and the nations with truth.

Lesson 2 ~ Titus 2:11-14

The letter to Titus points to the meaning of Christ's appearance.

¹¹ For the grace of God has appeared for the salvation of all, ¹²training us to renounce irreligion and worldly passions, and to live sober, upright, and godly lives in this world, ¹³awaiting our blessed hope, the appearing of the glory of our great God and Savior Jesus Christ, ¹⁴who gave up Christ's self for us to redeem us from all iniquity and to purify for Christ's self a chosen people who are zealous for good deeds.

Gospel ~ Luke 2:1-20

Luke describes the birth of Jesus.

¹ In those days a decree went out from Caesar Augustus that all the world should be enrolled. ²This was the first enrollment, when Quirinius was governor of Syria. ³And all went to be enrolled, each to their own city. ⁴And Joseph also went up from Galilee, from the city of Nazareth, to Judea, to the city of David, which is called Bethlehem, because he was of the house and lineage of David, ⁵to be enrolled with Mary, his betrothed, who was with child. ⁶And while they were there, the time came for her to be delivered. ⁷And she gave birth to her firstborn son, whom she wrapped in swaddling clothes and laid in a manger, because there was no place for them in the inn.

⁸ And in that region there were shepherds out in the field, keeping watch over their flock by night. ⁹And an angel of God [[*or* the Lord]] appeared to them, and the glory of God [[*or* the Lord]] shone around them, and they were filled with fear. ¹⁰And the angel said to them, "Be not afraid; for I bring you good news of a great joy which will come to all the people; ¹¹for to you is born this day in the city of David a Savior, who is Christ the Sovereign [[*or* Lord]]. ¹²And this will be a sign for you: you will find a baby wrapped in swaddling clothes and lying in a manger." ¹³And suddenly there was with the angel a multitude of the heavenly host praising God and saying,

¹⁴ "Glory to God in the highest,
   and on earth peace among those with whom God is pleased!"

¹⁵ When the angels went away from them into heaven, the shepherds said to one another, "Let us go over to Bethlehem and see this thing that has happened, which God [[*or* the Lord]] has made known to us." ¹⁶And they went with haste, and found Mary and Joseph, and the baby lying in a manger. ¹⁷And when they saw it they made known the saying which had been told them concerning this child; ¹⁸and all who heard it wondered at what the shepherds told them. ¹⁹But Mary kept all these things, pondering them in her heart. ²⁰And the shepherds returned, glorifying and praising God for all they had heard and seen, as it had been told them.

CHRISTMAS DAY, Additional Lections, First Set

Lesson 1 ~ Isaiah 62:6-7, 10-12

God sets watchers on the walls of Zion to contemplate the return of the exiles to the holy city.

> ⁶ Upon your walls, O Jerusalem,
>   I have set watchers;
>   all the day and all the night
>   they shall never be silent.
>   You who put GOD [[*or* the LORD]] in remembrance,
>   take no rest,
> ⁷ and give God no rest
>   until Jerusalem is established
>   and is made an object of praise on the earth.
> ¹⁰ Go through, go through the gates,
>   prepare the way for the people;
>   build up, build up the highway,
>   clear it of stones,
>   lift up an ensign over the peoples.
> ¹¹ GOD [[*or* The LORD]] has proclaimed
>   to the end of the earth:
>   Say to the children of Zion,
>   "Your salvation comes;
>   God's reward is with God,
>   and God's recompense goes before God."
> ¹² And they shall be called The holy people,
>   The redeemed of GOD [[*or* the LORD]];
>   and you shall be called Sought out,
>   a city not forsaken.

¹ GOD [[*or* The LORD]] reigns; let the earth rejoice;
  let the many coastlands be glad!
² Clouds and thick darkness are round about God;
  righteousness and justice are the foundation of God's throne.
³ Fire goes before God,
  and burns up God's adversaries round about.
⁴ God's lightnings lighten the world;
  the earth sees and trembles.
⁵ The mountains melt like wax before the SOVEREIGN [[*or* LORD]],
  before the God [[*or* Lord]] of all the earth.
⁶ The heavens proclaim God's righteousness;
  and all people behold God's glory.
⁷ All worshipers of images are put to shame,
  who make their boast in worthless idols;
  all gods bow down before God.
⁸ Zion hears and is glad,
  and the daughters of Judah rejoice,
  because of your judgments, O GOD [[*or* LORD]].
⁹ For you, O GOD [[*or* LORD]], are most high over all the earth;
  you are exalted far above all gods.
¹⁰ GOD [[*or* The LORD]] loves those who hate evil,
  preserves the lives of the saints,
  and delivers them from the hand of the wicked.
¹¹ Light dawns for the righteous,
  and joy for the upright in heart.
¹² Rejoice in GOD [[*or* the LORD]], O you righteous,
  and give thanks to God's holy name!

Lesson 2 ~ Titus 3:4-7

*In the letter to Titus we are told that all things are changed because of the
mercy of God.*

⁴ When the goodness and loving kindness of God our Savior appeared,
⁵ we were saved, not because of deeds done by us in righteousness, but in
virtue of God's own mercy, by the washing of regeneration and renewal in
the Holy Spirit, ⁶ which God poured out upon us richly through Jesus
Christ our Savior, ⁷ so that we might be justified by God's grace and
become heirs in hope of eternal life.

Luke describes the birth of Jesus.

8 And in that region there were shepherds out in the field, keeping watch over their flock by night. 9 And an angel of God [[*or* the Lord]] appeared to them, and the glory of God [[*or* the Lord]] shone around them, and they were filled with fear. 10 And the angel said to them, "Be not afraid; for I bring you good news of a great joy which will come to all the people; 11 for to you is born this day in the city of David a Savior, who is Christ the Sovereign [[*or* Lord]]. 12 And this will be a sign for you: you will find a baby wrapped in swaddling clothes and lying in a manger." 13 And suddenly there was with the angel a multitude of the heavenly host praising God and saying,

14 "Glory to God in the highest,
and on earth peace among those with whom God is pleased!"

15 When the angels went away from them into heaven, the shepherds said to one another, "Let us go over to Bethlehem and see this thing that has happened, which God [[*or* the Lord]] has made known to us." 16 And they went with haste, and found Mary and Joseph, and the baby lying in a manger. 17 And when they saw it they made known the saying which had been told them concerning this child; 18 and all who heard it wondered at what the shepherds told them. 19 But Mary kept all these things, pondering them in her heart. 20 And the shepherds returned, glorifying and praising God for all they had heard and seen, as it had been told them.

CHRISTMAS DAY, Additional Lections, Second Set

Lesson 1 ~ Isaiah 52:7-10

Isaiah proclaims God's word of comfort.

⁷ How beautiful upon the mountains
    are the feet of the one who brings good tidings,
who publishes peace, who brings good tidings of good,
    who publishes salvation,
    who says to Zion, "Your God reigns."
⁸ Hark, your watchers lift up their voice,
    together they sing for joy;
  for eye to eye they see
    the return of GOD ⟦*or* the LORD⟧ to Zion.
⁹ Break forth together into singing,
    you waste places of Jerusalem;
  for GOD ⟦*or* the LORD⟧ has comforted God's people,
    and has redeemed Jerusalem.
¹⁰ GOD ⟦*or* The LORD⟧ has bared God's holy arm
    before the eyes of all the nations;
  and all the ends of the earth shall see
    the salvation of our God.

Psalm 98

¹ O sing a new song to GOD ⟦*or* the LORD⟧,
    who has done marvelous things,
  whose right hand and holy arm
    have gained the victory!
² GOD ⟦*or* The LORD⟧ has made known the victory,
    and has revealed God's vindication in the sight of the nations.
³ God has remembered God's steadfast love and faithfulness
    to the house of Israel.
  All the ends of the earth have seen
    the victory of our God.
⁴ Make a joyful noise to GOD ⟦*or* the LORD⟧, all the earth;
    break forth into joyous song and sing praises!
⁵ Sing praises to GOD ⟦*or* the LORD⟧ with the lyre,
    with the lyre and the sound of melody!
⁶ With trumpets and the sound of the horn
    make a joyful noise before the Ruler,⬚ the SOVEREIGN ⟦*or* LORD⟧!

⬚RSV *King.* See Appendix.

⁷ Let the sea roar, and all that fills it;
    the world and those who dwell in it!
⁸ Let the floods clap their hands;
    let the hills sing together for joy
⁹ before GOD [[*or* the LORD]], who comes
        to judge the earth,
    to judge the world with righteousness,
        and the nations with equity.

Lesson 2 ~ Hebrews 1:1-12

The letter to the Hebrews begins by emphasizing that Jesus Christ is greater than the prophets and the angels.

¹ In many and various ways God spoke of old to our forebears by the prophets; ² but in these last days God has spoken to us by a Child,◇ whom God appointed the heir of all things, through whom also God created the world. ³ This Child, by whose word of power the universe is upheld, reflects the glory of God and bears the very stamp of God's nature. Having made purification for sins, the Child sat down at the right hand of the Majesty on high, ⁴ having become as much superior to angels as the name the Child has obtained is more excellent than theirs.

⁵ For to what angel did God ever say,

"You are my Child,◇
today I have begotten you"?

Or again,

"I will be to the Child a parent,
and the Child shall be my very own"?

⁶ And again, when bringing the firstborn into the world, God says,

"Let all the angels of God worship this Child."

⁷ Of the angels it is said,

"God makes the angels into winds,
and the servants of God into flames of fire."

⁸ But of the Child◇ it is said,

"Your throne, O God, is forever and ever,
the righteous scepter is the scepter of your dominion. ☆

◇RSV *Son*. See Appendix.
☆RSV *kingdom*. See Appendix.

⁹ You haved loved righteousness and hated lawlessness;
therefore God, your God, has anointed you
with the oil of gladness beyond your comrades."

¹⁰And,

"You, Sovereign [[or Lord]], founded the earth in the beginning,
and the heavens are the work of your hands;
¹¹ they will perish, but you remain;
they will all grow old like a garment,
¹² like a mantle you will roll them up,
and they will be changed.
But you are the same,
and your years will never end."

Gospel ~ John 1:1-14

The author of the Gospel of John unfolds the mystery of the incarnation.

¹ In the beginning was the Word, and the Word was with God, and the Word was God. ²The Word was in the beginning with God; ³all things were made through the Word, and without the Word was not anything made that was made. ⁴In the Word was life, and the life was the light of all. ⁵The light shines in the deepest night, and the night has not overcome it.

⁶ There was a man sent from God, whose name was John. ⁷John came for testimony, to bear witness to the light, that all might believe through him. ⁸John was not the light, but came to bear witness to the light.

⁹ The true light that enlightens everyone was coming into the world. ¹⁰The Word was in the world, and the world was made through the Word, yet the world did not know the Word. ¹¹The Word came to the Word's own home, but those to whom the Word came did not receive the Word. ¹²But to all who received the Word, who believed in the name of the Word, power was given to become children of God; ¹³who were born, not of blood nor of the will of the flesh nor of human will, but of God.

¹⁴ And the Word became flesh and dwelt among us, full of grace and truth; we have beheld the Word's glory, glory as of the only Child◇ from [*God*] the Father [*and Mother**].

◇RSV *Son*. See Appendix.
*Addition to the text. See "Metaphor" and "God the Father and Mother" in the Appendix.

CHRISTMAS 1

(Or the lections for Epiphany)

Lesson 1 ~ Isaiah 63:7-9

Isaiah writes of God's compassion.

7 I will recount the steadfast love of GOD [[*or* the LORD]],
    the praises of the SOVEREIGN [[*or* LORD]],
according to all that GOD [[*or* the LORD]] has granted us,
    and the great goodness to the house of Israel
which God has granted them according to God's mercy,
    according to the abundance of God's steadfast love.
8 For God said, Surely they are my people,
    children who will not deal falsely;
    and God became their Savior.
9 In all their affliction God was afflicted,
    and the angel of God's presence saved them;
in love and in pity God redeemed them,
    lifted them up and carried them all the days of old.

Psalm 111

1 Praise GOD [[*or* the LORD]]!
I will give thanks to GOD [[*or* the LORD]] with my whole heart,
    in the company of the upright, in the congregation.
2 Great are the works of GOD [[*or* the LORD]],
    studied by all who have pleasure in them.
3 Full of honor and majesty is God's work,
    and God's righteousness endures forever.
4 God has caused God's wonderful works to be remembered,
    and is gracious and merciful,
5 providing food for those who fear God
    and being ever mindful of the covenant.
6 God has shown God's people the power of God's works,
    in giving them the heritage of the nations.
7 The works of God's hands are faithful and just;
    all God's precepts are trustworthy,
8 they are established forever and ever,
    to be performed with faithfulness and uprightness.

^{9} God sent redemption to God's people,
  and has commanded the covenant forever.
  Holy and terrible is God's name!
^{10} The fear of GOD [[or the LORD]] is the beginning of wisdom;
  a good understanding have all those who practice it.
  God's praise endures forever!

Lesson 2 ~ Hebrews 2:10-18

Because Jesus has suffered and been tempted as we are, Jesus is able to deliver us.

^{10} For it was fitting that the one for whom and by whom all things exist, in bringing many sons and daughters to glory, should make the pioneer of their salvation perfect through suffering. ^{11} For the one who sanctifies and those who are sanctified have all one origin. That is why Jesus is not ashamed to call them brothers and sisters, ^{12} saying,

  "I will proclaim your name to my brothers and sisters,
  in the midst of the congregation I will praise you."

^{13} And again,

  "I will put my trust in God."

And again,

  "Here am I, and the children God has given me."

^{14} Since therefore the children share in flesh and blood, Jesus likewise partook of the same nature in order to destroy through death the one who has the power of death, that is, the devil, ^{15} and to deliver all those who through fear of death were subject to lifelong bondage. ^{16} For surely it is not with angels that Jesus is concerned but with the descendants of Abraham [and Sarah*]. ^{17} Therefore Jesus had to be made like human beings in every respect, in order to become a merciful and faithful high priest in the service of God, to make expiation for the sins of the people. ^{18} For because Jesus also has suffered and been tempted, Jesus is able to help those who are tempted.

---

*Addition to the text. See "Addition of Women's Names to the Text" in the Appendix.

After the visit of the magi, Joseph and Mary depart into Egypt with their child.

13 Now when the magi had departed, an angel of God [[*or* the Lord]] appeared to Joseph in a dream and said, "Rise, take the child and his mother, and flee to Egypt, and remain there till I tell you; for Herod is about to search for the child, to destroy him." 14 And Joseph rose and took the child and his mother by night, and departed to Egypt, 15 and remained there until the death of Herod. This was to fulfill what God [[*or* the Lord]] had spoken by the prophet, "Out of Egypt have I called my child."

19 But when Herod died, an angel of God [[*or* the Lord]] appeared in a dream to Joseph in Egypt, saying, 20 "Rise, take the child and his mother, and go to the land of Israel, for those who sought the child's life are dead." 21 And Joseph rose and took the child and his mother, and went to the land of Israel. 22 But hearing that Archelaus reigned over Judea in place of his father Herod, Joseph was afraid to go there, and being warned in a dream, withdrew to the district of Galilee. 23 And Joseph went and dwelt in a city called Nazareth, that what was spoken by the prophets might be fulfilled, "There shall come forth a Nazarene."

JANUARY 1 (New Year)

Lesson 1 ~ Deuteronomy 8:1-10

Israel is reminded that God provided care on their journey.

¹ All the commandment which I command you this day you shall be careful to do, that you may live and multiply, and go in and possess the land which GOD [[*or* the LORD]] swore to give to your ancestors. ² And you shall remember all the way which the SOVEREIGN [[*or* the LORD]] your God has led you these forty years in the wilderness, that God might humble you, testing you to know what was in your heart, whether you would keep God's commandments, or not. ³ And God humbled you and let you hunger, and fed you with manna, which you did not know, nor did your ancestors know; that God might make you know that one does not live by bread alone, but by everything that proceeds out of the mouth of GOD [[*or* the LORD]]. ⁴ Your clothing did not wear out upon you, and your foot did not swell, these forty years. ⁵ Know then in your heart that, as a parent disciplines a child, the SOVEREIGN [[*or* LORD]] your God disciplines you. ⁶ So you shall keep the commandments of the SOVEREIGN [[*or* LORD]] your God, by walking in God's ways and by fearing God. ⁷ For the SOVEREIGN [[*or* LORD]] your God is bringing you into a good land, a land of brooks of water, of fountains and springs, flowing forth in valleys and hills, ⁸ a land of wheat and barley, of vines and fig trees and pomegranates, a land of olive trees and honey, ⁹ a land in which you will eat bread without scarcity, in which you will lack nothing, a land whose stones are iron, and out of whose hills you can dig copper. ¹⁰ And you shall eat and be full, and you shall bless the SOVEREIGN [[*or* LORD]] your God for the good land God has given you.

Psalm 117

¹ Praise GOD [[*or* the LORD]], all nations!
    Extol God, all people!
² For great is God's steadfast love toward us;
    and the faithfulness of GOD [[*or* the LORD]] endures forever.
    Praise GOD [[*or* the LORD]]!

Lesson 2 ~ Revelation 21:1-6a

The seer envisions a new heaven and a new earth.

¹ Then I saw a new heaven and a new earth; for the first heaven and the first earth had passed away, and the sea was no more. ² And I saw the holy city, new Jerusalem, coming down out of heaven from God, prepared as a bride adorned for her husband; ³ and I heard a loud voice from the throne saying, "The dwelling of God is with human beings. God will dwell with them, and they shall be God's people, and God will indeed be with them. ⁴ God will wipe away every tear from their eyes, and death shall be no more, neither shall there be mourning nor crying nor pain anymore, for the former things have passed away."

⁵ And the one who sat upon the throne said, "See, I make all things new," to which was added, "Write this, for these words are trustworthy and true." ⁶ And the one who sat upon the throne said to me, "It is done! I am the Alpha and the Omega, the beginning and the end."

Jesus tells the parable of the last judgment.

31 When the Human One° comes in glory, with all the angels, then that one will sit on a glorious throne. 32 All the nations will be gathered before the Human One,° who will separate them one from another as a shepherd separates the sheep from the goats, 33 placing the sheep on the right, but the goats on the left. 34 Then the Ruler▢ will say to those on the right, "Come, O blessed of [*God*] my Father [*and Mother**], inherit the realm☆ prepared for you from the foundation of the world; 35 for I was hungry and you gave me food, I was thirsty and you gave me drink, I was a stranger and you welcomed me, 36 I was naked and you clothed me, I was sick and you visited me, I was in prison and you came to me." 37 Then the righteous will answer, "Sovereign [[*or* Lord]], when did we see you hungry and feed you, or thirsty and give you drink? 38 And when did we see you a stranger and welcome you, or naked and clothe you? 39 And when did we see you sick or in prison and visit you?" 40 And the Ruler▢ will answer them, "Truly, I say to you, as you did it to one of the least of these my sisters and brothers, you did it to me." 41 Then the Ruler will say to those on the left, "Depart from me, you cursed, into the eternal fire prepared for the devil and the devil's angels; 42 for I was hungry and you gave me no food, I was thirsty and you gave me no drink, 43 I was a stranger and you did not welcome me, naked and you did not clothe me, sick and in prison and you did not visit me." 44 Then they also will answer, "Sovereign [[*or* Lord]], when did we see you hungry or thirsty or a stranger or naked or sick or in prison, and did not minister to you?" 45 Then the Ruler will answer them, "Truly, I say to you, as you did it not to one of the least of these, you did it not to me." 46 And they will go away into eternal punishment, but the righteous into eternal life.

°RSV *Son of man*. See Appendix.
▢RSV *King*. See Appendix.
*Addition to the text. See "Metaphor" and "God the Father and Mother" in the Appendix.
☆RSV *kingdom*. See Appendix.

JANUARY 1 Holy Name of Jesus; Solemnity of Mary, Mother of God

Lesson 1 ~ Numbers 6:22-27

Moses learns how Aaron is to bless the people of Israel.

²² GOD [[*or* The LORD]] said to Moses, ²³ "Say to Aaron and his offspring, Thus you shall bless the people of Israel: you shall say to them,

²⁴ GOD [[*or* The LORD]] bless you and keep you:

²⁵ GOD [[*or* The LORD]] make God's face to shine upon you, and be gracious to you:

²⁶ GOD [[*or* The LORD]] lift up God's countenance upon you, and give you peace.

²⁷ "So shall they put my name upon the people of Israel, and I will bless them."

Psalm 67

¹ May God be gracious to us and bless us
    and make God's face to shine upon us,
² that your way may be known upon earth,
    and your saving power among all nations.
³ Let the people praise you, O God;
    let all the people praise you!
⁴ Let the nations be glad and sing for joy,
    for you judge the people with equity
    and guide the nations upon earth.
⁵ Let the people praise you, O God;
    let all the people praise you!
⁶ The earth has yielded its increase;
    God, our God, has blessed us.
⁷ God has blessed us;
    let all the ends of the earth fear God!

Lesson 2 ~ Galatians 4:4-7

Paul writes to the Galatians about the time of Christ's coming.

⁴ But when the time had fully come, God sent forth God's Child,◇ born of woman, born under the law, ⁵ to redeem those who were under the law, so that we might receive adoption as children of God. ⁶ And because you are children, God has sent the Spirit of the Child◇ into our hearts, crying, "[*God! my Mother and**] Father!" ⁷ So through God you are no longer a slave but a child, and if a child then an heir.

Lesson 2 (alternate) ~ Philippians 2:9-13

Paul reflects on Christ's example of humility.

⁹ Therefore God has highly exalted Jesus and bestowed on Jesus the name which is above every name, ¹⁰ that at the name of Jesus every knee should bow, in heaven and on earth and under the earth, ¹¹ and every tongue confess that Jesus Christ is Sovereign [[*or* Lord]], to the glory of God the Father [*and Mother**].

¹² Therefore, my beloved, as you have always obeyed, so now, not only as in my presence but much more in my absence, work out your own salvation with fear and trembling; ¹³ for God is at work in you, both to will and to work for God's good pleasure.

◇RSV *his Son.* See Appendix.
*Addition to the text. RSV Gal. 4:6 *"Abba!";* Phil. 2:11 *God the Father.* See "Metaphor" and "God the Father and Mother" in the Appendix.

Gospel ~ Luke 2:15-21

Luke describes the shepherds' visit to Bethlehem.

[15] When the angels went away from them into heaven, the shepherds said to one another, "Let us go over to Bethlehem and see this thing that has happened, which God [[*or* the Lord]] has made known to us." [16] And they went with haste, and found Mary and Joseph, and the baby lying in a manger. [17] And when they saw it they made known the saying which had been told them concerning this child; [18]and all who heard it wondered at what the shepherds told them. [19] But Mary kept all these things, pondering them in her heart. [20] And the shepherds returned, glorifying and praising God for all they had heard and seen, as it has been told them.

[21] And at the end of eight days, the child was circumcised and was called Jesus, the name given by the angel before the child was conceived in the womb.

CHRISTMAS 2

(Or the lections for Epiphany if not otherwise used)

Lesson 1 ~ Jeremiah 31:7-14

The prophet Jeremiah assures Israel that their despair shall be turned to joy.

⁷ For thus says the SOVEREIGN [*or* LORD]:
   "Sing aloud with gladness for Jacob,
      and raise shouts for the chief of the nations;
   proclaim, give praise, and say,
      'GOD [*or* The LORD] has saved the people,
      the remnant of Israel.'
⁸ I will bring them from the north country,
      and gather them from the farthest parts of the earth,
   among them those who are blind and those who are lame,
      the woman with child and the woman in travail, together;
      a great company, they shall return here.
⁹ With weeping they shall come,
      and with consolations I will lead them back,
   I will make them walk by brooks of water,
      in a straight path in which they shall not stumble;
   for I am a father [*and a mother**] to Israel,
      and Ephraim is my firstborn.
¹⁰ Hear the word of GOD [*or* the LORD], O nations,
      and declare it in the coastlands afar off;
   say, 'The one who scattered Israel will gather them,
      and will keep them as a shepherd keeps a flock.'
¹¹ For GOD [*or* the LORD] has ransomed Jacob,
      and has redeemed them from hands too strong for them.
¹² They shall come and sing aloud on the height of Zion,
      and they shall be radiant over the goodness of GOD [*or* the LORD],
   over the grain, the wine, and the oil,
      and over the young of the flock and the herd;
   their life shall be like a watered garden,
      and they shall languish no more.

---

*Addition to the text.

¹³ Then shall the women rejoice in the dance,
and the young men and the old shall be merry.
I will turn their mourning into joy,
I will comfort them, and give them gladness for sorrow.
¹⁴ I will feast the soul of the priests with abundance,
and my people shall be satisfied with my goodness,

says the SOVEREIGN [[or LORD]]."

Lesson 1 (alternate) ~ Ecclesiasticus (Sirach) 24:1-4, 12-16

Sirach sings the praises of Wisdom.

¹ Wisdom will praise herself,
and will glory in the midst of her people.
² In the assembly of the Most High she will open her mouth,
and in the presence of the host of the Most High she will glory:
³ "I came forth from the mouth of the Most High,
and covered the earth like a mist.
⁴ I dwelt in high places,
and my throne was in a pillar of cloud.
¹² So I took root in an honored people,
in the portion of God [[or the Lord]], who is their inheritance.
¹³ I grew tall like a cedar in Lebanon,
and like a cypress on the heights of Hermon.
¹⁴ I grew tall like a palm tree in En-gedi,
and like rose plants in Jericho;
like a beautiful olive tree in the field,
and like a plane tree I grew tall.
¹⁵ Like cassia and camel's thorn I gave forth the aroma of spices,
and like choice myrrh I spread a pleasant odor,
like galbanum, onycha, and stacte,
and like the fragrance of frankincense in the tabernacle.
¹⁶ Like a terebinth I spread out my branches,
and my branches are glorious and graceful."

Psalm 147:12-20

¹² Praise GOD [[or the LORD]], O Jerusalem!
Praise your God, O Zion,
¹³ for God strengthens the bars of your gates,
and blesses your children within you,

14 making peace in your borders,
    and filling you with the finest of the wheat.
15 God sends forth a command to the earth;
    God's word runs swiftly.
16 God gives snow like wool,
    scattering hoarfrost like ashes,
17 and casting forth ice like morsels;
    who can stand before God's cold?
18 God sends forth God's word, and melts them,
    making the wind blow, and the waters flow.
19 God declares God's word to Jacob,
    God's statutes and ordinances to Israel.
20 God has not dealt thus with any other nation;
    they do not know the ordinances.
    Praise GOD [or the LORD]!

Lesson 2 ~ Ephesians 1:3-6, 15-18

The writer of the letter to the Ephesians begins by praising God's grace in Jesus Christ.

3 Blessed be God the Father [and Mother*] of our Sovereign [or Lord] Jesus Christ, who has blessed us in Christ with every spiritual blessing in the heavenly places, 4 even as God chose us in Christ before the foundation of the world, that we should be holy and blameless before God, 5 who destined us in love to be God's children through Jesus Christ, according to the purpose of God's will, 6 to the praise of God's glorious grace freely bestowed on us in the Beloved.

15 For this reason, because I have heard of your faith in the Sovereign [or Lord] Jesus and your love toward all the saints, 16 I do not cease to give thanks for you, remembering you in my prayers, 17 that the God of our Sovereign [or Lord] Jesus Christ, the Father [and Mother*] of glory, may give you a spirit of wisdom and of revelation in the knowledge of God, 18 having the eyes of your hearts enlightened, that you may know what is the hope to which you have been called, what are the riches of God's glorious inheritance in the saints.

---

*Addition to the text. RSV Gal. 4:6 *"Abba!"*; Phil. 2:11 *God the Father.* See "Metaphor" and "God the Father and Mother" in the Appendix.

Gospel ~ John 1:1-18

The author of the Gospel of John unfolds the mystery of the incarnation.

[1] In the beginning was the Word, and the Word was with God, and the Word was God. [2] The Word was in the beginning with God; [3] all things were made through the Word, and without the Word was not anything made that was made. [4] In the Word was life, and the life was the light of all. [5] The light shines in the deepest night, and the night has not overcome it.

[6] There was a man sent from God, whose name was John. [7] John came for testimony, to bear witness to the light, that all might believe through him. [8] John was not the light, but came to bear witness to the light.

[9] The true light that enlightens everyone was coming into the world. [10] The Word was in the world, and the world was made through the Word, yet the world did not know the Word. [11] The Word came to the Word's own home, but those to whom the Word came did not receive the Word. [12] But to all who received the Word, who believed in the name of the Word, power was given to become children of God; [13] who were born, not of blood nor of the will of the flesh nor of human will, but of God.

[14] And the Word became flesh and dwelt among us, full of grace and truth; we have beheld the Word's glory, glory as of the only Child◇ from [*God*] the Father [*and Mother**]. [15] (John bore witness to the Child, and cried, "This was the person of whom I said, 'The one who comes after me ranks before me, for that one was before me.' ") [16] And from the fullness of the Child have we all received, grace upon grace. [17] For the law was given through Moses; grace and truth came through Jesus Christ. [18] No one has ever seen God; the only Child,◇ who is in the bosom of [*God*] the [*Mother and**] Father, that one has made God known.

◇RSV *Son*. See Appendix.
*Addition to the text. See "Metaphor" and "God the Father and Mother" in the Appendix.

EPIPHANY

Lesson 1 ~ Isaiah 60:1-6

Isaiah tells of the coming of God's glory to the people.

¹ Arise, shine; for your light has come,
   and the glory of GOD [[*or* the LORD]] has risen upon you.
² For shadows shall cover the earth,
   and thick shadow the nations;
  but GOD [[*or* the LORD]] will arise upon you,
   and the glory of God will be seen upon you.
³ And nations shall come to your light,
   and rulers□ to the brightness of your rising.
⁴ Lift up your eyes round about, and see;
   they all gather together, they come to you;
  your sons shall come from afar,
   and your daughters shall be carried in the arms.
⁵ Then you shall see and be radiant,
   your heart shall thrill and rejoice;
  because the abundance of the sea shall be turned to you,
   the wealth of the nations shall come to you.
⁶ A multitude of camels shall cover you,
   the young camels of Midian and Ephah;
  all those from Sheba shall come.
  They shall bring gold and frankincense,
   and shall proclaim the praise of GOD [[*or* the LORD]].

□RSV *kings*. See Appendix.

¹ Give the ruler▢ your justice, O God,
    and your righteousness to the royal heir!
² May the ruler judge your people with righteousness,
    and your poor with justice!
³ Let the mountains bear prosperity for the people,
    and the hills, in righteousness!
⁴ May the ruler defend the cause of the poor of the people,
        give deliverance to the needy,
    and crush the oppressor!
⁵ May the ruler live while the sun endures,
    and as long as the moon, throughout all generations!
⁶ May the ruler be like rain that falls on the mown grass,
    like showers that water the earth!
⁷ In the ruler's days may righteousness flourish,
    and peace abound, till the moon be no more!
⁸ May the ruler have dominion from sea to sea,
    and from the River to the end of the earth!
⁹ May the foes of the ruler bow down,
    and the enemies lick the dust!
¹⁰ May the kings of Tarshish and of the isles
        render tribute,
    may the kings of Sheba and Seba
        bring gifts!
¹¹ May all kings bow down
    and all nations serve the ruler!
¹² For the ruler delivers the needy when they call,
    the poor and those who have no helper,
¹³ and has pity on the weak and the needy,
    and saves the lives of the needy.
¹⁴ The ruler redeems their lives from oppression and violence,
    and their blood is precious in the ruler's sight.

Lesson 2 ~ Ephesians 3:1-12

The Ephesians learn about ministry that is rooted in Christ.

¹ For this reason I, Paul, a prisoner for Christ Jesus on behalf of you Gentiles— ²assuming that you have heard of the stewardship of God's grace that was given to me for you, ³how the mystery was made known to me by revelation, as I have written briefly. ⁴When you read this you can perceive my insight into the mystery of Christ, ⁵which was not made

---

▢RSV *king*. See Appendix.

known to the human race in other generations as it has now been revealed to Christ's holy apostles and prophets by the Spirit; [6] that is, how the Gentiles are joint heirs, members of the same body, and partakers of the promise in Christ Jesus through the gospel.

[7] Of this gospel I was made a minister according to the gift of God's grace which was given me by the working of God's power. [8] To me, though I am the very least of all the saints, this grace was given, to preach to the Gentiles the unsearchable riches of Christ, [9] and to make everyone see what is the plan of the mystery hidden for ages in God who created all things; [10] that through the church the manifold wisdom of God might now be made known to the principalities and powers in the heavenly places. [11] This was according to the eternal purpose which God has realized in Christ Jesus our Sovereign [[or Lord]], [12] in whom we have boldness and confidence of access through our faith in Christ.

Gospel ~ Matthew 2:1-12

Matthew describes the visit of the magi to the child.

[1] Now when Jesus was born in Bethlehem of Judea in the days of Herod the king, magi from the East came to Jerusalem, saying, [2] "Where is the one who has been born king of the Jews? For we have seen his star in the East, and have come to worship him." [3] And hearing this, Herod the king was troubled, and all Jerusalem as well; [4] and assembling all the chief priests and scribes of the people, he inquired of them where the Christ was to be born. [5] They told Herod, "In Bethlehem of Judea; for so it is written by the prophet:

[6] 'And you, O Bethlehem, in the land of Judah,
are by no means least among the rulers of Judah;
for from you shall come a ruler
who will govern my people Israel.' "

[7] Then Herod summoned the magi secretly, ascertained from them what time the star appeared, and [8] sent them to Bethlehem, saying, "Go and search diligently for the child, and when you have found him bring me word, that I too may come and worship him." [9] When they had heard the king they went their way; and the star which they had seen in the East went before them, till it came to rest over the place where the child was. [10] When they saw the star, they rejoiced exceedingly with great joy; [11] and going into the house they saw the child with Mary his mother, and they fell down and worshiped him. Then, opening their treasures, they offered the child gifts, gold and frankincense and myrrh. [12] And being warned in a dream not to return to Herod, they departed to their own country by another way.

BAPTISM OF JESUS

Lesson 1 ~ Isaiah 42:1-9

God speaks through the prophet Isaiah about God's servant.

1 Behold my servant, whom I uphold,
    my chosen, in whom my soul delights;
  I have put my Spirit upon my servant,
    who will bring forth justice to the nations.
2 My servant will not cry or speak out,
    nor be heard in the street;
3 my servant will not break a bruised reed,
    nor quench a dimly burning wick,
    but will faithfully bring forth justice.
4 My servant will not fail or be discouraged
    till justice has been established in the earth;
    and the coastlands wait for the servant's law.
5 Thus says God, the SOVEREIGN [[*or* LORD]],
    who created the heavens and stretched them out,
    who spread forth the earth and what comes from it,
  who gives breath to the people upon it
    and spirit to those who walk in it:
6 "I am the SOVEREIGN [[*or* LORD]], I have called you in righteousness,
    I have taken you by the hand and kept you;
  I have given you as a covenant to the people,
    a light to the nations,
7   to open the eyes that are blind,
  to bring out the prisoners from the dungeon,
    from the prison those who sit with no light.
8 I am the SOVEREIGN [[*or* LORD]], that is my name;
    my glory I give to no other,
    nor my praise to graven images.
9 Now the former things have come to pass,
    and new things I declare;
  before they spring forth
    I tell you of them."

Psalm 29

¹ Ascribe to GOD [[or the LORD]], O heavenly beings,
   ascribe to GOD [[or the LORD]] glory and strength.
² Ascribe to GOD [[or the LORD]] the glory of God's name;
   worship GOD [[or the LORD]] in holy array.
³ The voice of GOD [[or the LORD]] is upon the waters;
   the God of glory thunders,
   GOD [[or the LORD]], upon many waters.
⁴ The voice of GOD [[or the LORD]] is powerful,
   the voice of GOD [[or the LORD]] is full of majesty.
⁵ The voice of GOD [[or the LORD]] breaks the cedars,
   GOD [[or the LORD]] breaks the cedars of Lebanon,
⁶ making Lebanon to skip like a calf,
   and Sirion like a young wild ox.
⁷ The voice of GOD [[or the LORD]] flashes forth flames of fire.
⁸ The voice of GOD [[or the LORD]] shakes the wilderness,
   GOD [[or the LORD]] shakes the wilderness of Kadesh.
⁹ The voice of GOD [[or the LORD]] makes the oaks to whirl,
   and strips the forests bare;
   and in God's temple all cry, "Glory!"
¹⁰ GOD [[or The LORD]] sits enthroned over the flood;
   GOD [[or the LORD]] sits enthroned as ruler□ forever.
¹¹ May GOD [[or the LORD]] give strength to the people!
   May GOD [[or the LORD]] bless the people with peace!

□RSV *king*. See Appendix.

Lesson 2 ~ Acts 10:34-43

Peter preaches about Jesus' life, death, and resurrection.

34 Peter proclaimed, "Truly I perceive that God shows no partiality,
35 but in every nation anyone who fears God and does what is right is
acceptable to God. 36 You know the word which God sent to Israel,
preaching good news of peace by Jesus Christ (Christ is Sovereign [[or
Lord]] of all), 37 the word which was proclaimed throughout all Judea,
beginning from Galilee after the baptism which John preached: 38 how
God anointed Jesus of Nazareth with the Holy Spirit and with power; how
Jesus went about doing good and healing all that were oppressed by the
devil, for God was with him. 39 And we are witnesses to all that Jesus did
both in Judea and in Jerusalem. They put Jesus to death by hanging him
on a tree; 40 but God raised Jesus on the third day and made Jesus
manifest; 41 not to all the people but to us who were chosen by God as
witnesses, who ate and drank with Jesus after the resurrection from the
dead. 42 And Jesus commanded us to preach to the people, and to testify
that Jesus is the one ordained by God to be judge of the living and the
dead. 43 To this one all the prophets bear witness that everyone who
believes in Jesus Christ receives forgiveness of sins through Jesus' name."

Gospel ~ Matthew 3:13-17

*Matthew recounts what happened immediately after Jesus was baptized
by John.*

13 Then Jesus came from Galilee to the Jordan to be baptized by John.
14 John would have prevented Jesus, saying, "I need to be baptized by
you, and do you come to me?" 15 But Jesus answered, "Let it be so now;
for thus it is fitting for us to fulfill all righteousness." Then John con-
sented. 16 And having been baptized, Jesus went up immediately from the
water, and the heavens were opened and Jesus saw the Spirit of God
descending like a dove, and alighting on him; 17 and then a voice from
heaven, saying, "This is my beloved Child,◇ with whom I am well
pleased."

◇RSV *Son.* See Appendix.

EPIPHANY 2

Lesson 1 ~ Isaiah 49:1-7

The servant of God speaks through the prophet Isaiah.

¹ Listen to me, O coastlands,
  and hearken, you nations from afar.
 GOD [*or* The LORD] called me from the womb,
  and from the body of my mother God named my name.
² God made my mouth like a sharp sword,
  in the shadow of God's hand I was hidden;
 God made me a polished arrow,
  in the quiver I was hidden away.
³ And God said to me, "You are my servant,
  Israel, in whom I will be glorified."
⁴ But I said, "I have labored in vain,
  I have spent my strength for nothing and vanity;
 yet surely my right is with the SOVEREIGN [*or* LORD],
  and my recompense with my God."
⁵ And now GOD [*or* the LORD] says,
  who formed me from the womb to be God's servant,
 to bring Jacob back to God,
  and that Israel might be gathered to God,
 for I am honored in the eyes of the SOVEREIGN [*or* LORD],
  and my God has become my strength—
⁶ God says:
 "It is too light a thing that you should be my servant
  to raise up the tribes of Jacob
  and to restore the preserved of Israel;
 I will give you as a light to the nations,
  that my salvation may reach to the end of the earth."
⁷ Thus says the SOVEREIGN [*or* LORD],
  the Redeemer of Israel and Israel's Holy One,
 to one deeply despised, abhorred by the nations,
  the servant of rulers:
 "Monarchs□ shall see and arise;
  rulers, and they shall prostrate themselves;
 because of the SOVEREIGN [*or* LORD], who is faithful,
  the Holy One of Israel, who has chosen you."

□RSV *Kings.* See Appendix.

1 I waited patiently for GOD [[*or* the LORD]],
　　who inclined to me and heard my cry.
2 God drew me up from the desolate pit,
　　out of the miry bog,
　and set my feet upon a rock,
　　making my steps secure.
3 God put a new song in my mouth,
　　a song of praise to our God.
　Many will see and fear,
　　and put their trust in GOD [[*or* the LORD]].
4 Blessed is the one who
　　trusts in GOD [[*or* the LORD]],
　who does not turn to the proud,
　　to those who go astray after false gods!
5 You have multiplied, O SOVEREIGN [[*or* LORD]] my God,
　　your wondrous deeds and your thoughts toward us;
　　none can compare with you!
　Were I to proclaim and tell of them,
　　they would be more than can be numbered.
6 Sacrifice and offering you do not desire;
　　but you have given me an open ear.
　Burnt offering and sin offering
　　you have not required.
7 Then I said, "I am coming;
　　in the scroll of the book it is written of me;
8 I delight to do your will, O my God;
　　your law is within my heart."
9 I have told the glad news of deliverance
　　in the great congregation;
　I have not restrained my lips,
　　as you know, O GOD [[*or* LORD]].
10 I have not hid your saving help within my heart,
　　I have spoken of your faithfulness and your salvation;
　I have not concealed your steadfast love and your faithfulness
　　from the great congregation.

Lesson 2 ~ 1 Corinthians 1:1-9

Paul greets the Christians at Corinth.

¹ Paul, called by the will of God to be an apostle of Christ Jesus, and our brother Sosthenes,

² To the church of God which is at Corinth, to those sanctified in Christ Jesus, called to be saints together with all those who in every place call on the name of our Sovereign ⟦*or* Lord⟧ Jesus Christ, both their Sovereign ⟦*or* Lord⟧ and ours:

³ Grace to you and peace from God our Father [*and Mother**] and from the Sovereign ⟦*or* Lord⟧ Jesus Christ.

⁴ I give thanks to God always for you because of the grace of God which was given you in Christ Jesus, ⁵ that in every way you were enriched in Christ with all speech and all knowledge—⁶ even as the testimony to Christ was confirmed among you—⁷ so that you are not lacking in any spiritual gift, as you wait for the revealing of our Sovereign ⟦*or* Lord⟧ Jesus Christ, ⁸ who will sustain you to the end, guiltless in the day of our Sovereign ⟦*or* Lord⟧ Jesus Christ. ⁹ God is faithful, by whom you were called into the community of God's Child,◇ Jesus Christ our Sovereign ⟦*or* Lord⟧.

Gospel ~ John 1:29-34

John the Baptist identifies Jesus as the Lamb of God.

²⁹ John saw Jesus approaching, and said, "Behold, the Lamb of God, who takes away the sin of the world! ³⁰ This is the one of whom I said, 'After me comes a person who ranks before me, for that one was before me.' ³¹ I myself did not know who it was; but for this I came baptizing with water, that the one who was to come might be revealed to Israel." ³² And John bore witness, "I saw the Spirit descend as a dove from heaven, and it remained on Jesus. ³³ I myself did not know who it was; but the one who sent me to baptize with water said to me, 'The person on whom you see the Spirit descend and remain, this is the one who baptizes with the Holy Spirit.' ³⁴ And I have seen and have borne witness that this is the Child◇ of God."

---

*Addition to the text. See "Metaphor" and "God the Father and Mother" in the Appendix.
◇RSV 1 Cor. 1:9 *his Son;* John 1:34 *Son.* See Appendix.

EPIPHANY 3

Lesson 1 ~ Isaiah 9:1-4

Isaiah announces a great light for the people.

¹ But there will be no gloom for the land that was in anguish. In the former time God brought into contempt the land of Zebulun and the land of Naphtali, but in the latter time God will make glorious the way of the sea, the land beyond the Jordan, Galilee of the nations.

² The people who walked without light
  have seen a great light;
 those who dwelt in a land of deep shadows,
  on them has light shined.
³ You have multiplied the nation,
  you have increased its joy;
 they rejoice before you
  as with joy at the harvest,
  as victors rejoice when they divide the spoil.
⁴ For the yoke of Israel's burden,
  the staff for its shoulder,
  and the rod of its oppressor,
  you have broken as on the day of Midian.

Psalm 27:1-6

¹ GOD [*or* The LORD] is my light and my salvation;
  whom shall I fear?
 GOD [*or* The LORD] is the stronghold of my life;
  of whom shall I be afraid?
² When evildoers assail me,
  uttering slanders against me,
 my adversaries and foes,
  they shall stumble and fall.
³ Though a host encamp against me,
  my heart shall not fear;
 though war arise against me,
  yet I will be confident.

^{4} One thing have I asked of GOD [[*or* the LORD]],
   that will I seek after;
   that I may dwell in the house of GOD [[*or* the LORD]]
   all the days of my life,
   to behold the beauty of GOD [[*or* the LORD]],
   and to inquire in God's temple.
^{5} For God will hide me in a shelter
   in the day of trouble,
   and will conceal me under the cover of God's tent.
   God will set me high upon a rock.
^{6} And now my head shall be lifted up
   above my enemies round about me;
   and I will offer in God's tent
   sacrifices with shouts of joy;
   I will sing and make melody to GOD [[*or* the LORD]].

Lesson 2 ~ 1 Corinthians 1:10-17

Paul pleads with the Corinthians to agree with each other and not to follow party leaders in the church.

^{10} I appeal to you, sisters and brothers, by the name of our Sovereign [[*or* Lord]] Jesus Christ, that all of you agree and that there be no dissensions among you, but that you be united in the same mind and the same judgment. ^{11} For it has been reported to me by Chloe's people that there is quarreling among you, my friends. ^{12} What I mean is that each one of you says, "I belong to Paul," or "I belong to Apollos," or "I belong to Cephas," or "I belong to Christ." ^{13} Is Christ divided? Was Paul crucified for you? Or were you baptized in the name of Paul? ^{14} I am thankful that I baptized none of you except Crispus and Gaius; ^{15} lest anyone should say that you were baptized in my name. ^{16} (I did baptize also the household of Stephanas. Beyond that, I do not know whether I baptized anyone else.) ^{17} For Christ did not send me to baptize but to preach the gospel, and not with eloquent wisdom, lest the cross of Christ be emptied of its power.

Jesus has returned from the time of temptation in the wilderness and is about to begin his public ministry.

[12] Now having heard that John had been arrested, Jesus withdrew into Galilee; [13] and leaving Nazareth, he went and dwelt in Capernaum by the sea, in the territory of Zebulun and Naphtali, [14] that what was spoken by the prophet Isaiah might be fulfilled:

[15] "The land of Zebulun and the land of Naphtali,
   toward the sea, across the Jordan,
   Galilee of the Gentiles—
[16] the people who sat without light
   have seen a great light,
   and for those who sat in the region and shadow of death
   light has dawned."

[17] From that time Jesus began to preach, saying, "Repent, for the realm✩ of heaven is at hand."

[18] Then walking by the Sea of Galilee, Jesus saw two brothers, Simon who is called Peter and Andrew his brother, casting a net into the sea; for they were fishers. [19] And Jesus said to them, "Follow me, and I will make you fishers of women and men." [20] Immediately they left their nets and followed him. [21] And going on from there Jesus saw two other brothers, James the son of Zebedee and John his brother, in the boat with Zebedee their father, mending their nets, and Jesus called them. [22] Immediately they left the boat and their father, and followed Jesus.

[23] And Jesus went about all Galilee, teaching in their synagogues, preaching the gospel of the realm of heaven,✩ and healing every disease and every infirmity among the people.

✩RSV v. 17 *kingdom;* v. 23 *gospel of the kingdom.* See Appendix.

EPIPHANY 4

Lesson 1 ~ Micah 6:1-8

The God of Israel takes the people to task.

¹ Hear what GOD [[*or* the LORD]] says:
Arise, plead your case before the mountains,
and let the hills hear your voice.
² Hear, you mountains, the controversy of GOD [[*or* the LORD]],
and you enduring foundations of the earth;
for GOD [[*or* the LORD]] has a controversy with the people,
and will contend with Israel.
³ "O my people, what have I done to you?
In what have I wearied you? Answer me!
⁴ For I brought you up from the land of Egypt,
and redeemed you from the house of bondage;
and I sent before you Moses,
Aaron, and Miriam.
⁵ O my people, remember what Balak king of Moab devised,
and what Balaam the son of Beor answered Balak,
and what happened from Shittim to Gilgal,
that you may know the saving acts of GOD [[*or* the LORD]]."
⁶ "With what shall I come before the SOVEREIGN [[*or* LORD]],
and bow myself before God on high?
Shall I come before God with burnt offerings,
with calves a year old?
⁷ Will GOD [[*or* the LORD]] be pleased with thousands of rams,
with ten thousands of rivers of oil?
Shall I give my firstborn for my transgression,
the fruit of my body for the sin of my soul?"
⁸ God has showed you, O people, what is good;
and what does the SOVEREIGN [[*or* LORD]] require of you
but to do justice, and to love kindness,
and to walk humbly with your God?

Psalm 37:1-11

1 Fret not yourself because of the wicked,
    be not envious of wrongdoers!
2 For they will soon fade like the grass,
    and wither like the green herb.
3 Trust in GOD [*or* the LORD], and do good;
    so you will dwell in the land, and enjoy security.
4 Take delight in GOD [*or* the LORD],
    who will give you the desires of your heart.
5 Commit your way to GOD [*or* the LORD];
    trust in God, and God will act.
6 God will bring forth your vindication as the light,
    and your right as the noonday.
7 Be still before GOD [*or* the LORD], and wait patiently for God;
    fret not yourself over those who prosper in their way,
    over those who carry out evil devices!
8 Refrain from anger, and forsake wrath!
    Fret not yourself; it tends only to evil.
9 For the wicked shall be cut off;
    but those who wait for GOD [*or* the LORD] shall possess the land.
10 Yet a little while, and the wicked will be no more;
    though you look well at their place, they will not be there.
11 But the meek shall possess the land,
    and delight themselves in abundant prosperity.

Lesson 2 ~ 1 Corinthians 1:18-31

Paul writes to the Christians at Corinth about the wisdom of God.

18 For the word of the cross is folly to those who are perishing, but to us who are being saved it is the power of God. 19 For it is written,

"I will destroy the wisdom of the wise,
and the cleverness of the clever I will thwart."

20 Where is the wise one? Where is the scribe? Where is the debater of this age? Has not God made foolish the wisdom of the world? 21 For since, in the wisdom of God, the world did not know God through wisdom, it pleased God through the folly of what we preach to save those who believe. 22 For Jews demand signs and Greeks seek wisdom, 23 but we preach Christ crucified, a stumbling block to Jews and folly to Gentiles, 24 but to those who are called, both Jews and Greeks, Christ the power of God and the wisdom of God. 25 For the foolishness of God is wiser than human wisdom, and the weakness of God is stronger than human strength.

26 For consider your call, my friends; not many of you were wise according to worldly standards, not many were powerful, not many were of noble birth; 27 but God chose what is foolish in the world to shame the wise, God chose what is weak in the world to shame the strong, 28 God chose what is low and despised in the world, even things that are not, to bring to nothing things that are, 29 so that no human being might boast in the presence of God. 30 God is the source of your life in Christ Jesus, whom God made our wisdom, our righteousness and sanctification and redemption; 31 therefore, as it is written, "Let the one who boasts, boast of the Sovereign [[or Lord]]."

In the Sermon on the Mount, Jesus teaches about blessedness.

¹ Seeing the crowds, Jesus went up on the mountain and sat down; and the disciples came to him. ²And Jesus opened his mouth and taught them, saying:

³ "Blessed are the poor in spirit, for theirs is the realm☆ of heaven.

⁴ "Blessed are those who mourn, for they shall be comforted.

⁵ "Blessed are the meek, for they shall inherit the earth.

⁶ "Blessed are those who hunger and thirst for righteousness, for they shall be satisfied.

⁷ "Blessed are the merciful, for they shall obtain mercy.

⁸ "Blessed are the pure in heart, for they shall see God.

⁹ "Blessed are the peacemakers, for they shall be called children of God.

¹⁰ "Blessed are those who are persecuted for righteousness' sake, for theirs is the realm☆ of heaven.

¹¹ "Blessed are you when others revile you and persecute you and utter all kinds of evil against you falsely on my account. ¹²Rejoice and be glad, for your reward is great in heaven, for so they persecuted the prophets who were before you."

☆RSV *kingdom*. See Appendix.

EPIPHANY 5

Lesson 1 ~ Isaiah 58:3-9a

The people ask God what is required of them, and God responds.

3 "Why have we fasted, and you do not see it?
    Why have we humbled ourselves, and you do not acknowledge it?"
Listen: in the day of your fast you seek your own pleasure,
    and oppress all your workers.
4 You fast only to quarrel and to fight
    and to hit with a wicked fist.
Fasting like yours this day
    will not make your voice to be heard on high.
5 Is such the fast that I choose,
    a day for you to humble yourself?
Is it to bow down your head like a rush,
    and to spread sackcloth and ashes under you?
Will you call this a fast,
    and a day acceptable to GOD [[*or* the LORD]]?
6 Is not this the fast that I choose:
    to loose the bonds of wickedness,
    to undo the thongs of the yoke,
to let the oppressed go free,
    and to break every yoke?
7 Is it not to share your bread with the hungry,
    and bring the homeless poor into your house;
when you see the naked, to cover them,
    and not to hide yourself from your own flesh?
8 Then shall your light break forth like the dawn,
    and your healing shall spring up speedily;
your righteousness shall go before you,
    the glory of GOD [[*or* the LORD]] shall be your rear guard.
9 Then you shall call, and GOD [[*or* the LORD]] will answer;
    you shall cry, and God will say, Here I am.

⁴ Light illumines the darkness for the upright;
  GOD [[or the LORD]] is gracious, merciful, and righteous.
⁵ It is well with those who deal generously and lend,
  who conduct their affairs with justice.
⁶ For the righteous will never be moved;
  they will be remembered forever.
⁷ They are not afraid of evil tidings;
  their heart is firm, trusting in GOD [[or the LORD]].
⁸ Their heart is steady, they will not be afraid,
  until they see their desire on their adversaries.
⁹ They have distributed freely, and have given to the poor;
  their righteousness endures forever;
  their horn is exalted in honor.

Lesson 2 ~ 1 Corinthians 2:1-11

Paul writes about the manner of his preaching among the Corinthians.

¹ When I came to you, brothers and sisters, I did not come proclaiming to you the testimony of God in lofty words or wisdom. ² For I decided to know nothing among you except Jesus Christ, and Christ crucified. ³ And I was with you in weakness and in much fear and trembling; ⁴ and my speech and my message were not in plausible words of wisdom, but in demonstration of the Spirit and of power, ⁵ that your faith might not rest in human wisdom but in the power of God.

⁶ Yet among the mature we do impart wisdom, although it is not a wisdom of this age or of the rulers of this age, who are doomed to pass away. ⁷ But we impart a secret and hidden wisdom of God, which God decreed before the ages for our glorification. ⁸ Not one of the rulers of this age understood that; for if they had, they would not have crucified the Sovereign [[or Lord]] of glory. ⁹ But, as it is written,

  "What no eye has seen, nor ear heard,
  nor the human heart conceived,
  what God has prepared for those who love God,"

¹⁰ God has revealed to us through the Spirit. For the Spirit searches everything, even the depths of God. ¹¹ For who knows a person's thoughts except the person's own spirit which is within? So also no one comprehends the thoughts of God except the Spirit of God.

Gospel ~ Matthew 5:13-16

Jesus teaches about the righteousness of the realm of God.

¹³ You are the salt of the earth; but if salt has lost its taste, how shall its saltness be restored? It is no good for anything except to be thrown out and trodden under foot.

¹⁴ You are the light of the world. A city set on a hill cannot be hid. ¹⁵ No one lights a lamp and puts it under a bushel, but on a stand, and it gives light to all in the house. ¹⁶ Let your light so shine before others, that they may see your good works and give glory to [God] your Father [and Mother*] who is in heaven.

---

*Addition to the text. See "Metaphor" and "God the Father and Mother" in the Appendix.

EPIPHANY 6 Feb. 11

Lesson 1 ~ Deuteronomy 30:15-20

Israel must choose between good and evil, life and death.

15 See, I have set before you this day life and good, death and evil. 16 If you obey the commandments of the SOVEREIGN [*or* LORD] your God which I command you this day, by loving the SOVEREIGN [*or* LORD] your God, by walking in God's ways, and by keeping God's commandments and statutes and ordinances, then you shall live and multiply, and the SOVEREIGN [*or* LORD] your God will bless you in the land which you are entering to take possession of it. 17 But if your heart turns away, and you will not hear, but are drawn away to worship other gods and serve them, 18 I declare to you this day, that you shall perish; you shall not live long in the land which you are going over the Jordan to enter and possess. 19 I call heaven and earth to witness against you this day, that I have set before you life and death, a blessing and a curse; therefore choose life, that you and your descendants may live, 20 loving the SOVEREIGN [*or* LORD] your God, obeying God's voice, and cleaving to God; for that means life to you and length of days, that you may dwell in the land which GOD [*or* the LORD] swore to your ancestors, to Abraham [*and Sarah**], to Isaac [*and Rebecca**], and to Jacob, [*Leah, and Rachel,**] to give them.

Lesson 1 (alternate) ~ Ecclesiasticus (Sirach) 15:15-20

God gives the ability to choose between good and evil.

15 If you will, you can keep the commandments,
   and to act faithfully is a matter of your own choice.
16 God has placed before you fire and water:
   stretch out your hand for whichever you wish.
17 Before each one are life and death,
   and whichever is chosen, it will be given.
18 For great is the wisdom of God [*or* the Lord];
   God is mighty in power and sees everything;
19 God's eyes are on those who fear God,
   and God knows every human deed;
20 God has not commanded anyone to be ungodly,
   and has not given anyone permission to sin.

---

*Addition to the text. See "Addition of Women's Names to the Text" in the Appendix.

Psalm 119:1-8

[1] Blessed are those whose way is blameless,
    who walk in the law of GOD [[or the LORD]]!
[2] Blessed are those who keep God's testimonies,
    who seek God with their whole heart,
[3] who also do no wrong,
    but walk in God's ways!
[4] You have commanded your precepts to be kept diligently.
[5] O that my ways may be steadfast
    in keeping your statutes!
[6] Then I shall not be put to shame,
    having my eyes fixed on all your commandments.
[7] I will praise you with an upright heart,
    when I learn your righteous ordinances.
[8] I will observe your statutes;
    O forsake me not utterly!

Lesson 2 ~ 1 Corinthians 3:1-9

Paul explains that it is not he, or any other leader, who provides growth, but God alone.

[1] But I, sisters and brothers, could not address you as spiritual people, but as people of the flesh, as children in Christ. [2] I fed you with milk, not solid food; for you were not ready for it; and even yet you are not ready, [3] for you are still of the flesh. For while there is jealousy and strife among you, are you not of the flesh, and behaving in human ways? [4] For when one says, "I belong to Paul," and another, "I belong to Apollos," are you not merely human?

[5] What then is Apollos? What is Paul? Servants through whom you believed, as the Sovereign [[or Lord]] assigned to each. [6] I planted, Apollos watered, but God gave the growth. [7] So neither the one who plants nor the one who waters is anything, but only God who gives the growth. [8] The one who plants and the one who waters are equal, and shall receive wages according to their labor. [9] For we are God's co-workers; you are God's field, God's building.

Jesus describes the righteousness of the realm of heaven.

¹⁷ Think not that I have come to abolish the law and the prophets; I have come not to abolish them but to fulfill them. ¹⁸ For truly, I say to you, till heaven and earth pass away, not an iota, not a dot, will pass from the law until everything is accomplished. ¹⁹ Whoever then relaxes one of the least of these commandments and teaches others so, shall be called least in the realm✩ of heaven; but whoever does them and teaches them shall be called great in the realm✩ of heaven. ²⁰ For I tell you, unless your righteousness exceeds that of the scribes and Pharisees, you will never enter the realm✩ of heaven.

²¹ You have heard that it was said in ancient times, "You shall not kill; and whoever kills shall be liable to judgment." ²² But I say to you that everyone who is angry with a neighbor shall be liable to judgment; whoever insults a neighbor shall be liable to the council, and whoever says, "You fool!" shall be liable to the hell of fire. ²³ So if you are offering your gift at the altar, and there remember that your neighbor has something against you, ²⁴ leave your gift there before the altar and go; first be reconciled to your neighbor, and then come and offer your gift. ²⁵ Make friends quickly with your accuser, while you are going to court, lest your accuser hand you over to the judge, and the judge to the guard, and you be put in prison; ²⁶truly, I say to you, you will never get out till you have paid the last penny.

✩RSV *kingdom*. See Appendix.

EPIPHANY 7 — Feb. 18

Lesson 1 ~ Isaiah 49:8-13

The prophet Isaiah speaks of the servant of God.

⁸ Thus says the SOVEREIGN [[*or* LORD]]:
"In a time of favor I have answered you,
   in a day of salvation I have helped you;
I have kept you and given you
   as a covenant to the people,
to establish the land,
   to apportion the desolate heritages;
⁹ saying to the prisoners, 'Come forth,'
   to those who are in dungeons, 'Appear.'
They shall feed along the ways,
   on all bare heights shall be their pasture;
¹⁰ they shall not hunger or thirst,
   neither scorching wind nor sun shall smite them,
for the one who has pity on them will lead them,
   and by springs of water will guide them.
¹¹ And I will make all my mountains a way,
   and my highways shall be raised up.
¹² These shall come from afar,
   and these from the north and from the west,
   and these from the land of Syene."
¹³ Sing for joy, O heavens, and exult, O earth;
   break forth, O mountains, into singing!
For the SOVEREIGN [[*or* LORD]] has comforted the people,
   and will have compassion on the afflicted.

Psalm 62:5-12

⁵ For God alone my soul waits in silence,
   for my hope is from God,
⁶ who alone is my rock and my salvation,
   my fortress; I shall not be shaken.
⁷ On God rests my deliverance and my honor;
   my mighty rock, my refuge is God.
⁸ Trust in God at all times, O people;
   pour out your heart before God,
   who is a refuge for us.

9 Those of low estate are but a breath,
   those of high estate are a delusion;
  in the balances they go up;
   they are together lighter than a breath.
10 Put no confidence in extortion,
   set no vain hopes on robbery;
   if riches increase, set not your heart on them.
11 Once God has spoken;
   twice have I heard this:
  that power belongs to God;
12   and that to you, O God [[or Lord]], belongs steadfast love.
  For you repay all people
   according to their work.

Lesson 2 ~ 1 Corinthians 3:10-11, 16-23

Paul writes to the Corinthians that those who are Christ's are truly strong and wise.

10 According to the grace of God given to me, like an expert builder I laid a foundation, and another is building upon it. Let each one take care how it is built upon. 11 For no other foundation can anyone lay than that which is laid, which is Jesus Christ.

16 Do you not know that you are God's temple and that God's Spirit dwells in you? 17 Whoever destroys God's temple, God will destroy. For God's temple is holy, and you are that temple.

18 Let none deceive themselves. If any among you think that they are wise in this age, let them become fools that they may become wise. 19 For the wisdom of this world is folly with God. For it is written, "God catches the wise in their craftiness," 20 and again, "The Sovereign [[or Lord]] knows that the thoughts of the wise are futile." 21 So let no one boast of mere human beings. For all things are yours, 22 whether Paul or Apollos or Cephas or the world or life or death or the present or the future, all are yours; 23 and you are Christ's; and Christ is God's.

Jesus contrasts the ways of the world with the demands of God's rule.

27 You have heard that it was said, "You shall not commit adultery." 28 But I say to you that any one of you who looks at another lustfully has already committed adultery in your heart. 29 If your right eye causes you to sin, pluck it out and throw it away; it is better that you lose one of your members than that your whole body be thrown into hell. 30 And if your right hand causes you to sin, cut it off and throw it away; it is better that you lose one of your members than that your whole body go into hell.

31 It was also said, "Whoever divorces his wife, let him give her a certificate of divorce." 32 But I say to you that everyone who divorces his wife, except on the ground of unchastity, forces her into adultery; and whoever marries a divorced woman commits adultery.

33 Again you have heard that it was said in ancient times, "You shall not swear falsely, but shall perform to the Sovereign [or Lord] what you have sworn." 34 But I say to you, Do not swear at all, either by heaven, for it is the throne of God, 35 or by the earth, for it is God's footstool, or by Jerusalem, for it is the city of the great Ruler.□ 36 And do not swear by your head, for you cannot make one hair white or black. 37 Let what you say be simply "Yes" or "No"; anything more than this comes from evil.

□RSV *King*. See Appendix.

EPIPHANY 8 — February 25

Lesson 1 ~ Leviticus 19:1-2, 9-18

Moses learns that to know God is to do justice.

¹ And GOD [[*or* the LORD]] said to Moses, ² "Say to all the congregation of the people of Israel, You shall be holy; for I the SOVEREIGN [[*or* LORD]] your God am holy.

⁹ "When you reap the harvest of your land, you shall not reap your field to its very border, neither shall you gather the gleanings after your harvest. ¹⁰ And you shall not strip your vineyard bare, neither shall you gather the fallen grapes of your vineyard; you shall leave them for the poor and for the resident alien: I am the SOVEREIGN [[*or* LORD]] your God.

¹¹ "You shall not steal, nor deal falsely, nor lie to one another. ¹² And you shall not swear by my name falsely, and so profane the name of your God: I am the SOVEREIGN [[*or* LORD]].

¹³ "You shall not oppress or rob your neighbors. The wages of a hired servant shall not remain with you all night until the morning. ¹⁴ You shall not curse those who are deaf or put a stumbling block before those who are blind, but you shall fear your God: I am the SOVEREIGN [[*or* LORD]].

¹⁵ "You shall do no injustice in judgment; you shall not be partial to the poor or defer to the great, but in righteousness shall you judge your neighbor. ¹⁶ You shall not go up and down as a slanderer among your people, and you shall not stand forth against the life of your neighbor: I am the SOVEREIGN [[*or* LORD]].

¹⁷ "You shall not hate your neighbor in your heart, but you shall reason with your neighbor, lest you bear sin because of that neighbor. ¹⁸ You shall not take vengeance or bear any grudge against any of your own people, but you shall love your neighbor as yourself: I am the SOVEREIGN [[*or* LORD]]."

³³ Teach me, O GOD [[*or* LORD]], the way of your statutes;
and I will keep it to the end.
³⁴ Give me understanding, that I may keep your law
and observe it with my whole heart.
³⁵ Lead me in the path of your commandments,
for I delight in it.
³⁶ Incline my heart to your testimonies,
and not to gain!
³⁷ Turn my eyes from looking at vanities;
and give me life in your ways.
³⁸ Confirm to your servant your promise,
which is for those who fear you.
³⁹ Turn away the reproach which I dread;
for your ordinances are good.
⁴⁰ I long for your precepts;
in your righteousness give me life!

Lesson 2 ~ 1 Corinthians 4:1-5

Paul has become a fool for Christ's sake, that we might become wise.

¹ This is how one should regard us, as servants of Christ and stewards of the mysteries of God. ² Moreover it is required of stewards that they be found trustworthy. ³ But with me it is a very small thing that I should be judged by you or by any human court. I do not even judge myself. ⁴ I am not aware of anything against myself, but I am not thereby acquitted. It is the Sovereign [[*or* Lord]] who judges me. ⁵ Therefore do not pronounce judgment before the time, before the Sovereign [[*or* Lord]] comes, who will bring to light the things now hidden and will disclose the purposes of the heart. Then all will receive their commendation from God.

Jesus tells the disciples to be merciful as God is merciful.

38 You have heard that it was said, "An eye for an eye and a tooth for a tooth." 39 But I say to you, Do not resist one who is evil. But if anyone strikes you on the right cheek, turn the other also; 40 and if anyone would sue you and take your coat, give your cloak as well; 41 and if anyone forces you to go one mile, go two miles. 42 Give to the one who begs from you, and do not refuse anyone who would borrow from you.

43 You have heard that it was said, "You shall love your neighbor and hate your enemy." 44 But I say to you, Love your enemies and pray for those who persecute you, 45 so that you may be children of God⊗ who is in heaven; for God makes the sun rise on the evil and on the good, and sends rain on the just and on the unjust. 46 For if you love those who love you, what reward have you? Do not even the tax collectors do the same? 47 And if you salute only your neighbors, what more are you doing than others? Do not even the Gentiles do the same? 48 You, therefore, must be perfect, as [God] your heavenly Father [and Mother*] is perfect.

⊗RSV *sons of your Father.* See Appendix.
*Addition to the text. See "Metaphor" and "God the Father and Mother" in the Appendix.

EPIPHANY 9

Lesson 1 ~ Exodus 24:12-18

Moses goes to God on the mountain.

¹² GOD [[*or* The LORD]] said to Moses, "Come up to me on the mountain, and wait there; and I will give you the tables of stone, with the law and the commandment, which I have written for their instruction." ¹³ So Moses rose with his servant Joshua and went up into the mountain of God. ¹⁴ And Moses said to the elders, "Wait here for us, until we come to you again; and, behold, Aaron and Hur are with you; whoever has a cause should go to them."

¹⁵ Then Moses went up on the mountain, and the cloud covered the mountain. ¹⁶ The glory of GOD [[*or* the LORD]] settled on Mount Sinai, and the cloud covered it six days; and on the seventh day God [[*or* the Lord]] called to Moses out of the midst of the cloud. ¹⁷ Now the appearance of the glory of GOD [[*or* the LORD]] was like a devouring fire on the top of the mountain in the sight of the people of Israel. ¹⁸ And Moses entered the cloud, and went up on the mountain. And Moses was on the mountain forty days and forty nights.

Psalm 2:6-11

⁶ [God will say,] "I have set my ruler⊡
    on Zion, my holy hill."
⁷ I will tell of the decree of GOD [[*or* the LORD]]:
  God said to me, "You are my child,
    today I have begotten you.
⁸ Ask of me, and I will make the nations your heritage,
    and the ends of the earth your possession.
⁹ You shall break them with a rod of iron,
    and dash them in pieces like a potter's vessel."
¹⁰ Now therefore, O kings, be wise;
    be warned, O rulers of the earth.
¹¹ Serve GOD [[*or* the LORD]] with fear.

⊡RSV *king*. See Appendix.

Lesson 2 ~ 2 Peter 1:16-21

True prophecy comes not from myths but from the Holy Spirit.

16 For we did not follow cleverly devised myths when we made known to you the power and coming of our Sovereign [[or Lord]] Jesus Christ, but we were eyewitnesses of the Sovereign's [[or Lord's]] majesty. 17 For when Christ Jesus received honor and glory from God the [*Mother and**] Father and the voice was borne to Christ by the Majestic Glory, "This is my beloved Child,◇ with whom I am well pleased," 18 we heard this voice borne from heaven, for we were with Christ on the holy mountain. 19 And we have the prophetic word made more sure. You will do well to pay attention to this as to a lamp shining in a dark place, until the day dawns and the morning star rises in your hearts. 20 First of all you must understand this, that no prophecy of scripture is a matter of one's own interpretation, 21 because no prophecy ever came by human impulse, but people moved by the Holy Spirit spoke from God.

Gospel ~ Matthew 17:1-9

Peter, James, and John witness the transfiguration of Jesus.

1 And after six days Jesus took Peter and James and John his brother, and led them up a high mountain apart. 2 And Jesus was transfigured before them, and his face shone like the sun, and his garments became brilliant as light. 3 And there appeared to them Moses and Elijah, talking with Jesus. 4 And Peter said to Jesus, "Sovereign [[or Lord]], it is well that we are here; if you wish, I will make three booths here, one for you and one for Moses and one for Elijah." 5 Peter was still speaking, when a bright cloud overshadowed them, and a voice from the cloud said, "This is my beloved Child,◇ with whom I am well pleased; to this one you shall listen." 6 When the disciples heard this, they fell on their faces, and were filled with awe. 7 But Jesus came and touched them, saying, "Rise, and have no fear." 8 And when they lifted up their eyes, they saw no one but Jesus only.

9 And as they were coming down the mountain, Jesus commanded them, "Tell no one the vision, until the Human One○ is raised from the dead."

---

*Addition to the text. See "Metaphor" and "God the Father and Mother" in the Appendix.
◇RSV *Son*. See Appendix.
○RSV *Son of man*. See Appendix

ASH WEDNESDAY

Lesson 1 ~ Joel 2:1-2, 12-17a

God calls the people to fasting and repentance.

¹ Blow the trumpet in Zion;
    sound the alarm on my holy mountain!
  Let all the inhabitants of the land tremble,
    for the day of GOD [*or* the LORD] is coming, it is near,
² a day of shadow and gloom,
    a day of clouds and thick shadow!
  Like a blanket there is spread upon the mountains
    a great and powerful people;
  their like has never been from of old,
    nor will be again after them
    through the years of all generations.
¹² "Yet even now," says the SOVEREIGN [*or* LORD],
    "return to me with all your heart,
  with fasting, with weeping, and with mourning;
¹³   and rend your hearts and not your garments."
  Return to the SOVEREIGN [*or* LORD], your God,
    for God is gracious and merciful,
  slow to anger, and abounding in steadfast love,
    and repents of evil.
¹⁴ Who knows whether God will not turn and repent,
    and leave a blessing behind,
  a cereal offering and a drink offering
    for the SOVEREIGN [*or* LORD], your God?
¹⁵ Blow the trumpet in Zion;
    sanctify a fast;
  call a solemn assembly;
¹⁶   gather the people.
  Sanctify the congregation;
    assemble the elders;
  gather the children,
    even nursing infants.
  Let the bridegroom leave his room,
    and the bride her chamber.
¹⁷ Between the vestibule and the altar
    let the priests, the ministers of GOD [*or* the LORD], weep
  and say, "Spare your people, O SOVEREIGN [*or* LORD],
    and make not your heritage a reproach,
    a byword among the nations."

Psalm 51:1-12

1 Have mercy on me, O God, according to your steadfast love;
   according to your abundant mercy blot out my transgressions.
2 Wash me thoroughly from my iniquity,
   and cleanse me from my sin!
3 For I know my transgressions,
   and my sin is ever before me.
4 Against you, you only, have I sinned,
   and done that which is evil in your sight,
 so that you are justified in your sentence
   and blameless in your judgment.
5 I was brought forth in iniquity,
   and in sin did my mother conceive me.
6 You desire truth in the inward being;
   therefore teach me wisdom in my secret heart.
7 Purge me with hyssop, and I shall be clean;
   wash me, and I shall be cleaner than snow.
8 Fill me with joy and gladness;
   let the bones which you have broken rejoice.
9 Hide your face from my sins,
   and blot out all my iniquities.
10 Create in me a clean heart, O God,
   and put a new and right spirit within me.
11 Cast me not away from your presence,
   and take not your holy Spirit from me.
12 Restore to me the joy of your salvation,
   and uphold me with a willing spirit.

Lesson 2 ~ 2 Corinthians 5:20b–6:2 (3-10 optional)

Paul writes to the Corinthians of his ministry of reconciliation.

20 We beseech you on behalf of Christ, be reconciled to God. 21 For our sake God made to be sin the one who knew no sin, so that in this very one we might become the righteousness of God.

6:1 Working together with God, then, we entreat you not to accept the grace of God in vain. 2 For God says,

> "At the acceptable time I have listened to you,
> and helped you on the day of salvation."

Now is the acceptable time; now is the day of salvation. 3 We put no obstacle in anyone's way, so that no fault may be found with our ministry, 4 but as servants of God we commend ourselves in every way: through great endurance, in afflictions, hardships, calamities, 5 beatings, imprisonments, tumults, labors, watching, hunger; 6 by purity, knowledge, forbearance, kindness, the Holy Spirit, genuine love, 7 truthful speech, and the power of God; with the weapons of righteousness for the right hand and for the left; 8 in honor and dishonor, in ill repute and good repute. We are treated as impostors, and yet are true; 9 as unknown, and yet well known; as dying, and yet we live; as punished, and yet not killed; 10 as sorrowful, yet always rejoicing; as poor, yet making many rich; as having nothing, and yet possessing everything.

Jesus tells the disciples to lay up treasure in heaven.

¹ Beware of practicing your piety before others in order to be seen by them; for then you will have no reward from [*God*] your Father [*and Mother**] who is in heaven.

² Thus, when you give alms, sound no trumpet before you, as the hypocrites do in the synagogues and in the streets, that they may be praised by others. Truly, I say to you, they have received their reward. ³ But when you give alms, do not let your left hand know what your right hand is doing, ⁴ so that your alms may be in secret; and God⊗ who sees in secret will reward you.

⁵ And when you pray, you must not be like the hypocrites; for they love to stand and pray in the synagogues and at the street corners, that they may be seen by others. Truly, I say to you, they have received their reward. ⁶ But when you pray, go into your room and shut the door and pray to God⊗ who is in secret; and God⊗ who sees in secret will reward you.

¹⁶ And when you fast, do not look dismal, like the hypocrites, for they disfigure their faces that their fasting may be seen by others. Truly, I say to you, they have received their reward. ¹⁷ But when you fast, anoint your head and wash your face, ¹⁸ that your fasting may not be seen by others but by God⊗ who is in secret; and God⊗ who sees in secret will reward you.

¹⁹ Do not lay up for yourselves treasures on earth, where moth and rust consume and where thieves break in and steal, ²⁰ but lay up for yourselves treasures in heaven, where neither moth nor rust consumes and where thieves do not break in and steal. ²¹ For where your treasure is, there will your heart be also.

---

*Addition to the text. See "Metaphor" and "God the Father and Mother" in the Appendix.
⊗RSV *your Father*. See Appendix.

LENT 1 - March 4

Lesson 1 ~ Genesis 2:4b-9, 15-17, 25–3:7

God creates humankind.

⁴ In the day that the SOVEREIGN [[*or* LORD]] God made the earth and the heavens, ⁵when no plant of the field was yet in the earth and no herb of the field had yet sprung up—for the SOVEREIGN [[*or* LORD]] God had not caused it to rain upon the earth, and there was no one to till the ground; ⁶but a mist went up from the earth and watered the whole face of the ground— ⁷then the SOVEREIGN [[*or* LORD]] God formed a human creature of dust from the ground, and breathed into the creature's nostrils the breath of life; and the human creature became a living being. ⁸And the SOVEREIGN [[*or* LORD]] God planted a garden in Eden, in the east; and there God put the human being whom God had formed. ⁹And out of the ground the SOVEREIGN [[*or* LORD]] God made to grow every tree that is pleasant to the sight and good for food, the tree of life also in the midst of the garden, and the tree of the knowledge of good and evil. ¹⁵The SOVEREIGN [[*or* LORD]] God took and placed the human being in the garden of Eden to till it and keep it. ¹⁶And the SOVEREIGN [[*or* LORD]] God commanded the human being, saying, "You may freely eat of every tree of the garden; ¹⁷but of the tree of the knowledge of good and evil you shall not eat, for in the day that you eat of it you shall die."

²⁵And the man and the woman were both naked, and were not ashamed.

³:¹ Now the serpent was more subtle than any other wild creature that the SOVEREIGN [[*or* LORD]] God had made. The serpent said to the woman, "Did God say, 'You shall not eat of any tree of the garden'?" ²And the woman said to the serpent, "We may eat of the fruit of the trees of the garden; ³but God said, 'You shall not eat of the fruit of the tree which is in the midst of the garden, neither shall you touch it, lest you die.'" ⁴But the serpent said to the woman, "You will not die. ⁵For God knows that when you eat of it your eyes will be opened, and you will be like God, knowing good and evil." ⁶So when the woman saw that the tree was good for food, and that it was a delight to the eyes, and that the tree was to be desired to make one wise, she took of its fruit and ate; and she also gave some to her husband, and he ate. ⁷Then the eyes of both were opened, and they knew that they were naked; and they sewed fig leaves together and made themselves aprons.

¹ Out of the depths I cry to you, O GOD ⟦*or* LORD⟧!
²   God ⟦*or* Lord⟧, hear my voice!
  Let your ears be attentive
    to the voice of my supplications!
³ If you, O GOD ⟦*or* LORD⟧, should mark iniquities,
    God ⟦*or* Lord⟧, who could stand?
⁴ But there is forgiveness with you,
    that you may be feared.
⁵ I wait for GOD ⟦*or* the LORD⟧, my soul waits,
    and in God's word I hope;
⁶ my soul waits for GOD ⟦*or* the LORD⟧
    more than those who watch for the morning,
    more than those who watch for the morning.
⁷ O Israel, hope in GOD ⟦*or* the LORD⟧!
    For with GOD ⟦*or* the LORD⟧ there is steadfast love,
    and with God is plenteous redemption.
⁸ And God will redeem Israel
    from all their iniquities.

Lesson 2 ~ Romans 5:12-19

Paul writes of the trespass of Adam and of the grace of Jesus Christ.

¹² Therefore as sin came into the world through one human being and death through sin, and so death spread to all humankind because all sinned— ¹³ sin indeed was in the world before the law was given, but sin is not counted where there is no law. ¹⁴ Yet death reigned from Adam to Moses, even over those whose sins were not like the transgression of Adam, who was a type of the one who was to come.

¹⁵ But the free gift is not like the trespass. For if many died through the trespass of one, much more have the grace of God and the free gift in the grace of that one person Jesus Christ abounded for many. ¹⁶ And the free gift is not like the effect of that one person's sin. For the judgment following one trespass brought condemnation, but the free gift following many trespasses brings justification. ¹⁷ If, because of the trespass of one, death reigned through that one, much more will those who receive the abundance of grace and the free gift of righteousness reign in life through the one person Jesus Christ.

¹⁸ Then as the trespass of one led to condemnation for all, so the act of righteousness of one leads to acquittal and life for all. ¹⁹ For as by the disobedience of one many were made sinners, so by the obedience of one many will be made righteous.

Jesus is tempted by the devil.

¹ Then Jesus was led up by the Spirit into the wilderness to be tempted by the devil. ² Having fasted forty days and forty nights, Jesus was hungry. ³ And the tempter came and said to Jesus, "If you are the Child◇ of God, command these stones to become loaves of bread." ⁴ But Jesus answered, "It is written,

'One shall not live by bread alone,
  but by every word that proceeds from the mouth of God.'"

⁵ Then the devil took Jesus to the holy city, and set him on the pinnacle of the temple, ⁶ and said, "If you are the Child◇ of God, throw yourself down; for it is written,

'God will give the angels charge of you,'

and

'On their hands they will bear you up,
  lest you strike your foot against a stone.'"

⁷ Jesus said to the devil, "Again it is written, 'You shall not tempt the Sovereign [[*or* Lord]] your God.'" ⁸ Again, the devil took Jesus to a very high mountain, and showed him all the nations of the world and the glory of them; ⁹ and the devil said to Jesus, "All these I will give you, if you will fall down and worship me." ¹⁰ Then Jesus said to the devil, "Be gone, Satan! for it is written,

'You shall worship the Sovereign [[*or* Lord]] your God,
  and God only shall you serve.'"

¹¹ Then the devil left Jesus, and angels came and ministered to him.

◇RSV *Son*. See Appendix.

LENT 2

Lesson 1 ~ Genesis 12:1-4a (4b-8 optional)

Abram and Sarai are chosen to play a decisive role in God's purpose for history.

¹ Now GOD [[*or* the LORD]] said to Abram, "Go from your country and your kindred and your family's house to the land that I will show you. ² And I will make of you a great nation, and I will bless you, and make your name great, so that you will be a blessing. ³ I will bless those who bless you, and the one who curses you I will curse; and by you all the families of the earth shall bless themselves."

⁴ So Abram went, as GOD [[*or* the LORD]] had told him; and Lot went with him. Abram was seventy-five years old when he departed from Haran. ⁵ And Abram took Sarai his wife, and Lot his nephew, and all their possessions which they had gathered, and the persons that they had gotten in Haran; and they set forth to go to the land of Canaan. When they had come to the land of Canaan, ⁶ Abram passed through the land to the place at Shechem, to the oak of Moreh. At that time the Canaanites were in the land. ⁷ Then GOD [[*or* the LORD]] appeared to Abram, and said, "To your descendants I will give this land." So Abram built there an altar to GOD [[*or* the LORD]], who had appeared to him. ⁸ Then Abram went to the mountain on the east of Bethel, and pitched a tent, with Bethel on the west and Ai on the east; and there Abram built an altar to GOD [[*or* the LORD]] and called on the name of the SOVEREIGN [[*or* LORD]].

Psalm 33:18-22

¹⁸ The eye of the SOVEREIGN [[*or* LORD]] is on those who fear God,
    on those who hope in God's steadfast love,
¹⁹ that God may deliver their soul from death,
    and keep them alive in famine.
²⁰ Our soul waits for the SOVEREIGN [[*or* LORD]],
    who is our help and shield.
²¹ Indeed, our heart is glad in God,
    because we trust in God's holy name.
²² Let your steadfast love, O SOVEREIGN [[*or* LORD]], be upon us,
    even as we hope in you.

Lesson 2 ~ Romans 4:1-5 (6-12 optional), 13-17

The heirs of the promise are those who have faith.

[1] What then shall we say about Abraham, our ancestor according to the flesh? [2] For if Abraham was justified by works, he has something to boast about, but not before God. [3] For what does the scripture say? "Abraham believed God, and it was reckoned to him as righteousness." [4] Now to one who works, wages are not reckoned as a gift but as the worker's due. [5] And to one who does not work but trusts God who justifies the ungodly, faith is reckoned as righteousness. [6] So also David pronounces a blessing upon the one to whom God reckons righteousness apart from works:

> [7] "Blessed are those whose iniquities are forgiven, and whose sins are covered;
>
> [8] blessed are those against whom the Sovereign [or Lord] will not reckon their sin."

[9] Is this blessing pronounced only upon the Jews, or also upon the Gentiles? We say that faith was reckoned to Abraham as righteousness. [10] How then was it reckoned to Abraham? Was it before or after circumcision? It was not after, but before. [11] Abraham received circumcision as a sign or seal of the righteousness which he had by faith while still uncircumcised. The purpose was to make Abraham the ancestor of all uncircumcised believers, who have righteousness reckoned to them, [12] and likewise the ancestor of the circumcised believers who follow the example of the faith which our ancestor Abraham had before circumcision.

[13] The promise to Abraham and to the descendants of Abraham [and Sarah*], that they should inherit the world, did not come through the law but through the righteousness of faith. [14] If it is the adherents of the law who are to be the heirs, faith is null and the promise is void. [15] For the law brings wrath, but where there is no law there is no transgression.

[16] That is why it depends on faith, in order that the promise may rest on grace and be guaranteed to all their descendants—not only to the adherents of the law but also to those who share the faith of Abraham, who [with Sarah*] is the ancestor of us all; [17] as it is written, "I have made you the ancestor of many nations"—in the presence of the God in whom Abraham believed, who gives life to the dead and calls into existence the things that do not exist.

---

*Addition to the text. See "Addition of Women's Names to the Text" in the Appendix.

Gospel ~ John 3:1-17

Jesus tells Nicodemus about the work of the Spirit.

¹ Now there was a man of the Pharisees, named Nicodemus, a ruler of the Jews. ² Nicodemus came to Jesus by night and said, "Rabbi, we know that you are a teacher come from God; for no one can do these signs that you do, except by the power of God." ³ Jesus answered Nicodemus, "Truly, truly, I say to you, unless one is born anew,① one cannot see the realm☆ of God." ⁴ Nicodemus replied, "How can someone be born who is old? Can anyone enter the mother's womb a second time and be born?" ⁵ Jesus answered, "Truly, truly, I say to you, unless one is born of water and the Spirit, one cannot enter the realm☆ of God. ⁶ That which is born of the flesh is flesh, and that which is born of the Spirit is spirit. ⁷ Do not marvel that I said to you, 'You must be born anew.'① ⁸ The wind blows where it wills, and you hear the sound of it, but you do not know where it comes from or where it goes; so it is with everyone who is born of the Spirit." ⁹ Nicodemus said to Jesus, "How can this be?" ¹⁰ Jesus answered, "Are you a teacher of Israel, and yet you do not understand this? ¹¹ Truly, truly, I say to you, we speak of what we know, and bear witness to what we have seen; but you do not receive our testimony. ¹² If I have told you earthly things and you do not believe, how can you believe if I tell you heavenly things? ¹³ No one has ascended into heaven but the one who descended from heaven, the Human One.○ ¹⁴ And as Moses lifted up the serpent in the wilderness, so must the Human One○ be lifted up, ¹⁵ that whoever believes in that one may have eternal life."

¹⁶ For God so loved the world that God gave God's only Child,◇ that whoever believes in that Child should not perish but have eternal life. ¹⁷ For God sent that Child◇ into the world, not to condemn the world, but that through that Child the world might be saved.

---

① Or *from above.*
☆ RSV *kingdom.* See Appendix.
○ RSV *Son of man.* See Appendix.
◇ RSV v. 16 *Son;* v. 17 *the Son.* See Appendix.

Gospel (alternate) ∼ Matthew 17:1-9

Peter, James, and John witness the transfiguration of Jesus.

¹ And after six days Jesus took Peter and James and John his brother, and led them up a high mountain apart. ² And Jesus was transfigured before them, and his face shone like the sun, and his garments became brilliant as light. ³ And there appeared to them Moses and Elijah, talking with Jesus. ⁴ And Peter said to Jesus, "Sovereign [[*or* Lord]], it is well that we are here; if you wish, I will make three booths here, one for you and one for Moses and one for Elijah." ⁵ Peter was still speaking, when a bright cloud overshadowed them, and a voice from the cloud said, "This is my beloved Child,◇ with whom I am well pleased; to this one you shall listen." ⁶ When the disciples heard this, they fell on their faces, and were filled with awe. ⁷ But Jesus came and touched them, saying, "Rise, and have no fear." ⁸ And when they lifted up their eyes, they saw no one but Jesus only.

⁹ And as they were coming down the mountain, Jesus commanded them, "Tell no one the vision, until the Human One○ is raised from the dead."

◇RSV *Son*. See Appendix.
○RSV *Son of man*. See Appendix.

LENT 3

Lesson 1 ~ Exodus 17:3-7

Moses brings water from a rock at Massah.

³ But the people thirsted there for water, and the people murmured against Moses, and said, "Why did you bring us up out of Egypt, to kill us and our children and our cattle with thirst?" ⁴ So Moses cried to GOD ⟦*or* the LORD⟧, "What shall I do with this people? They are almost ready to stone me." ⁵ And GOD ⟦*or* the LORD⟧ said to Moses, "Pass on before the people, taking with you some of the elders of Israel; and take in your hand the rod with which you struck the Nile, and go. ⁶ Behold, I will stand before you there on the rock at Horeb; and you shall strike the rock, and water shall come out of it, that the people may drink." And Moses did so, in the sight of the elders of Israel. ⁷ And he called the name of the place Massah and Meribah, because of the faultfinding of the children of Israel, and because they put GOD ⟦*or* the LORD⟧ to the proof by saying, "Is GOD ⟦*or* the LORD⟧ among us or not?"

Psalm 95

¹ O come, let us sing to GOD ⟦*or* the LORD⟧;
   let us make a joyful noise to the rock of our salvation!
² Let us come into God's presence with thanksgiving;
   let us make a joyful noise to God with songs of praise!
³ For the SOVEREIGN ⟦*or* LORD⟧ is a great God,
   and a great Ruler□ above all gods.
⁴ The depths of the earth are in the hand of God;
   the heights of the mountains are God's also.
⁵ The sea belongs to God, for God made it;
   for God's hands formed the dry land.
⁶ O come, let us worship and bow down,
   let us kneel before GOD ⟦*or* the LORD⟧, our Maker!
⁷ For this is our God,
   and we are the people of God's pasture,
   and the sheep of God's hand.
  O that today you would hearken to the voice of God!
⁸   Harden not your hearts, as at Meribah,
   as on the day at Massah in the wilderness,
⁹ when your ancestors tested me,
   and put me to the proof, though they had seen my work.

□RSV *King*. See Appendix.

¹⁰ For forty years I loathed that generation
    and said, "They are a people who err in heart,
    and they do not regard my ways."
¹¹ Therefore I swore in my anger
    that they should not enter my rest.

Lesson 2 ~ Romans 5:1-11

Paul writes to the Christians at Rome about the greatness of God's love for us.

¹ Therefore, since we are justified by faith, we have peace with God through our Sovereign [*or* Lord] Jesus Christ, ² through whom we have obtained access to this grace in which we stand, and we rejoice in our hope of sharing the glory of God. ³ More than that, we rejoice in our sufferings, knowing that suffering produces endurance, ⁴ and endurance produces character, and character produces hope, ⁵ and hope does not disappoint us, because God's love has been poured into our hearts through the Holy Spirit who has been given to us.

⁶ While we were still weak, at the right time Christ died for the ungodly. ⁷ Why, one will hardly die for a righteous person—though perhaps for a good person one will dare even to die. ⁸ But God shows love for us in that while we were yet sinners, Christ died for us. ⁹ Since, therefore, we are now justified by the blood of Christ, much more shall we be saved by Christ from the wrath of God. ¹⁰ For if while we were enemies we were reconciled to God by the death of God's Child,◇ much more, now that we are reconciled, shall we be saved by the life of Christ. ¹¹ Not only so, but we also rejoice in God through our Sovereign [*or* Lord] Jesus Christ, through whom we have now received our reconciliation.

◇RSV *of his Son.* See Appendix.

Gospel ~ John 4:5-26 (27-42 optional)

A woman of Samaria meets Jesus at Jacob's well.

⁵ Jesus came to a city of Samaria, called Sychar, near the field that Jacob gave to his son Joseph. ⁶ Jacob's well was there, and so Jesus, wearied with the journey, sat down beside the well. It was about the sixth hour.

⁷ There came a woman of Samaria to draw water. Jesus said to her, "Give me a drink." ⁸ For the disciples had gone away into the city to buy food. ⁹ The Samaritan woman said to Jesus, "How is it that you, a Jew, ask a drink of me, a woman of Samaria?" For Jews have no dealings with Samaritans. ¹⁰ Jesus answered her, "If you knew the gift of God, and who it is that is saying to you, 'Give me a drink,' you would have asked that person, who would then have given you living water." ¹¹ The woman said to Jesus, "You have nothing to draw with, and the well is deep; where do you get that living water? ¹² Are you greater than our ancestor Jacob, who gave us the well, and drank from it, as did his children and animals?" ¹³ Jesus said to her, "Everyone who drinks of this water will thirst again, ¹⁴ but whoever drinks of the water that I shall give will never thirst; the water that I shall give will become in the one who drinks it a spring of water welling up to eternal life." ¹⁵ The woman said to Jesus, "Give me this water, that I may not thirst, nor come here to draw."

¹⁶ Jesus said to her, "Go, call your husband, and come here." ¹⁷ The woman answered, "I have no husband." Jesus said to her, "You are right in saying, 'I have no husband'; ¹⁸ for you have had five husbands, and he whom you now have is not your husband; this you said truly." ¹⁹ The woman said to Jesus, "I perceive that you are a prophet. ²⁰ Our ancestors worshiped on this mountain; and you say that in Jerusalem is the place where people ought to worship." ²¹ Jesus said to her, "Woman, believe me, the hour is coming when neither on this mountain nor in Jerusalem will you worship [God] the Father [and Mother*]. ²² You worship what you do not know; we worship what we know, for salvation is from the Jews. ²³ But the hour is coming, and now is, when the true worshipers will worship [God] the [Mother and*] Father in spirit and truth, for such are those whom God seeks as worshipers. ²⁴ God is spirit, and those who worship God must worship in spirit and truth." ²⁵ The woman said to Jesus, "I know that Messiah is coming (the one who is called Christ), who, having come, will show us all things." ²⁶ Jesus said to her, "I who speak to you am that very one."

²⁷ Just then the disciples came. They marveled that Jesus was talking with a woman, but none said, "What do you wish?" or, "Why are you talking with her?" ²⁸ So the woman left her water jar, and went away into

---

* Addition to the text. See "Metaphor" and "God the Father and Mother" in the Appendix.

the city, and said to the people, ²⁹"Come, see someone who told me all that I ever did. Can this be the Christ?" ³⁰They went out of the city and were coming to Jesus.

³¹ Meanwhile the disciples said to Jesus, "Rabbi, eat." ³² But Jesus said to them, "I have food to eat of which you do not know." ³³ So the disciples said to one another, "Has anyone brought Jesus food?" ³⁴ Jesus said to them, "My food is to do the will of God who sent me, and to accomplish God's work. ³⁵ Do you not say, 'There are yet four months, then comes the harvest'? I tell you, lift up your eyes, and see how the fields are already white for harvest. ³⁶ One who reaps receives wages, and gathers fruit for eternal life, so that sower and reaper may rejoice together. ³⁷ For here the saying holds true, 'One sows and another reaps.' ³⁸ I sent you to reap that for which you did not labor; others have labored, and you have entered into their labor."

³⁹ Many Samaritans from that city believed in Jesus because of the woman's testimony, "This person told me all that I ever did." ⁴⁰ So when the Samaritans approached, they asked Jesus to stay with them; and he stayed there two days. ⁴¹ And many more believed because of Jesus' word. ⁴² They said to the woman, "It is no longer because of your words that we believe, for we have heard for ourselves, and we know that this is indeed the Savior of the world."

LENT 4

Lesson 1 ~ 1 Samuel 16:1-13

Samuel anoints David to be king over Israel.

¹ GOD [*or* The LORD] said to Samuel, "How long will you grieve over Saul, seeing I have rejected him from being king over Israel? Fill your horn with oil, and go; I will send you to Jesse the Bethlehemite, for I have provided for myself a king among Jesse's sons." ² And Samuel said, "How can I go? If Saul hears it, he will kill me." And GOD [*or* the LORD] said, "Take a heifer with you, and say, 'I have come to sacrifice to GOD [*or* the LORD].' ³ And invite Jesse to the sacrifice, and I will show you what you shall do; and you shall anoint for me the one whom I name to you." ⁴ Samuel did what GOD [*or* the LORD] commanded, and came to Bethlehem. The elders of the city came to meet Samuel trembling, and said, "Do you come peaceably?" ⁵ And Samuel said, "Peaceably; I have come to sacrifice to GOD [*or* the LORD]; consecrate yourselves, and come with me to the sacrifice." And he consecrated Jesse and his sons, and invited them to the sacrifice.

⁶ When they came, Samuel looked on Eliab and thought, "Surely GOD's [*or* the LORD's] anointed is present." ⁷ But GOD [*or* the LORD] said to Samuel, "Do not look on Eliab's appearance or on the height of his stature, because I have rejected Eliab; for GOD [*or* the LORD] sees not as people see; people look on the outward appearance, but GOD [*or* the LORD] looks on the heart." ⁸ Then Jesse called Abinadab, and made Abinadab pass before Samuel. And Samuel said, "Neither has GOD [*or* the LORD] chosen this one." ⁹ Then Jesse made Shammah pass by. And Samuel said, "Neither has GOD [*or* the LORD] chosen this one." ¹⁰ And Jesse made seven of his sons pass before Samuel. And Samuel said to Jesse, "GOD [*or* The LORD] has not chosen these." ¹¹ And Samuel said to Jesse, "Are all your sons here?" And Jesse said, "There remains yet the youngest, but he is keeping the sheep." And Samuel said to Jesse, "Send and fetch him; for we will not sit down till he comes here." ¹² And Jesse sent, and brought David in. Now David was ruddy, and had beautiful eyes, and was handsome. And GOD [*or* the LORD] said, "Arise, anoint David; for this is the one." ¹³ Then Samuel took the horn of oil, and anointed David in the midst of his brothers; and the Spirit of GOD [*or* the LORD] came mightily upon David from that day forward. And Samuel rose up, and went to Ramah.

Psalm 23

[1] GOD [[or The LORD]] is my shepherd, I shall not want;
[2]   God makes me lie down in green pastures,
  and leads me beside still waters;
[3]   God restores my soul.
  God leads me in paths of righteousness
    for God's name's sake.
[4] Even though I walk through the valley of the shadow of death,
    I fear no evil;
  for you are with me;
    your rod and your staff,
    they comfort me.
[5] You prepare a table before me
    in the presence of my enemies;
  you anoint my head with oil,
    my cup overflows.
[6] Surely goodness and mercy shall follow me
    all the days of my life;
  and I shall dwell in the house of GOD [[or the LORD]]
    forever.

Lesson 2 ~ Ephesians 5:8-14

The Ephesians are exhorted to walk as children of light.

[8] For once you were stumbling in the night, but now you are light in the Sovereign [[or Lord]]; walk as children of light [9] (for the fruit of light is found in all that is good and right and true), [10] and try to learn what is pleasing to the Sovereign [[or Lord]]. [11] Take no part in unfruitful works, but instead expose them. [12] For it is a shame even to speak of the things that are done in secret; [13] but all things exposed by the light are revealed, for everything that is revealed is light. [14] Therefore it is said,

"Awake, O sleeper, and arise from the dead,
and Christ shall give you light."

Gospel ~ John 9:1-41

Jesus heals the one born blind.

¹ As Jesus passed by, he saw a person blind from birth. ² And the disciples asked Jesus, "Rabbi, who sinned, this person or the parents, that the child was born blind?" ³ Jesus answered, "It was not that this person sinned, or the parents, but that the works of God might be made manifest. ⁴ We must work the works of the one who sent me, while it is day; night comes, when no one can work. ⁵ As long as I am in the world, I am the light of the world." ⁶ As Jesus said this, he spat on the ground and made clay of the spittle and anointed with the clay the eyes of the person who was blind, ⁷ saying, "Go, wash in the pool of Siloam" (which means Sent). So the person who was blind went and washed and came back seeing. ⁸ The neighbors and those who had seen that person before as a beggar, said, "Is not this the one who used to sit and beg?" ⁹ Some said, "It is the one"; others said, "No, but they look alike." The one born blind said, "I am that person." ¹⁰ They said, "Then how were your eyes opened?" ¹¹ The answer came, "The one called Jesus made clay and anointed my eyes and said to me, 'Go to Siloam and wash'; so I went and washed and received my sight." ¹² They asked, "Where is he?" The one born blind said, "I do not know."

¹³ They brought to the Pharisees the person who had formerly been blind. ¹⁴ Now it was a sabbath day when Jesus made the clay and opened the blind one's eyes. ¹⁵ The Pharisees again asked that person how sight had been restored. And the answer came, "He put clay on my eyes, and I washed, and I see." ¹⁶ Some of the Pharisees said, "This one is not from God, for he does not keep the sabbath." But others said, "How can a person who is a sinner do such signs?" There was a division among them. ¹⁷ So they again said to the person born blind, "What do you say about him, since he has opened your eyes?" The answer came, "He is a prophet."

¹⁸ The Jews did not believe that the person had been blind and had received sight, until they called the parents of the one who had received sight, ¹⁹ and asked them, "Is this your child, who you say was born blind? How then does this one now see?" ²⁰ The parents answered, "We know that this is our child, who was born blind; ²¹ but how sight was given or how the eyes were opened we do not know. Ask our child, who is of age and will speak directly." ²² The parents said this because they feared the leaders of the synagogue, for the leaders had already agreed that anyone who confessed Jesus to be Christ would be put out of the synagogue. ²³ Therefore the parents said, "Ask our child, who is of age."

24 So for the second time they called the one who had been blind, and said, "Give God the praise; we know that this man is a sinner." 25 The one born blind answered, "Whether he is a sinner, I do not know; one thing I know, that though I was blind, now I see." 26 They said, "What did he do to you? How did he open your eyes?" 27 The answer came, "I have told you already, and you would not listen. Why do you want to hear it again? Do you too want to become Jesus' disciples?" 28 And they reviled the one born blind, saying, "You are his disciple, but we are disciples of Moses. 29 We know that God has spoken to Moses but as for this one, we do not know where he comes from." 30 The one who had been blind answered, "Why, this is a marvel! You do not know where he comes from, and yet he opened my eyes. 31 We know that God does not listen to sinners, but if anyone is a worshiper of God and does God's will, God listens. 32 Never since the world began has it been heard that anyone opened the eyes of a person born blind. 33 If this one were not from God, he could do nothing." 34 They answered, "You were born in utter sin, and would you teach us?" And they cast out the one who had been blind.

35 Jesus found the one who he heard had been cast out and said, "Do you believe in the Human One○?" 36 The one born blind answered, "And who is it, sir, so that I may believe in whoever it is?" 37 Jesus said, "You have seen who it is, and it is the very one who speaks to you." 38 The one who had been blind said, "Sovereign [or Lord], I believe," and worshiped Jesus. 39 Jesus said, "For judgment I came into this world, that those who do not see may see, and that those who see may become blind." 40 Some of the Pharisees nearby heard this, and they said to Jesus, "Are we also blind?" 41 Jesus said to them, "If you were blind, you would have no guilt; but now that you say, 'We see,' your guilt remains."

○RSV *Son of man*. See Appendix.

LENT 5

Lesson 1 ~ Ezekiel 37:1-14

Ezekiel sees a vision of the glorification of Israel.

¹ The hand of GOD [[*or* the LORD]] was upon me, and brought me out by the Spirit of GOD [[*or* the LORD]], and set me down in the midst of the valley; it was full of bones. ²And God led me round among them; and there were very many upon the valley; and they were very dry. ³And God said to me, "O mortal,○ can these bones live?" And I answered, "O Sovereign [[*or* Lord]] GOD, you know." ⁴Again God said to me, "Prophesy to these bones, and say to them, O dry bones, hear the word of GOD [[*or* the LORD]]. ⁵Thus says the Sovereign [[*or* Lord]] GOD to these bones: I will cause breath to enter you, and you shall live. ⁶And I will lay sinews upon you, and will cause flesh to come upon you, and cover you with skin, and put breath in you, and you shall live; and you shall know that I am GOD [[*or* the LORD]]."

⁷ So I prophesied as I was commanded; and as I prophesied, there was a noise and a rattling; and the bones came together, bone to its bone. ⁸And as I looked, there were sinews on them, and flesh had come upon them, and skin had covered them; but there was no breath in them. ⁹Then God said to me, "Prophesy to the breath, prophesy, O mortal,○ and say to the breath, Thus says the Sovereign [[*or* Lord]] GOD: Come from the four winds, O breath, and breathe upon these slain, that they may live." ¹⁰So I prophesied as God commanded me, and the breath came into them, and they lived, and stood upon their feet, an exceedingly great host.

¹¹Then God said to me, "O mortal,○ these bones are the whole house of Israel. They say, 'Our bones are dried up, and our hope is lost; we are clean cut off.' ¹²Therefore prophesy, and say to them, Thus says the Sovereign [[*or* Lord]] GOD: I will open your graves, and raise you from your graves, O my people; and I will bring you home into the land of Israel. ¹³And you shall know that I am GOD [[*or* the LORD]], when I open your graves, and raise you from your graves, O my people. ¹⁴And I will put my Spirit within you, and you shall live, and I will place you in your own land; then you shall know that I, the SOVEREIGN [[*or* LORD]], have spoken, and I have done it, says the SOVEREIGN [[*or* LORD]]."

○RSV vs. 3, 11 *Son of man;* v. 9 *son of man.* See Appendix.

Psalm 116:1-9

1 I love GOD [[or the LORD]], because God has heard
   my voice and my supplications.
2 Because God has listened to me,
   therefore I will call on God as long as I live.
3 The snares of death encompassed me;
   the pangs of Sheol laid hold on me;
   I suffered distress and anguish.
4 Then I called on the name of GOD [[or the LORD]]:
   "O GOD [[or LORD]], I beseech you, save my life!"
5 GOD [[or The LORD]] is gracious and righteous;
   our God is merciful.
6 GOD [[or The LORD]] preserves the simple;
   when I was brought low, God saved me.
7 Return, O my soul, to our rest;
   for GOD [[or the LORD]] has dealt bountifully with you.
8 For you have delivered my soul from death,
   my eyes from tears,
   my feet from stumbling;
9 I walk before GOD [[or the LORD]]
   in the land of the living.

Lesson 2 ~ Romans 8:6-11

Paul writes about the work of the Spirit.

6 To set the mind on the flesh is death, but to set the mind on the Spirit is life and peace. 7 For the mind that is set on the flesh is hostile to God; it does not submit to God's law, indeed it cannot; 8 and those who are in the flesh cannot please God.

9 But you are not in the flesh, you are in the Spirit, if in fact the Spirit of God dwells in you. Anyone who does not have the Spirit of Christ does not belong to Christ. 10 But if Christ is in you, although your bodies are dead because of sin, your spirits are alive because of righteousness. 11 If the Spirit of the one who raised Jesus from the dead dwells in you, the one who raised Christ Jesus from the dead will give life to your mortal bodies also through that same Spirit which dwells in you.

Jesus raises Lazarus from the dead.

¹ Now a certain person was ill, Lazarus of Bethany, the village of Mary and her sister Martha. ² It was Mary who anointed the Sovereign [[or Lord]] with ointment and wiped his feet with her hair, whose brother Lazarus was ill. ³ So the sisters sent to Jesus, saying, "Sovereign [[or Lord]], the one you love is ill." ⁴ But hearing it, Jesus said, "This illness is not unto death; it is for the glory of God, so that the Child◇ of God may be glorified by means of it."

⁵ Now Jesus loved Martha and her sister, Mary, and Lazarus. ⁶ And hearing that Lazarus was ill, Jesus stayed two days longer in the place where he was. ⁷ Then after this Jesus said to the disciples, "Let us go into Judea again." ⁸ The disciples replied, "Rabbi, the religious authorities▽ were but now seeking to stone you, and are you going there again?" ⁹ Jesus answered, "Are there not twelve hours in the day? Those who walk in the day do not stumble, because they see the light of this world. ¹⁰ But those who walk in the night stumble because the light is not in them."

¹¹ Thus Jesus spoke to the disciples, and then added, "Our friend Lazarus has fallen asleep, but I go to awaken him out of sleep." ¹² The disciples replied, "Sovereign [[or Lord]], if he has fallen asleep, he will recover." ¹³ Now Jesus had spoken of the death of Lazarus, but they thought that he meant taking rest in sleep. ¹⁴ Then Jesus told them plainly, "Lazarus is dead; ¹⁵ and for your sake I am glad I was not there, so that you may believe. But let us go to him." ¹⁶ Thomas, called the Twin, said to the other disciples, "Let us also go, that we may die with him."

¹⁷ Now when Jesus came, he found that Lazarus had already been in the tomb four days. ¹⁸ Bethany was near Jerusalem, about two miles off, ¹⁹ and many of the Jews had come to Martha and Mary to console them concerning their brother. ²⁰ When Martha heard that Jesus was coming, she went and met him, while Mary sat in the house. ²¹ Martha said to Jesus, "Sovereign [[or Lord]], if you had been here, my brother would not have died. ²² And even now I know that whatever you ask from God, God will give you." ²³ Jesus said to her, "Your brother will rise again." ²⁴ Martha replied, "I know that he will rise again in the resurrection at the last day." ²⁵ Jesus said to her, "I am the resurrection and the life; those who believe in me, though they die, yet shall they live, ²⁶ and whoever lives and believes in me shall never die. Do you believe this?" ²⁷ She said to Jesus, "Yes, Sovereign [[or Lord]], I believe that you are the Christ, the Child◇ of God, the one who is coming into the world."

²⁸ When Martha had said this, she went and called her sister Mary, saying quietly, "The Teacher is here and is calling for you." ²⁹ And when

---

◇RSV *Son*. See Appendix.
▽RSV *the Jews*. See Appendix.

Mary heard it, she rose quickly and went to him. ³⁰ Now Jesus had not yet come to the village, but was still in the place where Martha had met him. ³¹ When the Jews who were with her in the house, consoling her, saw Mary rise quickly and go out, they followed her, supposing that she was going to the tomb to weep there. ³² Then Mary, when she came and saw Jesus, fell at his feet, and said, "Sovereign [or Lord], if you had been here, my brother would not have died." ³³ When Jesus saw her weeping, and the Jews who came with her also weeping, he was indignant in spirit and troubled, ³⁴ and said, "Where have you laid Lazarus?" They answered, "Sovereign [or Lord], come and see." ³⁵ Jesus wept. ³⁶ So the Jews said, "See how Jesus loved him!" ³⁷ But some of them said, "Could not the one who opened the eyes of the person born blind have kept this one from dying?"

³⁸ Then Jesus, again indignant, came to the tomb; it was a cave, and a stone lay upon it. ³⁹ Jesus said, "Take away the stone." Martha, the sister of the one who had died, said to Jesus, "Sovereign [or Lord], by this time there will be an odor, for he has been dead four days." ⁴⁰ Jesus said to her, "Did I not tell you that if you would believe you would see the glory of God?" ⁴¹ So they took away the stone. And Jesus looked up and said, "[God, my Mother and*] Father, I thank you that you have heard me. ⁴²I already knew that you hear me always, but I have said this on account of the people standing by, that they may believe that you sent me." ⁴³ Having said this, Jesus cried with a loud voice, "Lazarus, come out." ⁴⁴ The dead man came out, his hands and feet bound with bandages, and his face wrapped with a cloth. Jesus said to them, "Unbind him, and let him go."

⁴⁵ Many of the Jews therefore, who had come with Mary and had seen what was done, believed in Jesus.

---

*Addition to the text. See "Metaphor" and "God the Father and Mother" in the Appendix.

LENT 6, PASSION SUNDAY

Lesson 1 ~ Isaiah 50:4-9a

The prophet Isaiah tells of the suffering of the one who obeys God.

⁴ The Sovereign [[*or* Lord]] GOD has given me
    the tongue of those who are taught,
  that I may know to sustain with a word
    one who is weary.
  Morning by morning God wakens,
    God wakens my ear
    to hear as those who are taught.
⁵ The Sovereign [[*or* Lord]] GOD has opened my ear,
    and I was not rebellious,
    I turned not backward.
⁶ I gave my back to the smiters,
    and my cheeks to those who pulled out my beard;
  I hid not my face
    from shame and spitting.
⁷ For the Sovereign [[*or* Lord]] GOD helps me;
    therefore I have not been confounded;
  therefore I have set my face like a flint,
    and I know that I shall not be put to shame;
⁸   the one who vindicates me is near.
  Who will contend with me?
    Let us stand together.
  Who are my adversaries?
    Let them come near to me.
⁹ The Sovereign [[*or* Lord]] GOD helps me;
    who will declare me guilty?

9 Be gracious to me, O GOD [or LORD], for I am in distress;
    my eye is wasted from grief,
    my soul and my body also.
10 For my life is spent with sorrow,
    and my years with sighing;
    my strength fails because of my misery,
    and my bones waste away.
11 I am the scorn of all my adversaries,
    a horror to my neighbors,
    an object of dread to my acquaintances;
    those who see me in the street flee from me.
12 I have passed out of mind like one who is dead;
    I have become like a broken vessel.
13 For I hear the whispering of many—
    terror on every side!—
    as they scheme together against me,
    as they plot to take my life.
14 But I trust in you, O GOD [or LORD],
    I say, "You are my God."
15 My times are in your hand;
    deliver me from the hand of my enemies and persecutors!
16 Let your face shine on your servant;
    save me in your steadfast love!

Lesson 2 ~ Philippians 2:5-11

Paul speaks about the Sovereign Jesus Christ.

5 Have this mind among yourselves, which is yours in Christ Jesus, 6 who, though being in the form of God, did not count equality with God a thing to be grasped, 7 but emptied Christ's self, taking the form of a servant, being born in the likeness of human beings. 8 And being found in human form, Christ humbled Christ's self and became obedient unto death, even death on a cross. 9 Therefore God has highly exalted Jesus and bestowed on Jesus the name which is above every name, 10 that at the name of Jesus every knee should bow, in heaven and on earth and under the earth, 11 and every tongue confess that Jesus Christ is Sovereign [or Lord], to the glory of God the Father [and Mother*].

*Addition to the text. See "Metaphor" and "God the Father and Mother" in the Appendix.

Matthew tells of the Last Supper and of Jesus' passion.

14 Then one of the twelve, who was called Judas Iscariot, went to the chief priests 15 and said, "What will you give me if I deliver Jesus to you?" And they paid Judas thirty pieces of silver. 16 And from that moment he sought an opportunity to betray Jesus.

17 Now on the first day of Unleavened Bread the disciples came to Jesus, saying, "Where will you have us prepare for you to eat the passover?" 18 Jesus replied, "Go into the city to a certain one, and say, 'The Teacher says, My time is at hand; I will keep the passover at your house with my disciples.'" 19 And the disciples did as Jesus had directed them, and they prepared the passover.

20 When it was evening, Jesus sat at table with the twelve disciples, 21 and as they were eating, said, "Truly, I say to you, one of you will betray me." 22 And they were very sorrowful, and began to say to Jesus one after another, "Is it I, Sovereign [[or Lord]]?" 23 Jesus answered, "The one who has dipped a hand in the dish with me, will betray me. 24 The Human One○ goes as it is written, but woe to that person by whom the Human One○ is betrayed! It would have been better for that one not to have been born." 25 Judas, who betrayed Jesus, said, "Is it I, Teacher?" Jesus said to him, "You have said so."

26 Now as they were eating, Jesus took bread, and blessed, and broke it, and gave it to the disciples and said, "Take, eat; this is my body." 27 Then taking a cup, and having given thanks, Jesus gave it to them, saying, "Drink of it, all of you; 28 for this is my blood of the covenant, which is poured out for many for the forgiveness of sins. 29 I tell you I shall not drink again of this fruit of the vine until that day when I drink it new with you in the realm✭ of God."

30 And when they had sung a hymn, they went out to the Mount of Olives. 31 Then Jesus said to them, "You will all fall away because of me this night; for it is written, 'I will strike the shepherd, and the sheep of the flock will be scattered.' 32 But after I am raised up, I will go before you to Galilee." 33 Peter declared to Jesus, "Though they all fall away because of you, I will never fall away." 34 Jesus said to him, "Truly, I say to you, this very night, before the cock crows, you will deny me three times." 35 Peter said to Jesus, "Even if I must die with you, I will not deny you." And so said all the disciples.

36 Then Jesus went with them to a place called Gethsemane, and said to the disciples, "Sit here, while I go yonder and pray." 37 And taking with him Peter and the two sons of Zebedee, he began to be sorrowful and

---

○RSV *Son of man*. See Appendix.
✭RSV *kingdom*. See Appendix.

troubled. ³⁸ Then he said to them, "My soul is very sorrowful, even to death; remain here, and watch with me." ³⁹ And going a little farther Jesus fell to the ground and prayed, "[God] my Father [and Mother*], if it be possible, let this cup pass from me; nevertheless, not as I will, but as you will." ⁴⁰ And he came and found them sleeping, and said to Peter, "So, could you not watch with me one hour? ⁴¹ Watch and pray that you may not enter into temptation; the spirit indeed is willing, but the flesh is weak." ⁴² Again, for the second time, Jesus went away and prayed, "[God] my Father [and Mother*], if this cannot pass unless I drink it, your will be done." ⁴³ And again he came and found them sleeping, for their eyes were heavy. ⁴⁴ So, leaving them again, he went away and prayed for the third time, saying the same words. ⁴⁵ Then coming to the disciples Jesus said to them, "Are you still sleeping and taking your rest? Behold, the hour is at hand, and the Human One° is betrayed into the hands of sinners. ⁴⁶ Rise, let us be going; see, my betrayer is at hand."

⁴⁷ While Jesus was still speaking, Judas came, one of the twelve, and with him a great crowd with swords and clubs, from the chief priests and the elders of the people. ⁴⁸ Now the betrayer had given them a sign, saying, "The one I shall kiss is the person; seize him." ⁴⁹ And Judas came up to Jesus at once and said, "Hail, Teacher!" And Judas kissed him. ⁵⁰ Jesus said to Judas, "Friend, why are you here?" Then they came up and laid hands on Jesus and seized him. ⁵¹ And one of those who were with Jesus stretched out his hand and drew a sword, and struck the slave of the high priest, and cut off his ear. ⁵² Then Jesus said to the disciple, "Put your sword back into its place; for all who take the sword will perish by the sword. ⁵³ Do you think that I cannot appeal to [God] my Father [and Mother*], who will at once send me more than twelve legions of angels? ⁵⁴ But how then should the scriptures be fulfilled, that it must be so?" ⁵⁵ At that hour Jesus said to the crowds, "Have you come out as against a robber, with swords and clubs to capture me? Day after day I sat in the temple teaching, and you did not seize me. ⁵⁶ But all this has taken place, that the scriptures of the prophets might be fulfilled." Then all the disciples forsook him and fled.

⁵⁷ Then those who had seized Jesus led him to Caiaphas the high priest, where the scribes and the elders had gathered. ⁵⁸ But Peter followed Jesus at a distance, as far as the courtyard of the high priest, and going inside, Peter sat with the guards to see the end. ⁵⁹ Now the chief priests and the whole council sought false testimony against Jesus that they might put him to death, ⁶⁰ but they found none, though many false witnesses came forward. At last two came forward ⁶¹ and said, "This person said, 'I am able to destroy the temple of God, and to build it in three days.'" ⁶² And the high priest stood up and said, "Have you no answer to make? What is it

---

*Addition to the text. See "Metaphor" and "God the Father and Mother" in the Appendix.
°RSV Son of man. See Appendix.

that these people testify against you?" 63 But Jesus was silent. And the high priest said to him, "I adjure you by the living God, tell us if you are the Christ, the Child◇ of God." 64 Jesus replied, "You have said so. But I tell you, hereafter you will see the Human One○ seated at the right hand of Power, and coming on the clouds of heaven." 65 Then the high priest tore his robes, and said, "He has uttered blasphemy. Why do we still need witnesses? You have now heard the blasphemy. 66 What is your judgment?" They answered, "He deserves death." 67 Then they spat in Jesus' face, and struck him; and some slapped him, 68 saying, "Prophesy to us, you Christ! Who is it that struck you?"

69 Now Peter was sitting outside in the courtyard. And a maid came up and said, "You also were with Jesus the Galilean." 70 But Peter denied it before them all, saying, "I do not know what you mean." 71 And when Peter went out to the porch, another maid saw him, and she said to the bystanders, "This one was with Jesus of Nazareth." 72 And again Peter denied it with an oath, "I do not know the man." 73 After a little while the bystanders came up and said to Peter, "Certainly you are also one of them, for your accent betrays you." 74 Then Peter began to invoke a curse on himself and to swear, "I do not know the man." And immediately the cock crowed. 75 And Peter remembered the saying of Jesus, "Before the cock crows, you will deny me three times." And Peter went out and wept bitterly.

27:1 When the morning came, all the chief priests and the elders of the people took counsel against Jesus to put him to death; 2 and they bound him and led him away and delivered him to Pilate the governor.

3 When Judas, the betrayer, saw that Jesus was condemned, Judas repented and brought back the thirty pieces of silver to the chief priests and the elders, 4 saying, "I have sinned in betraying innocent blood." They said, "What is that to us? See to it yourself." 5 And throwing down the pieces of silver in the temple, Judas departed, and went and hanged himself. 6 But the chief priests, taking the pieces of silver, said, "It is not lawful to put them into the treasury, since they are blood money." 7 So they took counsel, and bought with them the potter's field, to bury strangers in. 8 Therefore that field has been called the Field of Blood to this day. 9 Then was fulfilled what had been spoken by the prophet Jeremiah, saying, "And they took the thirty pieces of silver, the price of the one on whom a price had been set by some of the children of Israel, 10 and they gave them for the potter's field, as the Sovereign [or Lord] directed me."

11 Now Jesus stood before the governor; and the governor asked, "Are you the King of the Jews?" Jesus said, "You have said so." 12 But when accused by the chief priests and elders, Jesus made no answer. 13 Then Pilate said to him, "Do you not hear how many things they testify against

◇RSV Son. See Appendix.
○RSV Son of man. See Appendix.

you?" ¹⁴ But Jesus gave Pilate no answer, not even to a single charge; so that the governor wondered greatly.

¹⁵ Now at the feast the governor was accustomed to release for the crowd any one prisoner whom they wanted. ¹⁶ And they had then a notorious prisoner, called Barabbas. ¹⁷ So when they had gathered, Pilate said to them, "Whom do you want me to release for you, Barabbas or Jesus who is called Christ?" ¹⁸ For Pilate knew that it was out of envy that they had delivered up Jesus. ¹⁹ Besides, while Pilate was sitting on the judgment seat, his wife sent word, "Have nothing to do with that righteous person, for I have suffered much over him today in a dream." ²⁰ Now the chief priests and the elders persuaded the people to ask for Barabbas and destroy Jesus. ²¹ The governor again said to them, "Which of the two do you want me to release for you?" And they said, "Barabbas." ²² Pilate said to them, "Then what shall I do with Jesus who is called Christ?" They all said, "Let him be crucified." ²³ And Pilate said, "Why, what evil has he done?" But they shouted all the more, "Let him be crucified."

²⁴ So when Pilate saw that nothing was being gained, but rather that a riot was beginning, he took water and washed his hands before the crowd, saying, "I am innocent of this one's blood; see to it yourselves." ²⁵ And all the people answered, "His blood be on us and on our children!" ²⁶ Then Pilate released for them Barabbas, and having scourged Jesus, delivered him to be crucified.

²⁷ Then the soldiers of the governor took Jesus into the praetorium, and they gathered the whole battalion before him. ²⁸ And they stripped him and put a scarlet robe upon him, ²⁹ and plaiting a crown of thorns they put it on his head, and put a reed in his right hand. And kneeling down, they mocked Jesus, saying, "Hail, King of the Jews!" ³⁰ And they spat upon him, and took the reed and struck him on the head. ³¹ And when they had mocked Jesus, they stripped him of the robe, and put his own clothes on him, and led him away to be crucified.

³² As they went out, they came upon a Cyrenian, Simon by name, whom they compelled to carry Jesus' cross. ³³ And when they came to a place called Golgotha (which means the place of a skull), ³⁴ they offered Jesus wine to drink, mingled with gall; but after tasting it, he would not drink it. ³⁵ And when they had crucified him, they divided his garments among them by casting lots; ³⁶ then they sat down and kept watch over him there. ³⁷ And over Jesus' head they put the charge against him, which read, "This is Jesus the King of the Jews." ³⁸ Then two robbers were crucified with him, one on the right and one on the left. ³⁹ And those who passed by derided him, wagging their heads ⁴⁰ and saying, "You who would destroy the temple and build it in three days, save yourself! If you are the Child◇ of God, come down from the cross." ⁴¹ So also the chief priests, with the scribes and elders, mocked Jesus, saying, ⁴² "This one

---

◇RSV *Son*. See Appendix.

saved others, but cannot save himself. He is the King of Israel; let him come down now from the cross, and we will believe in him. ⁴³ He trusts in God; let God deliver him now, if God desires to; for he said, 'I am the Child◇ of God.'" ⁴⁴ And the robbers who were crucified with him also reviled him in the same way.

⁴⁵ Now from the sixth hour there was darkness over all the land until the ninth hour. ⁴⁶ And about the ninth hour Jesus cried with a loud voice, "Eli, Eli, lama sabachthani?" that is, "My God, my God, why have you forsaken me?" ⁴⁷ And some of the bystanders hearing it said, "He is calling Elijah." ⁴⁸ And one of them at once ran and took a sponge, filled it with vinegar, and put it on a reed, and gave it to Jesus to drink. ⁴⁹ But the others said, "Wait, let us see whether Elijah will come to save him." ⁵⁰ And Jesus cried again with a loud voice and yielded up his spirit.

⁵¹ And with that, the curtain of the temple was torn in two, from top to bottom; and the earth shook, and the rocks were split; ⁵² the tombs also were opened, and many bodies of the saints who had fallen asleep were raised, ⁵³ and coming out of the tombs after Jesus' resurrection they went into the holy city and appeared to many. ⁵⁴ When the centurion and those who were with him, keeping watch over Jesus, saw the earthquake and what took place, they were filled with awe, and said, "Truly this was the Child◇ of God!"

⁵⁵ There were also many women there, looking on from afar, who had followed Jesus from Galilee, ministering to him; ⁵⁶ among whom were Mary Magdalene, and Mary the mother of James and Joseph, and the mother of the sons of Zebedee.

⁵⁷ When it was evening, there came a rich man from Arimathea, named Joseph, who also was a disciple of Jesus. ⁵⁸ Joseph went to Pilate and asked for the body of Jesus. Then Pilate ordered it to be given to him. ⁵⁹ And Joseph took the body, and wrapped it in a clean linen shroud, ⁶⁰ and laid it in his own new tomb, which he had hewn in the rock; and he rolled a great stone to the door of the tomb, and departed. ⁶¹ Mary Magdalene and the other Mary were there, sitting opposite the sepulchre.

⁶² Next day, that is, after the day of Preparation, the chief priests and the Pharisees gathered before Pilate ⁶³ and said, "Sir, we remember how that impostor, while still alive, said, 'After three days I will rise again.' ⁶⁴ Therefore order the sepulchre to be made secure until the third day, lest the disciples go and steal the body, and tell the people, 'He has risen from the dead,' and the last fraud will be worse than the first." ⁶⁵ Pilate said to them, "You have a guard of soldiers; go, make it as secure as you can." ⁶⁶ So they went and made the sepulchre secure by sealing the stone and setting a guard.

◇RSV *Son*. See Appendix.

LENT 6, PALM SUNDAY

Lesson 1 ~ Isaiah 50:4-9a

The prophet Isaiah tells of the suffering of the one who obeys God.

⁴ The Sovereign [[*or* Lord]] GOD has given me
    the tongue of those who are taught,
  that I may know how to sustain with a word
    one who is weary.
Morning by morning God wakens,
    God wakens my ear
  to hear as those who are taught.
⁵ The Sovereign [[*or* Lord]] GOD has opened my ear,
    and I was not rebellious,
  I turned not backward.
⁶ I gave my back to the smiters,
    and my cheeks to those who pulled out my beard;
  I hid not my face
    from shame and spitting.
⁷ For the Sovereign [[*or* Lord]] GOD helps me;
    therefore I have not been confounded;
  therefore I have set my face like a flint,
    and I know that I shall not be put to shame;
⁸   the one who vindicates me is near.
Who will contend with me?
    Let us stand together,
Who are my adversaries?
    Let them come near to me.
⁹ The Sovereign [[*or* Lord]] GOD helps me;
  who will declare me guilty?

Psalm 118:19-29

¹⁹ Open to me the gates of righteousness,
    that I may enter through them
    and give thanks to GOD [[*or* the LORD]].
²⁰ This is the gate of GOD [[*or* the LORD]];
    the righteous shall enter through it.
²¹ I thank you that you have answered me
    and have become my salvation.

22 The stone which the builders rejected
　　has become the head of the corner.
23 This is GOD's [[*or* the LORD's]] doing;
　　it is marvelous in our eyes.
24 This is the day which GOD [[*or* the LORD]] has made;
　　let us rejoice and be glad in it.
25 Save us, we beseech you, O GOD [[*or* LORD]]!
　　O GOD [[*or* LORD]], we beseech you, give us success!
26 Blessed be the one who enters in the name of GOD [[*or* the LORD]]!
　　We bless you from the house of GOD [[*or* the LORD]].
27 The SOVEREIGN [[*or* LORD]] is God,
　　who has caused light to shine upon us.
　Bind the festal procession with branches,
　　up to the horns of the altar!
28 You are my God, and I will give thanks to you;
　　you are my God, I will extol you.
29 O give thanks to GOD [[*or* the LORD]], for God is good;
　　for God's steadfast love endures forever!

Lesson 2 ~ Philippians 2:5-11

Paul speaks about the Sovereign Jesus Christ.

5 Have this mind among yourselves, which is yours in Christ Jesus,
6 who, though being in the form of God, did not count equality with God a
thing to be grasped, 7 but emptied Christ's self, taking the form of a
servant, being born in the likeness of human beings. 8 And being found in
human form, Christ humbled Christ's self and became obedient unto
death, even death on a cross. 9 Therefore God has highly exalted Jesus and
bestowed on Jesus the name which is above every name, 10 that at the
name of Jesus every knee should bow, in heaven and on earth and under
the earth, 11 and every tongue confess that Jesus Christ is Sovereign [[*or*
Lord]], to the glory of God the Father [*and Mother**].

---

*Addition to the text. See "Metaphor" and "God the Father and Mother" in the Appendix.

Matthew describes the triumphal entry of Jesus into Jerusalem.

¹ And when they drew near to Jerusalem and came to Bethphage, to the Mount of Olives, then Jesus sent two disciples, ² saying to them, "Go into the village opposite you, and immediately you will find a donkey tied, and a colt with it; untie them and bring them to me. ³ If anyone says anything to you, you shall say, 'The Sovereign [[or Lord]] has need of them,' and they will be sent immediately." ⁴ This took place to fulfill what was spoken by the prophet, saying,

⁵ "Tell this to Zion,
Your ruler□ is coming to you,
humble, and mounted on a donkey,
and on a colt, the foal of a donkey."

⁶ The disciples went and did as Jesus had directed them; ⁷ they brought the donkey and the colt, and put their garments on them, and Jesus sat thereon. ⁸ Most of the crowd spread their garments on the road, and others cut branches from the trees and spread them on the road. ⁹ And the crowds that went before Jesus and that followed shouted, "Hosanna to the Son of David! Blessed is the one who comes in the name of the Soveréign [[or Lord]]! Hosanna in the highest!" ¹⁰ And when Jesus entered Jerusalem, all the city was stirred, saying, "Who is this?" ¹¹ And the crowds said, "This is the prophet Jesus from Nazareth of Galilee."

□RSV *king*. See Appendix.

MONDAY OF HOLY WEEK

Lesson 1 ～ Isaiah 42:1-9

God speaks through the prophet Isaiah about God's servant.

¹ Here is my servant, whom I uphold,
    my chosen, in whom my soul delights;
  I have put my Spirit upon my servant,
    who will bring forth justice to the nations.
² My servant will not cry or speak out,
    nor be heard in the street;
³ my servant will not break a bruised reed,
    nor quench a dimly burning wick,
    but will faithfully bring forth justice.
⁴ My servant will not fail or be discouraged
    till justice has been established in the earth;
    and the coastlands wait for the servant's law.
⁵ Thus says God, the SOVEREIGN [[or LORD]],
    who created the heavens and stretched them out,
    who spread forth the earth and what comes from it,
  who gives breath to the people upon it
    and spirit to those who walk in it:
⁶ "I am the SOVEREIGN [[or LORD]], I have called you in righteousness,
    I have taken you by the hand and kept you;
  I have given you as a covenant to the people,
    a light to the nations,
⁷   to open the eyes that are blind,
  to bring out the prisoners from the dungeon,
    from the prison those who sit with no light.
⁸ I am the SOVEREIGN [[or LORD]], that is my name;
    my glory I give to no other,
    nor my praise to graven images.
⁹ Now the former things have come to pass,
    and new things I declare;
  before they spring forth
    I tell you of them."

⁵ Your steadfast love, O GOD [[or LORD]], extends to the heavens,
   your faithfulness to the clouds.
⁶ Your righteousness is like the mountains of God,
   your judgments are like the great deep;
   all living things you save, O GOD [[or LORD]].
⁷ How precious is your steadfast love, O God!
   All people take refuge in the shadow of your wings.
⁸ They feast on the abundance of your house,
   and you give them drink from the river of your delights.
⁹ For with you is the fountain of life;
   in your light do we see light.
¹⁰ O continue your steadfast love to those who know you,
   and your salvation to the upright of heart!

Lesson 2 ∼ Hebrews 9:11-15

Christ is the mediator of a new covenant.

¹¹ But when Christ appeared as a high priest of the good things that have come, then through the greater and more perfect tent (not made with hands, that is, not of this creation) ¹² Christ entered once for all into the Holy Place, taking not the blood of goats and calves but Christ's own blood, thus securing an eternal redemption. ¹³ For if the sprinkling of defiled persons with the blood of goats and bulls and with the ashes of a heifer sanctifies for the purification of the flesh, ¹⁴ how much more shall the blood of Christ—who through the eternal Spirit offered Christ's self as an unblemished sacrifice to God—purify your conscience from dead works to serve the living God.

¹⁵ Therefore Christ is the mediator of a new covenant, so that those who are called may receive the promised eternal inheritance, since a death has occurred which redeems them from the transgressions under the first covenant.

Mary of Bethany anoints the feet of Jesus.

¹ Six days before the Passover, Jesus came to Bethany, where Lazarus was, whom Jesus had raised from the dead. ²There they made Jesus a supper; Martha served, and Lazarus was one of those at the table. ³Mary took a pound of costly ointment of pure nard and anointed the feet of Jesus and wiped them with her hair; and the house was filled with the fragrance of the ointment. ⁴But Judas Iscariot, one of the disciples (the one who was to betray Jesus), said, ⁵"Why was this ointment not sold for three hundred denarii and given to the poor?" ⁶This Judas said, not that he cared for the poor but because he was a thief, and having the money box, he used to take what was put into it. ⁷Jesus said, "Let her alone, let her keep it for the day of my burial. ⁸The poor you always have with you, but you do not always have me."

⁹When the great crowd of the Jews learned that Jesus was there, they came, not only on account of Jesus but also to see Lazarus, whom Jesus had raised from the dead. ¹⁰So the chief priests planned to put Lazarus also to death, ¹¹because on account of him many of the Jews were going away and believing in Jesus.

TUESDAY OF HOLY WEEK

Lesson 1 ~ Isaiah 49:1-7

The servant of God speaks through the prophet Isaiah.

¹ Listen to me, O coastlands,
  and hearken, you nations from afar.
GOD [*or* The LORD] called me from the womb,
  and from the body of my mother God named my name.
² God made my mouth like a sharp sword,
  in the shadow of God's hand I was hidden;
God made me a polished arrow,
  in the quiver I was hidden away.
³ And God said to me, "You are my servant,
  Israel, in whom I will be glorified."
⁴ But I said, "I have labored in vain,
  I have spent my strength for nothing and vanity;
yet surely my right is with the SOVEREIGN [*or* LORD],
  and my recompense with my God."
⁵ And now GOD [*or* the LORD] says,
  who formed me from the womb to be God's servant,
to bring Jacob back to God,
  and that Israel might be gathered to God,
for I am honored in the eyes of the SOVEREIGN [*or* LORD],
  and my God has become my strength—
⁶ God says:
"It is too light a thing that you should be my servant
  to raise up the tribes of Jacob
  and to restore the preserved of Israel;
I will give you as a light to the nations,
  that my salvation may reach to the end of the earth."
⁷ Thus says the SOVEREIGN [*or* LORD],
  the Redeemer of Israel and Israel's Holy One,
to one deeply despised, abhorred by the nations,
  the servant of rulers:
"Monarchs□ shall see and arise;
  rulers, and they shall prostrate themselves;
because of the SOVEREIGN [*or* LORD], who is faithful,
  the Holy One of Israel, who has chosen you."

□RSV *Kings*. See Appendix.

1 In you, O GOD [[*or* LORD]], do I take refuge;
   let me never be put to shame!
2 In your righteousness deliver me and rescue me;
   incline your ear to me, and save me!
3 Be to me a rock of refuge,
   a strong fortress, to save me,
   for you are my rock and my fortress.
4 Rescue me, O my God, from the hand of the wicked,
   from the grasp of the unjust and the cruel.
5 For you, O God [[*or* Lord]], are my hope,
   my trust, O GOD [[*or* LORD]], from my youth.
6 Upon you I have leaned from my birth;
   you are the one who took me from my mother's womb.
  My praise is continually of you.
7 I have been as a portent to many;
   but you are my strong refuge.
8 My mouth is filled with your praise,
   and with your glory all the day.
9 Do not cast me off in the time of old age;
   forsake me not when my strength is spent.
10 For my enemies speak concerning me,
   those who watch for my life consult together,
11 and say, "God has forsaken the one who trusted;
   pursue and seize the forsaken one,
   for there is no one to give deliverance."
12 O God, be not far from me;
   O my God, make haste to help me!

Lesson 2 ~ 1 Corinthians 1:18-31

Paul writes to the Christians at Corinth about the wisdom of God.

[18] For the word of the cross is folly to those who are perishing, but to us who are being saved it is the power of God. [19] For it is written,

"I will destroy the wisdom of the wise,
and the cleverness of the clever I will thwart."

[20] Where is the wise one? Where is the scribe? Where is the debater of this age? Has not God made foolish the wisdom of the world? [21] For since, in the wisdom of God, the world did not know God through wisdom, it pleased God through the folly of what we preach to save those who believe. [22] For Jews demand signs and Greeks seek wisdom, [23] but we preach Christ crucified, a stumbling block to Jews and folly to Gentiles, [24] but to those who are called, both Jews and Greeks, Christ the power of God and the wisdom of God. [25] For the foolishness of God is wiser than human wisdom, and the weakness of God is stronger than human strength.

[26] For consider your call, my friends; not many of you were wise according to worldly standards, not many were powerful, not many were of noble birth; [27] but God chose what is foolish in the world to shame the wise, God chose what is weak in the world to shame the strong, [28] God chose what is low and despised in the world, even things that are not, to bring to nothing things that are, [29] so that no human being might boast in the presence of God. [30] God is the source of your life in Christ Jesus, whom God made our wisdom, our righteousness and sanctification and redemption; [31] therefore, as it is written, "Let the one who boasts, boast of the Sovereign [[or Lord]]."

Jesus speaks of the glorification of the Human One.

20 Now among those who went up to worship at the feast were some Greeks. 21 So these came to Philip, who was from Bethsaida in Galilee, and said, "Sir, we wish to see Jesus." 22 Philip went and told Andrew; Andrew went with Philip and they told Jesus. 23 And Jesus answered them, "The hour has come for the Human One○ to be glorified. 24 Truly, truly, I say to you, unless a grain of wheat falls into the earth and dies, it remains alone; but if it dies, it bears much fruit. 25 Whoever loves their life loses it, and whoever hates their life in this world will keep it for eternal life. 26 Anyone who serves me must follow me; and where I am, there shall my servant be also; anyone who serves me will be honored by [*God*] the Father [*and Mother**].

27 "Now is my soul troubled. And what shall I say? 'God,⊗ save me from this hour'? No, for this purpose I have come to this hour. 28 God,⊗ glorify your name." Then a voice came from heaven, "I have glorified it, and I will glorify it again." 29 The crowd standing by heard it and said that it had thundered. Others said, "An angel has spoken to him." 30 Jesus answered, "This voice has come for your sake, not for mine. 31 Now is the judgment of this world, now shall the ruler of this world be cast out; 32 and I, when I am lifted up from the earth, will draw all people to myself." 33 Jesus said this to show by what death he was to die. 34 The crowd answered, "We have heard from the law that the Christ remains forever. How can you say that the Human One○ must be lifted up? Who is this Human One○?" 35 Jesus said to them, "The light is with you for a little longer. Walk while you have the light, lest the night overtake you; those who walk in the night do not know where they are going. 36 While you have the light, believe in the light, that you may become children of light."

Having said this, Jesus departed and hid from them.

○RSV *Son of man*. See Appendix.
*Addition to the text. See "Metaphor" and "God the Father and Mother" in the Appendix.
⊗RSV *Father*. See Appendix.

WEDNESDAY OF HOLY WEEK

Lesson 1 ~ Isaiah 50:4-9a

The prophet Isaiah tells of the suffering of the one who obeys God.

⁴ The Sovereign [[or Lord]] GOD has given me
  the tongue of those who are taught,
that I may know how to sustain with a word
  one who is weary.
Morning by morning God wakens,
  God wakens my ear
  to hear as those who are taught.
⁵ The Sovereign [[or Lord]] GOD has opened my ear,
  and I was not rebellious,
  I turned not backward.
⁶ I gave my back to the smiters,
  and my cheeks to those who pulled out my beard;
I hid not my face
  from shame and spitting.
⁷ For the Sovereign [[or Lord]] GOD helps me;
  therefore I have not been confounded;
therefore I have set my face like a flint,
  and I know that I shall not be put to shame;
⁸   the one who vindicates me is near.
Who will contend with me?
  Let us stand together.
Who are my adversaries?
  Let them come near to me.
⁹ The Sovereign [[or Lord]] GOD helps me;
  who will declare me guilty?

Psalm 70

¹ Be pleased, O God, to deliver me!
O GOD [[*or* LORD]], make haste to help me!
² Let them be put to shame and confusion
who seek my life!
Let them be turned back and brought to dishonor
who desire my hurt!
³ Let them be appalled because of their shame
who say, "Aha, Aha!"
⁴ May all who seek you
rejoice and be glad in you!
May those who love your salvation
say evermore, "God is great!"
⁵ But I am poor and needy;
hasten to me, O God!
You are my help and my deliverer;
O GOD [[*or* LORD]], do not tarry!

Lesson 2 ~ Hebrews 12:1-3

Jesus is the pioneer and perfecter of our faith.

¹ Therefore, since we are surrounded by so great a cloud of witnesses, let us also lay aside every weight, and sin which clings so closely, and let us run with perseverance the race that is set before us, ² looking to Jesus the pioneer and perfecter of our faith, who for the joy that was set before him endured the cross, despising the shame, and is seated at the right hand of the throne of God.

³ Consider the one who endured from sinners such hostility against himself, so that you may not grow weary or fainthearted.

Judas is identified as the one who will betray Jesus.

²¹ Having spoken thus, Jesus was troubled in spirit, and testified, "Truly, truly, I say to you, one of you will betray me." ²²The disciples looked at one another, uncertain of whom he spoke. ²³One of the disciples, whom Jesus loved, was lying close to his breast; ²⁴so Simon Peter beckoned to that disciple and said, "Tell us who it is of whom he speaks." ²⁵So lying thus, close to the breast of Jesus, the one whom Jesus loved said to him, "Sovereign [[or Lord]], who is it?" ²⁶Jesus answered, "It is the one to whom I shall give this morsel when I have dipped it." Having dipped the morsel, he gave it to Judas, the son of Simon Iscariot. ²⁷Then after the morsel, Satan entered into Judas. Jesus said to him, "What you are going to do, do quickly." ²⁸Now no one at the table knew why Jesus said this to Judas. ²⁹Some thought that, because Judas had the money box, Jesus was telling him, "Buy what we need for the feast," or that Judas should give something to the poor. ³⁰So, after receiving the morsel, Judas immediately went out; and it was night.

MAUNDY THURSDAY

Lesson 1 ~ Exodus 12:1-14

God instructs Israel about keeping the Passover.

¹ GOD [[*or* The LORD]] said to Moses and Aaron in the land of Egypt, ² "This month shall be for you the beginning of months; it shall be the first month of the year for you. ³ Tell all the congregation of Israel that on the tenth day of this month each of them shall take a lamb according to their families' houses, a lamb for a household; ⁴ and if the household is too small for a lamb, two households shall take according to the number of persons; according to what each can eat you shall make your count for the lamb. ⁵ Your lamb shall be without blemish, a male a year old; you shall take it from the sheep or from the goats; ⁶ and you shall keep it until the fourteenth day of this month, when the whole assembly of the congregation of Israel shall kill their lambs in the evening. ⁷ Then they shall take some of the blood, and put it on the two doorposts and the lintel of the houses in which they eat them. ⁸ They shall eat the flesh that night, roasted; with unleavened bread and bitter herbs they shall eat it. ⁹ Do not eat any of it raw or boiled with water, but roasted, its head with its legs and its inner parts. ¹⁰ And you shall let none of it remain until the morning, anything that remains until the morning you shall burn. ¹¹ In this manner you shall eat it: your loins girded, your sandals on your feet, and your staff in your hand; and you shall eat it in haste. It is the passover of GOD [[*or* the LORD]]. ¹² For I will pass through the land of Egypt that night, and I will smite all the firstborn in the land of Egypt, both human and animal; and on all the gods of Egypt I will execute judgments: I am the SOVEREIGN [[*or* LORD]]. ¹³ The blood shall be a sign for you, upon the houses where you are; and when I see the blood, I will pass over you, and no plague shall fall upon you to destroy you, when I smite the land of Egypt.

¹⁴ "This day shall be for you a memorial day, and you shall keep it as a feast to GOD [[*or* the LORD]]; throughout your generations you shall observe it as an ordinance forever."

Psalm 116:12-19

(Psalm 116:12-19 is used at the Eucharist on Maundy [Holy] Thursday. Psalm 89:20–21, 24, 26, below, is used at the Chrism service.)

12 What shall I render to GOD [[*or* the LORD]]
    for all God's bounty to me?
13 I will lift up the cup of salvation
    and call on the name of GOD [[*or* the LORD]],
14 I will pay my vows to GOD [[*or* the LORD]]
    in the presence of all God's people.
15 Precious in the sight of GOD [[*or* the LORD]]
    is the death of the saints.
16 O GOD [[*or* LORD]], I am your servant;
    I am your servant, the child of your womanservant.
    You have loosed my bonds.
17 I will offer to you the sacrifice of thanksgiving
    and call on the name of GOD [[*or* the LORD]].
18 I will pay my vows to GOD [[*or* the LORD]]
    in the presence of all God's people,
19 in the courts of the house of GOD [[*or* the LORD]],
    in your midst, O Jerusalem.
    Praise GOD [[*or* the LORD]]!

Psalm 89:20-21, 24, 26

20 I have found David, my servant;
    with my holy oil I have anointed him;
21 so that my hand shall ever abide with David,
    my arm also shall strengthen him.
24 My faithfulness and my steadfast love shall be with him,
    and in my name shall David's horn be exalted.
26 He shall cry to me, "You are my Parent,
    my God, and the Rock of my salvation."

Lesson 2 ~ 1 Corinthians 11:23-26

Paul writes to the Corinthians concerning the Last Supper.

23 For I received from the Sovereign [[or Lord]] what I also delivered to you, that the Sovereign [[or Lord]] Jesus on the night of the betrayal took bread, 24 and after giving thanks, broke it, and said, "This is my body which is for you. Do this in remembrance of me." 25 In the same way also the cup, after supper, saying, "This cup is the new covenant in my blood. Do this, as often as you drink it, in remembrance of me." 26 For as often as you eat this bread and drink the cup, you proclaim the Sovereign's [[or Lord's]] death until the Sovereign [[or Lord]] comes.

Gospel ~ John 13:1-15

Jesus washes the disciples' feet.

1 Now before the feast of the Passover, when Jesus knew that the hour had come to depart out of this world to [God] the Father [and Mother*], having loved his own who were in the world, he loved them to the end. 2 And during supper, when the devil had already put it into the heart of Judas Iscariot, Simon's son, to betray him, 3 Jesus, knowing that God⊗ had given all things into Jesus' own hands and that he had come from God and was going to God, 4 rose from supper, laid aside his garments, and girded himself with a towel. 5 Then Jesus poured water into a basin, and began to wash the disciples' feet, and to wipe them with the towel with which he was girded. 6 He came to Simon Peter; and Peter said to him, "Sovereign [[or Lord]], do you wash my feet?" 7 Jesus answered, "What I am doing you do not know now, but afterward you will understand." 8 Peter said to him, "You shall never wash my feet." Jesus answered, "If I do not wash you, you have no part in me." 9 Simon Peter said to Jesus, "Sovereign [[or Lord]], not my feet only but also my hands and my head!" 10 Jesus replied, "One who has bathed does not need to wash, except for the feet, but is clean all over; and you are clean, but not every one of you." 11 For he knew who was to betray him; that was why Jesus said, "You are not all clean."

12 Having washed their feet, and put on his garments, and returned to the table, Jesus said to them, "Do you know what I have done to you? 13 You call me Teacher and Sovereign [[or Lord]]; and you are right, for so I am. 14 If I then, your Sovereign [[or Lord]] and Teacher, have washed your feet, you also ought to wash one another's feet. 15 For I have given you an example, that you also should do as I have done to you."

---

*Addition to the text. See "Metaphor" and "God the Father and Mother" in the Appendix.
⊗RSV *the Father*. See Appendix.

GOOD FRIDAY

Lesson 1 ~ Isaiah 52:13–53:12

Isaiah writes of the Suffering Servant.

¹³ My servant shall prosper,
  shall be exalted and lifted up,
  and shall be very high.
¹⁴ As many were astonished at the one
  whose appearance was so marred, beyond human semblance,
  and whose form beyond that of human beings,
¹⁵ so many nations will be startled;
  rulers[□] shall shut their mouths because of my servant;
 for that which has not been told them they shall see,
  and that which they have not heard they shall understand.
^{53:1} Who has believed what we have heard?
  And to whom has the arm of GOD [[or the LORD]] been revealed?
² For the servant grew up before God like a young plant,
  and like a root out of dry ground,
 with no form or comeliness that we should admire,
  and no beauty that we should desire.
³ The servant was despised and rejected by everyone,
  was full of sorrows, and acquainted with grief,
 and as one from whom people hide their faces,
  was despised and not esteemed by us.
⁴ Surely this one has borne our griefs
  and carried our sorrows;
 yet we esteemed the servant stricken,
  smitten by God, and afflicted.
⁵ But this servant was wounded for our transgressions,
  was bruised for our iniquities,
 bore the chastisement that made us whole
  and the stripes by which we are healed.
⁶ All we like sheep have gone astray;
  we have turned everyone to our own way;
 and GOD [[or the LORD]] has laid on this one
  the iniquity of us all.
⁷ The servant was oppressed, and was afflicted,
  yet did not say a word;
 like a lamb that is led to the slaughter,
  and like a ewe that before her shearers is dumb,
  the servant did not say a word.

□RSV *kings*. See Appendix.

⁸ By oppression and judgment the servant was taken away;
    and as for that one's generation, who considered
  that the servant was cut off out of the land of the living,
    stricken for the transgression of my people?
⁹ Although the servant had done no violence
    and had spoken no deceit,
  the servant was buried with the wicked,
    and with the rich in death.
¹⁰ Yet it was the will of GOD ⟦or the LORD⟧ to bruise
    and put to grief this one,
  who, after choosing to become an offering for sin,
    shall see offspring, and enjoy long life;
  the will of GOD ⟦or the LORD⟧ shall prosper in the servant's hand;
¹¹   my servant shall see the fruit of the soul's travail and be satisfied;
  by knowledge shall the righteous one, my servant,
    make many to be accounted righteous,
    and shall bear their iniquities.
¹² Therefore I will divide for this one a portion with the great,
    and my servant shall divide the spoil with the strong,
  because my servant poured out life and died,
    and was numbered with the transgressors,
  yet bore the sin of many,
    and made intercession for the transgressors.

Psalm 22:1-18

1 My God, my God, why have you forsaken me?
   Why are you so far from helping me, from the words of my
     groaning?
2 O my God, I cry by day, but you do not answer;
   and by night, but find no rest.
3 Yet you are holy,
   enthroned on the praises of Israel.
4 In you our ancestors trusted;
   they trusted, and you delivered them.
5 To you they cried, and were saved;
   in you they trusted, and were not disappointed.
6 But I am a worm, not human at all;
   scorned by everyone, and despised by the people.
7 All who see me mock at me,
   they make mouths at me, they wag their heads and say,
8 "You trusted in GOD [or the LORD]; let God deliver you,
   let God rescue you, for God delights in you!"
9 Yet you, O God, are the one who took me from the womb;
   you kept me safe upon my mother's breasts.
10 Upon you I was cast from my birth,
   and since my mother bore me you have been my God.
11 Be not far from me,
   for trouble is near
   and there is none to help.
12 Many bulls encompass me,
   strong bulls of Bashan surround me;
13 they open wide their mouths at me,
   like a ravening and roaring lion.
14 I am poured out like water,
   and all my bones are out of joint;
 my heart is like wax,
   it is melted within my breast;
15 my strength is dried up like a potsherd,
   and my tongue cleaves to my jaws;
   you lay me in the dust of death.
16 Even dogs are round about me;
   a company of evildoers encircle me;
   they have pierced my hands and feet—
17 I can count all my bones—
   they stare and gloat over me;
18 they divide my garments among them,
   and for my raiment they cast lots.

Lesson 2 ~ Hebrews 4:14-16; 5:7-9

Jesus the high priest learns obedience through suffering.

[14] Since then we have a great high priest who has passed through the heavens, Jesus, the Child◇ of God, let us hold fast our confession. [15] For we have not a high priest who is unable to sympathize with our weaknesses, but one who in every respect has been tempted as we are, yet without sin. [16] Let us then with confidence draw near to the throne of grace, that we may receive mercy and find grace to help in time of need.

[5:7] While in the flesh, Jesus offered up prayers and supplications, with loud cries and tears, to the one who was able to save him from death, and was heard for his godly fear. [8] Although a Child◇ [*of God**], Jesus learned obedience through suffering, [9] and being made perfect, became the source of eternal salvation to all who obey Jesus.

Gospel ~ John 18–19 (or 19:17-30)

John tells of the arrest and crucifixion of Jesus.

[1] After praying for the disciples, Jesus went forth with them across the Kidron valley, where there was a garden, which they entered. [2] Now Judas, who betrayed him, also knew the place; for Jesus often met there with the disciples. [3] So Judas, procuring a band of soldiers and some officers from the chief priests and the Pharisees, went there with lanterns and torches and weapons. [4] Then Jesus, knowing all that was to befall him, came forward and said to them, "Whom do you seek?" [5] They answered, "Jesus of Nazareth." Jesus said to them, "I am the one." Judas, the betrayer, was standing with them. [6] When Jesus said to them, "I am the one," they drew back and fell to the ground. [7] Again Jesus asked them, "Whom do you seek?" And they said, "Jesus of Nazareth." [8] He answered, "I told you that I am the one; so, if you seek me, let these others go." [9] This was to fulfill the word which he had spoken, "Of those whom you gave me I lost not one." [10] Then Simon Peter, having a sword, drew it and struck the high priest's slave and cut off his right ear. The slave's name was Malchus. [11] Jesus said to Peter, "Put your sword into its sheath; shall I not drink the cup which [*God*] the Father [*and Mother***] has given me?"

[12] So the band of soldiers and their captain and the officers of the religious authorities▽ seized and bound Jesus. [13] First they led him to Annas, who was the father-in-law of Caiaphas, the high priest that year.

◇RSV 4:14 *Son;* 5:8 *Although he was a Son.* See Appendix.
* Addition to the text.
**Addition to the text. See "Metaphor" and "God the Father and Mother" in the Appendix.
▽RSV *the Jews.* See Appendix.

¹⁴It was Caiaphas who had given counsel to the religious authorities▽ that it was expedient that one person should die for the people.

¹⁵ Simon Peter followed Jesus, and so did another disciple, who was known to the high priest, and who entered the court of the high priest along with Jesus, ¹⁶while Peter stood outside at the door. So the other disciple, who was known to the high priest, went out and spoke to the maid who kept the door, and brought Peter in. ¹⁷The maid who kept the door said to Peter, "Are not you also one of this man's disciples?" Peter said, "I am not." ¹⁸Now the servants and officers had made a charcoal fire, because it was cold, and they were standing and warming themselves; Peter also was with them, standing and warming himself.

¹⁹The high priest then questioned Jesus about his disciples and teaching. ²⁰Jesus answered the high priest, "I have spoken openly to the world; I have always taught in synagogues and in the temple, where all Jews come together; I have said nothing secretly. ²¹Why do you ask me? Ask those who have heard me, what I said to them; they know what I said." ²²When Jesus had said this, one of the officers standing by struck him with his hand, saying, "Is that how you answer the high priest?" ²³Jesus answered the officer, "If I have spoken wrongly, bear witness to the wrong; but if I have spoken rightly, why do you strike me?" ²⁴Annas then sent Jesus bound to Caiaphas the high priest.

²⁵Now Simon Peter was standing and warming himself. They said to him, "Are not you also one of his disciples?" He denied it and said, "I am not." ²⁶One of the servants of the high priest, a relative of the slave whose ear Peter had cut off, asked, "Did I not see you in the garden with him?" ²⁷Peter again denied it; and at once the cock crowed.

²⁸Then they led Jesus from the house of Caiaphas to the praetorium. It was early. They themselves did not enter the praetorium, so that they might not be defiled, but might eat the passover. ²⁹So Pilate went out to them and said, "What accusation do you bring against this person?" ³⁰They answered Pilate, "If this one were not an evildoer, we would not have handed him over." ³¹Pilate said to them, "Take him yourselves and make judgment by your own law." The religious authorities▽ said to Pilate, "It is not lawful for us to put anyone to death." ³²This was to fulfill the word which Jesus had spoken to show by what death he was to die.

³³Pilate entered the praetorium again and called Jesus, and said, "Are you the King of the Jews?" ³⁴Jesus answered, "Do you say this of your own accord, or did others say it to you about me?" ³⁵Pilate answered, "Am I one of you?① Your own nation and the chief priests have handed you over to me; what have you done?" ³⁶Jesus answered, "My dominion☆ is not of

---

▽RSV v. 14 *the Jews;* v. 31 *The Jews.* See Appendix.
①RSV *"Am I a Jew?"*
☆RSV *kingship.* See Appendix.

this world; if my dominion☆ were of this world, my servants would fight, that I might not be handed over to the religious authorities;▽ but my dominion☆ is not from the world." ³⁷Pilate said to Jesus, "So you are a king?" Jesus answered, "You say that I am a king. For this I was born, and for this I have come into the world, to bear witness to the truth. Everyone who is of the truth hears my voice." ³⁸Pilate said to him, "What is truth?"

And having said this, Pilate went out to the religious authorities▽ again, and told them, "I find no crime in this person. ³⁹But you have a custom that I should release someone for you at the Passover; will you have me release for you the King of the Jews?" ⁴⁰They cried out again, "Not Jesus, but Barabbas!" Now Barabbas was a robber.

¹⁹:¹Then Pilate had Jesus scourged. ²And the soldiers plaited a crown of thorns, and put it on Jesus' head, and arrayed him in a purple robe; ³they came up, saying, "Hail, King of the Jews!" and struck him with their hands. ⁴Pilate went out again, and said to them, "See, I am bringing him out to you, that you may know that I find no crime in him." ⁵So Jesus came out, wearing the crown of thorns and the purple robe. Pilate said to them, "Here he is!" ⁶When the chief priests and the officers saw Jesus, they cried out, "Crucify, crucify!" Pilate said to them, "Take him yourselves and crucify him, for I find no crime in him." ⁷The religious authorities▽ answered Pilate, "We have a law, and by that law Jesus ought to die, because he has made himself the Child◇ of God." ⁸Hearing these words, Pilate was the more afraid. ⁹Pilate entered the praetorium again and said to Jesus, "Where are you from?" But Jesus gave no answer. ¹⁰Pilate therefore said to him, "You will not speak to me? Do you not know that I have power to release you, and power to crucify you?" ¹¹Jesus replied, "You would have no power over me unless it had been given you from above; therefore the one who delivered me to you has the greater sin."

¹²Upon this Pilate sought to release Jesus, but the religious authorities▽ cried out, "If you release this person, you are not Caesar's friend; everyone who claims to be a king opposes Caesar." ¹³Hearing these words, Pilate brought Jesus out and sat down on the judgment seat at a place called The Pavement, and in Hebrew, Gabbatha. ¹⁴Now it was the day of Preparation of the Passover; it was about the sixth hour. Pilate said to the Jews, "Behold your King!" ¹⁵They cried out, "Away, away with him, crucify him!" Pilate said to them, "Shall I crucify your King?" The chief priests answered, "We have no king but Caesar." ¹⁶Then Pilate handed him over to them to be crucified.

☆RSV *kingship*. See Appendix.
▽RSV 18:36, 38; 19:12 *the Jews;* 19:7 *The Jews*. See Appendix.
◇RSV *Son*. See Appendix.

¹⁷ So they took Jesus, who went out bearing his own cross, to the place called the place of a skull, which is called in Hebrew Golgotha. ¹⁸ There they crucified him, along with two others, one on either side, and Jesus between them. ¹⁹ Pilate also wrote a title and put it on the cross; it read, "Jesus of Nazareth, the King of the Jews." ²⁰ Many of the Jews read this title, for the place where Jesus was crucified was near the city; and it was written in Hebrew, in Latin, and in Greek. ²¹ The chief priests of the Jews then said to Pilate, "Do not write, 'The King of the Jews,' but, 'This one said, I am King of the Jews.'" ²² Pilate answered, "What I have written I have written."

²³ When the soldiers had crucified Jesus they took his garments and made four parts, one for each soldier; also his tunic. But the tunic was without seam, woven from top to bottom; ²⁴ so they said to one another, "Let us not tear it, but cast lots for it to see whose it shall be." This was to fulfill the scripture,

"They parted my garments among them,
and for my clothing they cast lots."

²⁵ So the soldiers did this. But standing by the cross of Jesus were his mother, and his mother's sister, Mary the wife of Clopas, and Mary Magdalene. ²⁶ When Jesus saw his mother, and the disciple whom he loved standing near, he said to his mother, "Woman, behold, your child!" ²⁷ Then Jesus said to the disciple, "Behold, your mother!" And from that hour the disciple took her home.

²⁸ After this, Jesus, knowing that all was now finished, said (to fulfill the scripture), "I thirst." ²⁹ A bowl full of vinegar stood there; so they put a sponge full of the vinegar on hyssop and held it to his mouth. ³⁰ After receiving the vinegar, Jesus said, "It is finished," and bowed his head and gave up the spirit.

³¹ Since it was the day of Preparation, in order to prevent the bodies from remaining on the cross on the sabbath (for that sabbath was a high day), the religious authorities[▽] asked Pilate that their legs might be broken, and that they might be taken away. ³² So the soldiers came and broke the legs of the first, and of the other who had been crucified with Jesus; ³³ but when they came to Jesus and saw that he was already dead, they did not break his legs. ³⁴ But one of the soldiers pierced Jesus' side with a spear, and at once there came out blood and water. ³⁵ The one who saw it has borne witness—this testimony is true, and the witness knows that it is the truth—that you also may believe. ³⁶ For these things took place that the scripture might be fulfilled, "Not a bone of him shall be broken." ³⁷ And again another scripture says, "They shall look on the one whom they have pierced."

▽RSV *the Jews*. See Appendix.

^{38} After this Joseph of Arimathea, who was a disciple of Jesus, but secretly, for fear of the religious authorities,$^\triangledown$ asked Pilate for permission to take away the body of Jesus, and Pilate granted it. So Joseph came and took away Jesus' body. ^{39} Nicodemus also, who had at first come to Jesus by night, came bringing a mixture of myrrh and aloes, about a hundred pounds' weight. ^{40} They took the body of Jesus, and bound it in linen cloths with the spices, as is the burial custom of the Jews. ^{41} Now in the place where Jesus was crucified there was a garden, and in the garden a new tomb where no one had ever been laid. ^{42} So because of the Jewish day of Preparation, as the tomb was close at hand, they laid Jesus there.

$^\triangledown$RSV *the Jews*. See Appendix.

EASTER

(If the first lesson is read from the Old Testament, the lection from Acts should be read as Lesson 2.)

Lesson 1 ~ Acts 10:34-43

Peter preaches about Jesus' life, death, and resurrection.

34 Peter proclaimed, "Truly I perceive that God shows no partiality, 35 but in every nation anyone who fears God and does what is right is acceptable to God. 36 You know the word which God sent to Israel, preaching good news of peace by Jesus Christ (Christ is Sovereign [or Lord] of all), 37 the word which was proclaimed throughout all Judea, beginning from Galilee after the baptism which John preached: 38 how God anointed Jesus of Nazareth with the Holy Spirit and with power; how Jesus went about doing good and healing all that were oppressed by the devil, for God was with him. 39 And we are witnesses to all that Jesus did both in Judea and in Jerusalem. They put Jesus to death by hanging him on a tree; 40 but God raised Jesus on the third day and made Jesus manifest; 41 not to all the people but to us who were chosen by God as witnesses, who ate and drank with Jesus after the resurrection from the dead. 42 And Jesus commanded us to preach to the people, and to testify that Jesus is the one ordained by God to be judge of the living and the dead. 43 To this one all the prophets bear witness that everyone who believes in Jesus Christ receives forgiveness of sins through Jesus' name."

Lesson 1 (alternate) ~ Jeremiah 31:1-6

The prophet asserts God's everlasting love for the people of Israel.

1 "At that time, says the SOVEREIGN [or LORD], I will be the God of all the families of Israel, and they shall be my people."

2 Thus says the SOVEREIGN [or LORD]:
"The people who survived the sword
found grace in the wilderness;
when Israel sought for rest,
3 GOD [or the LORD] appeared to them from afar.
I have loved you with an everlasting love;
therefore I have continued my faithfulness to you.

⁴ Again I will build you, and you shall be built,
    O faithful Israel!
  Again you shall adorn yourself with timbrels,
    and shall go forth in the dance of the merrymakers.
⁵ Again you shall plant vineyards
    upon the mountains of Samaria;
  the planters shall plant,
    and shall enjoy the fruit.
⁶ For there shall be a day when those who watch will call
    in the hill country of Ephraim:
  'Arise, and let us go up to Zion,
    to the SOVEREIGN [[*or* LORD]] our God.'"

Psalm 118:14-24

¹⁴ GOD [[*or* The LORD]] is my strength and my song,
    and has become my salvation.
¹⁵ Hark, glad songs of victory
    in the tents of the righteous:
  "The right hand of GOD [[*or* the LORD]] does valiantly,
¹⁶   the right hand of GOD [[*or* the LORD]] is exalted,
    the right hand of GOD [[*or* the LORD]] does valiantly!"
¹⁷ I shall not die, but I shall live,
    and recount the deeds of GOD [[*or* the LORD]].
¹⁸ GOD [[*or* The LORD]] has chastened me sorely,
    but has not given me over to death.
¹⁹ Open to me the gates of righteousness,
    that I may enter through them
    and give thanks to GOD [[*or* the LORD]].
²⁰ This is the gate of GOD [[*or* the LORD]];
    the righteous shall enter through it.
²¹ I thank you that you have answered me
    and have become my salvation.
²² The stone which the builders rejected
    has become the head of the corner.
²³ This is GOD'S [[*or* the LORD'S]] doing;
    it is marvelous in our eyes.
²⁴ This is the day which GOD [[*or* the LORD]] has made;
    let us rejoice and be glad in it.

Lesson 2 ~ Colossians 3:1-4

(If Jeremiah 31:1-6 is read as the first lesson, Acts 10:34-43 should be read as Lesson 2.)

The Colossians learn about their new life in Christ.

¹ If then you have been raised with Christ, seek the things that are above, where Christ is, seated at the right hand of God. ² Set your minds on things that are above, not on things that are on earth. ³ For you have died, and your life is hid with Christ in God. ⁴ When Christ who is our life appears, then you also will appear with Christ in glory.

Gospel ~ John 20:1-18

The risen Christ appears to Mary Magdalene.

¹ Now on the first day of the week Mary Magdalene came to the tomb early, while it was still dark, and saw that the stone had been taken away from the tomb. ² So she ran, and went to Simon Peter and the other disciple, the one whom Jesus loved, and said to them, "They have taken the Sovereign [[or Lord]] out of the tomb, and we do not know where they have laid him." ³ Peter then came out with the other disciple, and they went toward the tomb. ⁴ They both ran, but the other disciple outran Peter, reached the tomb first, ⁵ and stooping to look in, saw the linen cloths lying there, but did not go in. ⁶ Then Simon Peter came, following after, and went into the tomb; Peter saw the linen cloths lying, ⁷ and the napkin, which had been on Jesus' head, not lying with the linen cloths but rolled up in a place by itself. ⁸ Then the other disciple, who reached the tomb first, also went in, and saw and believed; ⁹ for as yet they did not know the scripture, that Jesus must rise from the dead. ¹⁰ Then the disciples went back to their homes.

¹¹ But Mary stood weeping outside the tomb, and as she wept she stooped to look into the tomb; ¹² and she saw two angels in white, sitting where the body of Jesus had lain, one at the head and one at the feet. ¹³ They said to her, "Woman, why are you weeping?" She said to them, "Because they have taken away my Sovereign [[or Lord]], and I do not know where they have laid him." ¹⁴ Saying this, she turned round and saw Jesus standing, but she did not know that it was Jesus. ¹⁵ Jesus said to her, "Woman, why are you weeping? Whom do you seek?" Supposing Jesus to be the gardener, she answered, "Sir, if you have carried Jesus away, tell me where you have laid him, and I will take him away." ¹⁶ Jesus said to her, "Mary." She turned and responded in Hebrew, "Rabboni!" (which

means Teacher). [17] Jesus said to her, "Do not hold me, for I have not yet ascended to God; but go to my friends and say to them, I am ascending to [*God*] my Father [*and Mother**] and your Father [*and Mother**], to my God and your God." [18] Mary Magdalene went and said to the disciples, "I have seen the Sovereign [[*or* Lord]]"; and she told them that Jesus had said these things to her.

Gospel (alternate) ~ Matthew 28:1-10

Jesus appears to Mary Magdalene and the other Mary.

[1] Now after the sabbath, toward the dawn of the first day of the week, Mary Magdalene and the other Mary went to see the sepulchre. [2] And there was a great earthquake; for an angel of God descended from heaven and came and rolled back the stone, and sat upon it. [3] The angel's appearance was like lightning, and its raiment white as snow. [4] And for fear of the angel the guards trembled and became like dead people. [5] But the angel said to the women, "Do not be afraid; for I know that you seek Jesus who was crucified. [6] Jesus is not here, but has risen, as he said. Come, see the place where Jesus lay. [7] Then go quickly and tell the disciples that Jesus has risen from the dead, and even now is going before you to Galilee. There you will see Jesus. Indeed, I have told you." [8] So they departed quickly from the tomb with fear and great joy, and ran to tell the disciples. [9] And then Jesus met them and said, "Hail!" And they came up and took hold of Jesus' feet and worshiped Jesus. [10] Then Jesus said to them, "Do not be afraid; go and tell my followers to go to Galilee, and there they will see me."

---

*Addition to the text. See "Metaphor" and "God the Father and Mother" in the Appendix.

EASTER EVENING

(If the first lesson is read from the Old Testament, the lection from Acts should be read as Lesson 2.)

Lesson 1 ~ Acts 5:29-32

Peter and the apostles bear witness to the risen Christ.

29 But Peter and the apostles answered, "We must obey God rather than human beings. 30 The God of our ancestors raised Jesus, whom you killed by hanging on a tree. 31 God exalted this Jesus at God's right hand as Leader and Savior, to give repentance to Israel and forgiveness of sins. 32 And we are witnesses to these things, and so is the Holy Spirit whom God has given to those who obey God."

Lesson 1 (alternate) ~ Daniel 12:1-3

Daniel prophesies the events of the end time.

1 At that time shall arise Michael, the great prince who has charge of your people. And there shall be a time of trouble, such as never has been since there was a nation till that time; but at that time your people shall be delivered, everyone whose name shall be found written in the book. 2 And many of those who sleep in the dust of the earth shall awake, some to everlasting life, and some to shame and everlasting contempt. 3 And those who are wise shall shine like the brightness of the firmament; and those who turn many to righteousness, like the stars forever and ever.

Psalm 150

1 Praise GOD [[*or* the LORD]]!
  Praise God in the sanctuary;
    praise God in the mighty firmament!
2 Praise God for mighty deeds;
    praise God according to God's exceeding greatness!
3 Praise God with trumpet sound;
    praise God with lute and harp!
4 Praise God with timbrel and dance;
    praise God with strings and pipe!
5 Praise God with sounding cymbals;
    praise God with loud clashing cymbals!
6 Let everything that breathes praise GOD [[*or* the LORD]]!
  Praise GOD [[*or* the LORD]]!

Lesson 2 ~ 1 Corinthians 5:6-8

(If Daniel 12:1-3 is read as the first lesson, Acts 5:29-32 should be read as Lesson 2.)

Paul writes about the bread of the new passover.

⁶ Your boasting is not good. Do you not know that a little leaven leavens the whole lump? ⁷ Cleanse out the old leaven that you may be a new lump, as you really are unleavened. For Christ, our paschal lamb, has been sacrificed. ⁸ Let us, therefore, celebrate the festival, not with the old leaven, the leaven of malice and evil, but with the unleavened bread of sincerity and truth.

Gospel ~ Luke 24:13-49

Jesus meets two disciples on the road to Emmaus.

¹³ That very day two of the disciples were going to a village named Emmaus, about seven miles from Jerusalem, ¹⁴ and talking with each other about all these things that had happened. ¹⁵ While they were talking and discussing together, Jesus drew near and went with them. ¹⁶ But their eyes were kept from recognizing Jesus. ¹⁷ And Jesus said to them, "What is this conversation which you are holding with each other as you walk?" And they stood still, looking sad. ¹⁸ Then one of them, named Cleopas, answered, "Are you the only visitor to Jerusalem who does not know the things that have happened there in these days?" ¹⁹ And Jesus said to them, "What things?" And they said, "Concerning Jesus of Nazareth, who was a prophet mighty in deed and word before God and all the people, ²⁰ and how our chief priests and rulers delivered up this Jesus to be condemned to death, and crucified him. ²¹ But we had hoped that Jesus was the one to redeem Israel. Yes, and besides all this, it is now the third day since this happened. ²² Moreover, some women of our company amazed us. They were at the tomb early in the morning ²³ and did not find Jesus' body; and they came back saying that they had even seen a vision of angels, who said that Jesus was alive. ²⁴ Some of those who were with us went to the tomb, and found it just as the women had said; but Jesus they did not see." ²⁵ And Jesus said to them, "O foolish ones, and slow of heart to believe all that the prophets have spoken! ²⁶ Was it not necessary that the Christ should suffer these things and be glorified?" ²⁷ And beginning with Moses and all the prophets, Jesus interpreted to them in all the scriptures the things concerning the Christ.

²⁸ So they drew near to the village to which they were going. Jesus appeared to be going further, ²⁹ but they urged against it, saying, "Stay with us, for it is toward evening and the day is now far spent." So Jesus

went in to stay with them. [30] While at table with them, Jesus took the bread and blessed, and broke it, and gave it to them. [31] And their eyes were opened and they recognized Jesus, who then vanished out of their sight. [32] They said to each other, "Did not our hearts burn within us while Jesus talked to us on the road, and opened to us the scriptures?" [33] And they rose that same hour and returned to Jerusalem; and they found the eleven gathered together and those who were with them, [34] who said, "The Sovereign [or Lord] has risen indeed, and has appeared to Simon!" [35] Then they told what had happened on the road, and how Jesus was known to them in the breaking of the bread.

[36] As they were saying this, that very Jesus stood among them. [37] But they were startled and frightened, and supposed that they saw a spirit. [38] And Jesus said to them, "Why are you troubled, and why do questionings rise in your hearts? [39] See my hands and my feet, that it is I myself; handle me, and see; for a spirit has not flesh and bones as you see that I have." [41] And while they still disbelieved for joy, and wondered, Jesus said to them, "Have you anything here to eat?" [42] They gave Jesus a piece of broiled fish, [43] and Jesus took it and ate before them.

[44] Then Jesus said to them, "These are my words which I spoke to you, while I was still with you, that everything written about me in the law of Moses and the prophets and the psalms must be fulfilled." [45] Then Jesus opened their minds to understand the scriptures, [46] and said to them, "Thus it is written, that the Christ should suffer and on the third day rise from the dead, [47] and that repentance and forgiveness of sins should be preached in Christ's name to all nations, beginning from Jerusalem. [48] You are witnesses of these things. [49] And I am sending the promise of [God] my Father [and Mother*] upon you; but stay in the city until you are clothed with power from on high."

---

*Addition to the text. See "Metaphor" and "God the Father and Mother" in the Appendix.

EASTER 2

Lesson 1 ~ Acts 2:14a, 22-32

Peter preaches at Pentecost.

14 Peter, standing with the eleven, addressed the Judeans:
22 "People of Israel, hear these words: Jesus of Nazareth, attested to you by God with mighty works and wonders and signs which God did through him in your midst, as you yourselves know— 23 this Jesus, delivered up according to the definite plan and foreknowledge of God, you crucified and killed by the hands of lawless people. 24 But God raised Jesus, having loosed the pangs of death, because it was not possible for Jesus to be held by it. 25 For David says, concerning Jesus,

'I saw the Sovereign [[*or* Lord]] always before me,
who is at my right hand that I may not be shaken;
26 therefore my heart was glad, and my tongue rejoiced;
moreover my flesh will dwell in hope.
27 For you will not abandon my soul to Hades,
nor let your Holy One see corruption.
28 You have made known to me the ways of life;
you will make me full of gladness with your presence.'

29 "Brothers and sisters, I may say to you confidently that David both died and was buried, and his tomb is with us to this day. 30 Being therefore a prophet, and knowing that God had sworn to set one of David's own descendants upon the throne, 31 David foresaw and spoke of the resurrection of the Christ, who was not abandoned to Hades, and whose flesh did not see corruption. 32 This Jesus God raised, and of that we all are witnesses."

⁵ GOD [[or The LORD]] is my chosen portion and my cup;
  you hold my lot.
⁶ The lines have fallen for me in pleasant places;
  I have a goodly heritage.
⁷ I bless GOD [[or the LORD]] who gives me counsel;
  in the night also my heart instructs me.
⁸ I keep GOD [[or the LORD]] always before me;
  because God is beside me, I shall not be moved.
⁹ Therefore my heart is glad, and my soul rejoices;
  my body also dwells secure.
¹⁰ For you do not give me up to Sheol,
  or let your godly one see the Pit.
¹¹ You show me the path of life;
  in your presence there is fullness of joy,
  in your right hand are pleasures forevermore.

Lesson 2 ~ 1 Peter 1:3-9

Peter speaks of God's great mercy in raising Christ from the dead.

³ Blessed be God, the Father [*and Mother**] of our Sovereign [[or Lord]] Jesus Christ! By God's great mercy we have been born anew to a living hope through the resurrection of Jesus Christ from the dead, ⁴ and to an inheritance which is imperishable, undefiled, and unfading, kept in heaven for you, ⁵ who by God's power are guarded through faith for a salvation ready to be revealed in the last time. ⁶ In this you rejoice, though now for a little while you may have to suffer various trials, ⁷ so that the genuineness of your faith, more precious than gold which though perishable is tested by fire, may redound to praise and glory and honor at the revelation of Jesus Christ, ⁸ whom not having seen, you love; and whom, though you do not now see, you yet believe in, and rejoice with unutterable and exalted joy. ⁹ As the outcome of your faith you obtain the salvation of your souls.

---

*Addition to the text. See "Metaphor" and "God the Father and Mother" in the Appendix.

The risen Christ appears to Thomas.

¹⁹ On the evening of that day, the first day of the week, the doors being shut where the disciples were, for fear of the religious authorities,▽ Jesus came and stood among them and said to them, "Peace be with you." ²⁰ Having said this, Jesus showed them Jesus' hands and side. Then the disciples were glad when they saw the Sovereign [[*or* Lord]]. ²¹ Jesus said to them again, "Peace be with you. As [*God*] the Father [*and Mother**] has sent me, even so I send you." ²² Having said this, Jesus breathed on them, and said to them, "Receive the Holy Spirit. ²³ If you forgive the sins of any, they are forgiven; if you retain the sins of any, they are retained."

²⁴ Now Thomas, one of the twelve, called the Twin, was not with them when Jesus came. ²⁵ So the other disciples told him, "We have seen the Sovereign [[*or* Lord]]." But Thomas said to them, "Unless I see in Jesus' hands the print of the nails, and place my finger in the mark of the nails, and place my hand in Jesus' side, I will not believe."

²⁶ Eight days later, the disciples were again in the house, and Thomas was with them. The doors were shut, but Jesus came and stood among them, and said, "Peace be with you." ²⁷ Then Jesus said to Thomas, "Put your finger here, and see my hands; and put out your hand, and place it in my side; do not be faithless, but believing." ²⁸ Thomas answered, "My Sovereign [[*or* Lord]] and my God!" ²⁹ Jesus said to Thomas, "Have you believed because you have seen me? Blessed are those who have not seen and yet believe."

³⁰ Now Jesus did many other signs in the presence of the disciples, which are not written in this book; ³¹ but these are written that you may believe that Jesus is the Christ, the Child◇ of God, and that believing you may have life in Christ's name.

▽RSV *the Jews.* See Appendix.
*Addition to the text. See "Metaphor" and "God the Father and Mother" in the Appendix.
◇RSV *Son.* See Appendix.

EASTER 3

Lesson 1 ~ Acts 2:14a, 36-41

Peter's preaching leads to the conversion of many.

¹⁴ Peter, standing with the eleven, addressed the Judeans:

³⁶ "Let all the house of Israel therefore know assuredly that God has made this Jesus whom you crucified both Sovereign [[or Lord]] and Christ."

³⁷ Now when the Judeans heard this they were cut to the heart, and said to Peter and the rest of the apostles, "Brothers and sisters, what shall we do?" ³⁸ And Peter said to them, "Repent, and be baptized every one of you in the name of Jesus Christ for the forgiveness of your sins; and you shall receive the gift of the Holy Spirit. ³⁹ For the promise is to you and to your children and to all that are far off, everyone whom the Sovereign [[or Lord]] our God calls." ⁴⁰ And Peter testified with many other words and exhorted them, saying, "Save yourselves from this crooked generation." ⁴¹ So those who received Peter's word were baptized, and there were added that day about three thousand souls.

Psalm 116:12-19

¹² What shall I render to GOD [[or the LORD]]
    for all God's bounty to me?
¹³ I will lift up the cup of salvation
    and call on the name of GOD [[or the LORD]],
¹⁴ I will pay my vows to GOD [[or the LORD]]
    in the presence of all God's people.
¹⁵ Precious in the sight of GOD [[or the LORD]]
    is the death of the saints.
¹⁶ O GOD [[or LORD]], I am your servant;
    I am your servant, the child of your womanservant.
    You have loosed my bonds.
¹⁷ I will offer to you the sacrifice of thanksgiving
    and call on the name of GOD [[or the LORD]].
¹⁸ I will pay my vows to GOD [[or the LORD]]
    in the presence of all God's people,
¹⁹ in the courts of the house of GOD [[or the LORD]],
    in your midst, O Jerusalem.
    Praise GOD [[or the LORD]]!

The power of the risen Christ transforms human lives.

[17] And if you invoke as Father [*and Mother**] the God who judges each one impartially according to their deeds, conduct yourselves with fear throughout the time of your exile. [18] You know that you were ransomed from the futile ways inherited from your ancestors, not with perishable things such as silver or gold, [19] but with the precious blood of Christ, like that of a lamb without blemish or spot. [20] Christ was destined before the foundation of the world but was made manifest at the end of the times for your sake. [21] You have confidence in God through Christ, whom God raised from the dead and glorified so that your faith and hope are in God.

[22] Having purified your souls by your obedience to the truth for a sincere love of each other, love one another earnestly from the heart. [23] You have been born anew, not of perishable seed but of imperishable, through the living and abiding word of God.

---

*Addition to the text. See "Metaphor" and "God the Father and Mother" in the Appendix.

Gospel ~ Luke 24:13-35

Jesus meets two disciples on the road to Emmaus.

13 That very day two of the disciples were going to a village named Emmaus, about seven miles from Jerusalem, 14 and talking with each other about all these things that had happened. 15 While they were talking and discussing together, Jesus drew near and went with them. 16 But their eyes were kept from recognizing Jesus. 17 And Jesus said to them, "What is this conversation which you are holding with each other as you walk?" And they stood still, looking sad. 18 Then one of them, named Cleopas, answered, "Are you the only visitor to Jerusalem who does not know the things that have happened there in these days?" 19 And Jesus said to them, "What things?" And they said, "Concerning Jesus of Nazareth, who was a prophet mighty in deed and word before God and all the people, 20 and how our chief priests and rulers delivered up this Jesus to be condemned to death, and crucified him. 21 But we had hoped that Jesus was the one to redeem Israel. Yes, and besides all this, it is now the third day since this happened. 22 Moreover, some women of our company amazed us. They were at the tomb early in the morning 23 and did not find Jesus' body; and they came back saying that they had even seen a vision of angels, who said that Jesus was alive. 24 Some of those who were with us went to the tomb, and found it just as the women had said; but Jesus they did not see." 25 And Jesus said to them, "O foolish ones, and slow of heart to believe all that the prophets have spoken! 26 Was it not necessary that the Christ should suffer these things and be glorified?" 27 And beginning with Moses and all the prophets, Jesus interpreted to them in all the scriptures the things concerning the Christ.

28 So they drew near to the village to which they were going. Jesus appeared to be going further, 29 but they urged against it, saying, "Stay with us, for it is toward evening and the day is now far spent." So Jesus went in to stay with them. 30 While at table with them, Jesus took the bread and blessed, and broke it, and gave it to them. 31 And their eyes were opened and they recognized Jesus, who then vanished out of their sight. 32 They said to each other, "Did not our hearts burn within us while Jesus talked to us on the road, and opened to us the scriptures?" 33 And they rose that same hour and returned to Jerusalem; and they found the eleven gathered together and those who were with them, 34 who said, "The Sovereign [or Lord] has risen indeed, and has appeared to Simon!" 35 Then they told what had happened on the road, and how Jesus was known to them in the breaking of the bread.

EASTER 4

Lesson 1 ~ Acts 2:42-47

The early Christians attract others by their manner of living.

⁴² And they devoted themselves to the teaching of the apostles and to community life, to the breaking of bread and to the prayers.

⁴³ And fear came upon every soul; and many wonders and signs were done through the apostles. ⁴⁴ And all who believed were together and had all things in common; ⁴⁵ and they sold their possessions and goods and distributed them to all, as any had need. ⁴⁶ And day by day, attending the temple together and breaking bread in their homes, they partook of food with glad and generous hearts, ⁴⁷ praising God and having favor with all the people. And the Sovereign [[*or* Lord]] added to their number day by day those who were being saved.

Psalm 23

¹ GOD [[*or* The LORD]] is my shepherd, I shall not want;
²   God makes me lie down in green pastures,
  and leads me beside still waters;
³   God restores my soul.
  God leads me in paths of righteousness
    for God's name's sake.
⁴ Even though I walk through the valley of the shadow of death,
    I fear no evil;
  for you are with me;
    your rod and your staff,
    they comfort me.
⁵ You prepare a table before me
    in the presence of my enemies;
  you anoint my head with oil,
    my cup overflows.
⁶ Surely goodness and mercy shall follow me
    all the days of my life;
  and I shall dwell in the house of GOD [[*or* the LORD]]
    forever.

Lesson 2 ~ 1 Peter 2:19-25

Jesus, who suffered and died for our sins, trusted in God who judges justly.

[19] For you are approved if, mindful of God, you endure pain while suffering unjustly. [20] For what credit is it, if when you do wrong and are beaten for it you take it patiently? But if when you do right and suffer for it you take it patiently, you have God's approval. [21] For to this you have been called, because Christ also suffered for you, leaving you an example, that you should follow in Christ's steps. [22] Christ committed no sin, and spoke without guile. [23] Though reviled, Christ did not revile in return; while suffering, Christ did not threaten, but trusted in God who judges justly, [24] bearing our sins in Christ's own body on the tree, that we might die to sin and live to righteousness. By Christ's wounds you have been healed. [25] For you were straying like sheep, but have now returned to the Shepherd and Guardian of your souls.

Gospel ~ John 10:1-10

Jesus tells the disciples the parable of the good shepherd.

[1] "Truly, truly, I say to you, anyone who does not enter the sheepfold by the door but climbs in by another way, is a thief and a robber; [2] but the one who enters by the door is the shepherd of the sheep. [3] To this one the gatekeeper opens; the sheep hear the voice of the shepherd who calls them by name and leads them out. [4] After bringing all of them out, the shepherd goes before them, and the sheep follow, for they know the shepherd's voice. [5] A stranger they will not follow, but they will flee away, for they do not know the voice of strangers." [6] This figure Jesus used with the disciples, but they did not understand what he was saying to them.

[7] So Jesus said again, "Truly, truly, I say to you, I am the door of the sheep. [8] All who came before me are thieves and robbers; but the sheep did not heed them. [9] I am the door; whoever enters by me will be saved, and will go in and out and find pasture. [10] The thief comes only to steal and kill and destroy; I came that they may have life, and have it abundantly."

EASTER 5

Lesson 1 ~ Acts 7:55-60

The witness of Stephen leads to his martyrdom.

⁵⁵ But Stephen, full of the Holy Spirit, gazed into heaven and saw the glory of God, and Jesus standing at the right hand of God; ⁵⁶ and Stephen said, "Behold, I see the heavens opened, and the Human One° standing at the right hand of God." ⁵⁷ But they cried out with a loud voice and stopped their ears and rushed together upon him. ⁵⁸ Then they cast him out of the city and stoned him; and the witnesses laid down their garments at the feet of a young man named Saul. ⁵⁹ And as they were stoning Stephen, he prayed, "Sovereign ⟦*or* Lord⟧ Jesus, receive my spirit." ⁶⁰ And he knelt down and cried with a loud voice, "Sovereign ⟦*or* Lord⟧, do not hold this sin against them." And when Stephen had said this, he died.

Lesson 1 (alternate) ~ Acts 17:1-12

Paul preaches in Thessalonica.

¹ Now when Paul and Silas had passed through Amphipolis and Apollonia, they came to Thessalonica, where there was a synagogue of the Jews. ² And Paul went in, as was his custom, and for three weeks argued with them from the scriptures, ³ explaining and proving that it was necessary for the Christ to suffer and to rise from the dead, and saying, "This Jesus, whom I proclaim to you, is the Christ." ⁴ And some of them were persuaded, and joined Paul and Silas; as did a great many of the devout Greeks and not a few of the leading women. ⁵ But the Jews were jealous, and taking a gang from the marketplace, they gathered a crowd, set the city in an uproar, and attacked the house of Jason, seeking to bring Paul and Silas out to the people. ⁶ And when the Jews could not find Paul and Silas, they dragged Jason and some of the other believers before the city authorities, crying, "These people who have turned the world upside down have come here also, ⁷ and Jason has received them, and they are all acting against the decrees of Caesar, saying that there is another ruler,▢ Jesus." ⁸ And the people and the city authorities were disturbed when they heard this. ⁹ And having taken security from Jason and the rest, the authorities let them go.

° RSV *Son of man*. See Appendix.
▢ RSV *king*. See Appendix.

¹⁰ The community immediately sent Paul and Silas away by night to Beroea; and when they arrived they went into the Jewish synagogue. ¹¹ Now these Jews were more noble than those in Thessalonica, for they received the word with all eagerness, examining the scriptures daily to see if these things were so. ¹² Many of them therefore believed, with not a few Greek women of high standing as well as men.

Psalm 31:1-8

¹ In you, O GOD [[*or* LORD]], do I seek refuge;
    let me never be put to shame;
    in your righteousness deliver me!
² Incline your ear to me,
    rescue me speedily!
  Be a rock of refuge for me,
    a strong fortress to save me!
³ You are my rock and my fortress;
    for your name's sake lead me and guide me,
⁴ take me out of the net which is hidden for me,
    for you are my refuge.
⁵ Into your hand I commit my spirit;
    you have redeemed me, O SOVEREIGN [[*or* LORD]], faithful God.
⁶ You hate those who pay regard to vain idols;
    but I trust in GOD [[*or* the LORD]].
⁷ I will rejoice and be glad for your steadfast love,
    because you have seen my affliction,
    you have taken heed of my adversities,
⁸ and have not delivered me into the hand of the enemy;
    you have set my feet in a broad place.

Christ is the living stone, precious to God.

2 Like newborn babies, long for the pure spiritual milk, that by it you may grow up to salvation; 3for you have tasted the kindness of the Sovereign [[or Lord]].

4 Come to Christ, to that living stone, rejected by human beings but in God's sight chosen and precious; 5and like living stones be yourselves built into a spiritual house, to be a holy priesthood, to offer spiritual sacrifices acceptable to God through Jesus Christ. 6For it stands in scripture:

> "I am laying in Zion a stone, a cornerstone chosen and precious,
> and whoever believes in Christ will not be put to shame."

7The honor, then, is for you who believe, but for those who do not believe,

> "The very stone which the builders rejected
> has become the head of the corner,"

8and

> "A stone of stumbling,
> and a rock of offense";

for they stumble because they disobey the word, as they were destined to do.

9 But you are a chosen race, a royal priesthood, a holy nation, God's own people, that you may declare the wonderful deeds of God who called you out of the night into God's marvelous light. 10Once you were no people but now you are God's people; once you had not received mercy but now you have received mercy.

Jesus is the way, the truth, and the life.

¹ "Let not your hearts be troubled; believe in God, believe also in me. ² In the house of [God] my Father [and Mother*] are many rooms; if it were not so, would I have told you that I go to prepare a place for you? ³ And when I go and prepare a place for you, I will come again and will take you to myself, that where I am you may be also. ⁴ And you know the way where I am going." ⁵ Thomas said to Jesus, "Sovereign [[or Lord]], we do not know where you are going; how can we know the way?" ⁶ Jesus said to Thomas, "I am the way, and the truth, and the life; no one comes to God,⊗ but by me. ⁷ If you had known me, you would have known God⊗ also; henceforth you know God and have seen God."

⁸ Philip said to Jesus, "Sovereign [[or Lord]], show us God,⊗ and we shall be satisfied." ⁹ Jesus replied, "Have I been with you so long, and yet you do not know me, Philip? Whoever has seen me has seen God;⊗ how can you say, 'Show us God'⊗? ¹⁰ Do you not believe that I am in God⊗ and God⊗ in me? The words that I say to you I do not speak on my own authority; but God⊗ who dwells in me does God's works. ¹¹ Believe me that I am in God⊗ and God⊗ in me; or else believe me for the sake of the works themselves.

¹² "Truly, truly, I say to you, all who believe in me will also do the works that I do; and greater works than these will they do, because I go to God.⊗ ¹³ Whatever you ask in my name, I will do it, that [God] the Father [and Mother*] may be glorified in the Child◇ [of God**]; ¹⁴ if you ask anything in my name, I will do it."

---

*Addition to the text. See "Metaphor" and "God the Father and Mother" in the Appendix.
⊗RSV vs. 6, 8, 9, 10, 11, 12 *the Father;* v. 7 *my Father.* See Appendix.
◇RSV *Son.* See Appendix.
**Addition to the text.

EASTER 6

Lesson 1 ~ Acts 17:22-31

Paul preaches to the Athenians.

[22] Paul, standing in the middle of the Areopagus, said: "People of Athens, I perceive that in every way you are very religious. [23] For as I passed along, and observed the objects of your worship, I found also an altar with this inscription, 'To an unknown god.' What therefore you worship as unknown, this I proclaim to you. [24] The God who made the world and everything in it, being Sovereign [[or Lord]] of heaven and earth, does not live in shrines made by human hands, [25] and is not served by human hands, as though God needed anything, since God alone gives to all people life and breath and everything. [26] And God made from one all the nations to live on the face of the whole earth, having determined allotted periods and the boundaries of their habitation, [27] that they should seek God, in the hope that they might feel after and find God, who is not far from each one of us, [28] for

'In this one we live and move and have our being';

as even some of your poets have said,

'For we are indeed the offspring of God.'

[29] Being then God's offspring, we ought not to think that the Deity is like gold, or silver, or stone, a representation by human art and imagination. [30] The times of ignorance God overlooked, but now God commands all people everywhere to repent, [31] because the day has been fixed on which God will judge the world in righteousness by a human being whom God has appointed, and of this God has given assurance to all by raising that one from the dead."

Psalm 66:8-20

8 Bless our God, O nations,
    let the sound of God's praise be heard,
9 who has kept us among the living,
    and has not let our feet slip.
10 For you, O God, have tested us;
    you have tried us as silver is tried.
11 You brought us into the net;
    you laid affliction on our loins;
12 you let people ride over our heads;
    we went through fire and through water;
yet you brought us forth to a spacious place.
13 I will come into your house with burnt offerings;
    I will pay you my vows,
14 that which my lips uttered
    and my mouth promised when I was in trouble.
15 I will offer to you burnt offerings of fatlings,
    with the smoke of the sacrifice of rams;
I will make an offering of bulls and goats.
16 Come and hear, all you who fear God,
    and I will tell what God has done for me.
17 I cried aloud to God,
    and God was extolled with my tongue.
18 If I had cherished iniquity in my heart,
    God [[or the Lord]] would not have listened.
19 But truly God has listened
    and has given heed to the voice of my prayer.
20 Blessed be God!
    You have not rejected my prayer
    nor removed your steadfast love from me!

Lesson 2 ~ 1 Peter 3:13-22

We are admonished not to fear suffering for righteousness' sake.

[13] Now who is there to harm you if you are zealous for what is right? [14] But even if you do suffer for righteousness' sake, you will be blessed. Have no fear of them, nor be troubled, [15] but in your hearts reverence Christ as Sovereign [or Lord]. Always be prepared to make a defense to anyone who calls you to account for the hope that is in you, yet do it with gentleness and reverence; [16] and keep your conscience clear, so that, when you are abused, those who revile your good behavior in Christ may be put to shame. [17] For it is better to suffer for doing right, if that should be God's will, than for doing wrong. [18] For Christ also died for sins once for all, the righteous for the unrighteous, in order to bring us to God, being put to death in the flesh but made alive in the spirit, [19] in which Christ went and preached to the spirits in prison. [20] They formerly did not obey, when God's patience waited in the days of Noah, during the building of the ark, in which a few, that is, eight persons, were saved through water. [21] Baptism, which corresponds to this, now saves you, not as a removal of dirt from the body but as an appeal to God for a clear conscience, through the resurrection of Jesus Christ, [22] who has gone into heaven and is at the right hand of God, to rule over angels, authorities, and powers.

Gospel ~ John 14:15-21

The one who loves Jesus keeps Jesus' commandments.

[15] If you love me, you will keep my commandments. [16] And I will pray [to God] the [Mother and*] Father, who will give you another Counselor, to be with you forever—[17] the Spirit of truth, whom the world cannot receive, because it neither sees nor knows this Spirit. But you know the Spirit, who dwells with you, and will be in you.

[18] I will not leave you desolate; I will come to you. [19] Yet a little while, and the world will see me no more, but you will see me; because I live, you also will live. [20] In that day, you will know that I am in God,⊗ and you in me, and I in you. [21] Whoever has my commandments and keeps them, that is the one who loves me; and all who love me will be loved by God,⊗ and I will love them and manifest myself to them.

---

*Addition to the text. See "Metaphor" and "God the Father and Mother" in the Appendix.
⊗RSV *my Father*. See Appendix.

ASCENSION

(Or on Easter 7)

Lesson 1 ~ Acts 1:1-11

The risen Jesus is taken up into heaven.

¹ In the first book, O Theophilus, I have dealt with all that Jesus began to do and teach, ²until the day when Jesus was taken up, having given commandment through the Holy Spirit to the apostles whom Jesus had chosen. ³After the passion Jesus was seen alive by the apostles through many proofs, appearing to them during forty days, and speaking of the realm☆ of God. ⁴And while staying with the apostles, Jesus charged them not to depart from Jerusalem, but to wait for the promise of God,⊗ which, Jesus said, "you heard from me, ⁵for John baptized with water, but before many days you shall be baptized with the Holy Spirit."

⁶ So when the apostles had come together, they asked Jesus, "Sovereign [or Lord], will you at this time restore the realm☆ to Israel?" ⁷Jesus said, "It is not for you to know times or seasons which have been fixed by God's⊗ own authority. ⁸But you shall receive power when the Holy Spirit has come upon you; and you shall be my witnesses in Jerusalem and in all Judea and Samaria and to the end of the earth." ⁹And having said this, as the apostles were looking on, Jesus was lifted up and carried on a cloud out of their sight. ¹⁰And while they were gazing into heaven as Jesus went, two figures stood by them in white robes, ¹¹and said, "People of Galilee, why do you stand looking into heaven? This Jesus, who was taken up from you into heaven, will come in the same way as you saw Jesus go into heaven."

Psalm 47

¹ Clap your hands, all you people!
　　Shout to God with loud songs of joy!
² For GOD [or the LORD], the Most High, is terrible,
　　a great ruler⊡ over all the earth,
³ subduing all people under us,
　　and nations under our feet,
⁴ choosing our heritage for us,
　　the pride of Jacob whom God loves.

☆RSV *kingdom.* See Appendix.
⊗RSV v. 4 *the Father;* v. 7 *which the Father has fixed by his own authority.* See Appendix.
⊡RSV *king.* See Appendix.

⁵ God has gone up with a shout,
    the SOVEREIGN ⟦*or* LORD⟧ with the sound of a trumpet.
⁶ Sing praises to God, sing praises!
    Sing praises to our Ruler,▢ sing praises!
⁷ For God is the ruler▢ of all the earth;
    sing praises with a psalm!
⁸ God reigns over the nations,
    God sits on the holy throne.
⁹ The nobles of the nations gather
    as the people of the God of Abraham.
For the shields of the earth belong to God
    who is highly exalted!

Lesson 2 ~ Ephesians 1:15-23

The risen Christ is exalted as head over all.

¹⁵ For this reason, because I have heard of your faith in the Sovereign ⟦*or* Lord⟧ Jesus and your love toward all the saints, ¹⁶ I do not cease to give thanks for you, remembering you in my prayers, ¹⁷ that the God of our Sovereign ⟦*or* Lord⟧ Jesus Christ, the Father [*and Mother**] of glory, may give you a spirit of wisdom and of revelation in the knowledge of God, ¹⁸ having the eyes of your hearts enlightened, that you may know what is the hope to which you have been called, what are the riches of God's glorious inheritance in the saints, ¹⁹ and what is the immeasurable greatness of God's power in us who believe, according to the working of God's great might ²⁰ which was accomplished in Christ when God raised Christ from the dead and made Christ sit at God's right hand in the heavenly places, ²¹ far above all rule and authority and power and dominion, and above every name that is named, not only in this age but also in that which is to come; ²² and God has put all things under Christ's feet and has made Christ the head over all things for the church, ²³ which is Christ's body, the fullness of the one who fills all in all.

▢RSV v. 6 *King;* v. 7 *king.* See Appendix.
*Addition to the text. See "Metaphor" and "God the Father and Mother" in the Appendix.

Gospel ~ Luke 24:46-53

Jesus commissions the disciples and is parted from them.

⁴⁶ And Jesus said to them, "Thus it is written, that the Christ should suffer and on the third day rise from the dead, ⁴⁷ and that repentance and forgiveness of sins should be preached in Christ's name to all nations, beginning from Jerusalem. ⁴⁸ You are witnesses of these things. ⁴⁹ And I am sending the promise of [*God*] my Father [*and Mother**] upon you; but stay in the city until you are clothed with power from on high."

⁵⁰ Then Jesus led them out as far as Bethany, and with uplifted hands blessed them. ⁵¹ While blessing them, Jesus parted from them, and was carried up into heaven. ⁵² And they returned to Jerusalem with great joy, ⁵³ and were continually in the temple blessing God.

Gospel (alternate) ~ Mark 16:9-16, 19-20

The risen Jesus appears first to Mary Magdalene and then to others, sending the disciples to preach the gospel.

⁹ Now having risen early on the first day of the week, Jesus appeared first to Mary Magdalene, from whom Jesus had cast out seven demons. ¹⁰ She went and told those who had been with Jesus, as they mourned and wept. ¹¹ But when they heard that Jesus was alive and had been seen by her, they would not believe it.

¹² After this Jesus appeared in another form to two of them, as they were walking into the country. ¹³ And they went back and told the rest, but they did not believe them.

¹⁴ Afterward Jesus appeared to the eleven themselves as they sat at table, and upbraided them for their unbelief and hardness of heart, because they had not believed those who saw Jesus after Jesus had risen. ¹⁵ And Jesus said to them, "Go into all the world and preach the gospel to the whole creation. ¹⁶ Whoever believes and is baptized will be saved; but whoever does not believe will be condemned."

¹⁹ So then the Sovereign [*or* Lord] Jesus, after speaking to them, was taken up into heaven, and sat down at the right hand of God. ²⁰ And they went forth and preached everywhere, while the Sovereign [*or* Lord] worked with them and confirmed the message by the signs that attended it. Amen.

---

*Addition to the text. See "Metaphor" and "God the Father and Mother" in the Appendix.

EASTER 7

Lesson 1 ~ Acts 1:6-14

The risen Jesus is taken up into heaven.

⁶ So when the apostles had come together, they asked Jesus, "Sovereign ⟦*or* Lord⟧, will you at this time restore the realm☆ to Israel?" ⁷ Jesus said, "It is not for you to know times or seasons which have been fixed by God's⊗ own authority. ⁸ But you shall receive power when the Holy Spirit has come upon you; and you shall be my witnesses in Jerusalem and in all Judea and Samaria and to the end of the earth." ⁹ And having said this, as the apostles were looking on, Jesus was lifted up and carried on a cloud out of their sight. ¹⁰ And while they were gazing into heaven as Jesus went, two figures stood by them in white robes, ¹¹ and said, "People of Galilee, why do you stand looking into heaven? This Jesus, who was taken up from you into heaven, will come in the same way as you saw Jesus go into heaven."

¹² Then the apostles returned to Jerusalem from the mount called Olivet, which is near Jerusalem, a sabbath day's journey away; ¹³ and when they had entered, they went up to the upper room, where they were staying, Peter and John and James and Andrew, Philip and Thomas, Bartholomew and Matthew, James the son of Alphaeus and Simon the Zealot and Judas the son of James. ¹⁴ All these with one accord devoted themselves to prayer, together with the women and Mary the mother of Jesus, and with Jesus' brothers.

Psalm 68:1-10

¹ Let God arise, let God's enemies be scattered;
    let those who hate God flee before God!
² As smoke is driven away, so drive them away;
    as wax melts before fire,
    let the wicked perish before God!
³ But let the righteous be joyful;
    let them exult before God;
    let them be jubilant with joy!
⁴ Sing to God, sing praises to God's name;
    lift up a song to the one who rides upon the clouds,
    whose name is SOVEREIGN ⟦*or* the LORD⟧, exult before God!

☆RSV *kingdom.* See Appendix.
⊗RSV *which the Father has fixed by his own authority.* See Appendix.

⁵ Parent of the orphan and protector of widows
    is God in God's holy habitation.
⁶ God gives the desolate a home in which to dwell,
    and leads out the prisoners to prosperity;
    but the rebellious dwell in a parched land.
⁷ O God, when you went forth before your people,
    when you marched through the wilderness,
⁸ the earth quaked, the heavens poured down rain,
    at the presence of God;
Sinai quaked at the presence of God,
    the God of Israel.
⁹ Rain in abundance, O God, you shed abroad;
    you restored your heritage as it languished;
¹⁰ your flock found a dwelling in it;
    in your goodness, O God, you provided for the needy.

Lesson 2 ~ 1 Peter 4:12-14; 5:6-11

Those suffering persecution are to do right.

¹² Beloved, do not be surprised at the fiery ordeal which comes upon you to prove you, as though something strange were happening to you. ¹³ But rejoice in so far as you share Christ's sufferings, that you may also rejoice and be glad when Christ's glory is revealed. ¹⁴ If you are reproached for the name of Christ, you are blessed, because the spirit of glory and of God rests upon you.

5:6 Humble yourselves therefore under the mighty hand of God, that in due time God may exalt you. ⁷ Cast all your anxieties on God, for God cares about you. ⁸ Be sober, be watchful. Your adversary the devil prowls around like a roaring lion, seeking someone to devour. ⁹ Resist the devil, firm in your faith, knowing that the same experience of suffering is required of the Christian community throughout the world. ¹⁰ And after you have suffered a little while, the God of all grace, who has called you to eternal glory in Christ, will restore, establish, and strengthen you. ¹¹ To God be the dominion forever and ever. Amen.

Gospel ~ John 17:1-11

Jesus prays for the disciples.

¹ Having spoken these words, Jesus looked up to heaven and said, "[*God my Mother and**] Father, the hour has come; glorify your Child,[◇] so that the Child[◇] may glorify you, ² since you have given that Child power over all flesh, to give eternal life to all whom you have given your Child. ³ And this is eternal life, that they know you the only true God, and Jesus Christ whom you have sent. ⁴ I glorified you on earth, having accomplished the work which you gave me to do; ⁵ and now, [*God my*] Father [*and Mother**], glorify me in your own presence with the glory which I had with you before the world was made.

⁶ "I have manifested your name to those whom you gave me out of the world; yours they were, and you gave them to me, and they have kept your word. ⁷ Now they know that everything that you have given me is from you; ⁸ for I have given them the words which you gave me, and they have received them and know in truth that I came from you; and they have believed that you sent me. ⁹ I am praying for them; I am not praying for the world but for those whom you have given me, for they are yours; ¹⁰ all mine are yours, and yours are mine, and I am glorified in them. ¹¹ And now I am no more in the world, but they are in the world, and I am coming to you. Holy [*God my Mother and**] Father, keep them in your name, which you have given me, that they may be one, even as we are one."

---

*Addition to the text. See "Metaphor" and "God the Father and Mother" in the Appendix.
◇RSV *Son*. See Appendix.

PENTECOST

(If the first lesson is read from the Old Testament, the lection from Acts should be read as Lesson 2.)

Lesson 1 ~ Acts 2:1-21

Luke describes the day of Pentecost, when worshipers were filled with the Holy Spirit.

[1] When the day of Pentecost had come, they were all together in one place. [2] And suddenly a sound came from heaven like the rush of a mighty wind, and it filled all the house where they were sitting. [3] And there appeared to them tongues as of fire, distributed and resting on each one of them. [4] And they were all filled with the Holy Spirit and began to speak in other tongues, as the Spirit gave them utterance.

[5] Now there were dwelling in Jerusalem devout Jews from every nation under heaven. [6] And at this sound the multitude came together, and they were bewildered, because they heard them speaking each in their own language. [7] And they were amazed and wondered, saying, "Are not all these who are speaking Galileans? [8] And how is it that we hear, each of us in our own native language? [9] Parthians and Medes and Elamites and residents of Mesopotamia, Judea and Cappadocia, Pontus and Asia, [10] Phrygia and Pamphylia, Egypt and the parts of Libya belonging to Cyrene, and visitors from Rome, both Jews and proselytes, [11] Cretans and Arabians, we hear them telling in our own tongues the mighty works of God." [12] And all were amazed and perplexed, saying to one another, "What does this mean?" [13] But others mocking said, "They are filled with new wine."

[14] But Peter, standing with the eleven, lifted up his voice and addressed them, "People of Judea and all who dwell in Jerusalem, let this be known to you, and give ear to my words. [15] For these people are not drunk, as you suppose, since it is only the third hour of the day; [16] but this is what was spoken by the prophet Joel:

[17] 'And in the last days it shall be, God declares,
  that I will pour out my Spirit upon all flesh,
  and your sons and your daughters shall prophesy,
  and the young shall see visions,
  and the old shall dream dreams;
[18] and in those days I will pour out my Spirit
  on my servants, both men and women; and they shall prophesy.
[19] And I will show wonders in the heaven above
  and signs on the earth beneath,
  blood, and fire, and vapor of smoke;

²⁰ the sun shall be turned into night
and the moon into blood,
before the day of the Sovereign ⟦*or* Lord⟧ comes,
the great and manifest day.
²¹ And it shall be that whoever calls on the name of the Sovereign ⟦*or*
Lord⟧ shall be saved.'"

Lesson 1 (alternate) ~ Isaiah 44:1-8

God, the Redeemer, proclaims: "I am the first and the last." No one is to be afraid.

¹ "But now hear, O Jacob my servant,
Israel whom I have chosen!
² Thus says the GOD ⟦*or* LORD⟧ who made you,
who formed you from the womb and will help you:
Fear not, O Jacob my servant,
Jeshurun whom I have chosen.
³ For I will pour water on the thirsty land,
and streams on the dry ground;
I will pour my Spirit upon your descendants,
and my blessing on your offspring.
⁴ They shall spring up like grass amid waters,
like willows by flowing streams.
⁵ This one will say, 'I am GOD's ⟦*or* the LORD's⟧,'
another will say, 'my name is Jacob,'
and another will write on their hand, 'GOD's ⟦*or* The LORD's⟧,'
and say, 'my family name is Israel.'"
⁶ Thus says GOD ⟦*or* the LORD⟧, the Ruler[□] and Redeemer of Israel,
the GOD ⟦*or* LORD⟧ of hosts:
"I am the first and I am the last;
besides me there is no god.
⁷ Who is like me? Let them proclaim it,
let them declare and set it forth before me.
Who has announced from of old the things to come?
Let them tell us what is yet to be.
⁸ Fear not, nor be afraid;
have I not told you from of old and declared it?
And you are my witnesses!
Is there a God besides me?
There is no Rock; I know not any."

□RSV *King*. See Appendix.

24 O GOD [or LORD], how manifold are your works!
  In wisdom you have made them all;
  the earth is full of your creatures.
25 Yonder is the sea, great and wide,
  which teems with things innumerable,
  living things both small and great.
26 There go the ships,
  and Leviathan which you formed to sport in it.
27 These all look to you,
  to give them their food in due season.
28 When you give to them, they gather it up;
  when you open your hand, they are filled with good things.
29 When you hide your face, they are dismayed;
  when you take away their breath, they die
  and return to their dust.
30 When you send forth your Spirit, they are created;
  and you renew the face of the ground.
31 May the glory of GOD [or the LORD] endure forever,
  may GOD [or the LORD] rejoice in God's works,
32 who looks on the earth and it trembles,
  who touches the mountains and they smoke!
33 I will sing to GOD [or the LORD] as long as I live;
  I will sing praise to my God while I have being.
34 May my meditation be pleasing to God,
  in whom I rejoice.

Lesson 2 ~ 1 Corinthians 12:3b-13

(If Isaiah 44:1-8 is read as the first lesson, Acts 2:1-21 should be read as Lesson 2.)

Paul writes to the Corinthians about spiritual gifts.

3 No one speaking by the Spirit of God ever says "Jesus be cursed!" and no one can say "Jesus is Sovereign [or Lord]" except by the Holy Spirit.

4 Now there are varieties of gifts, but the same Spirit; 5 and there are varieties of service, but the same Sovereign [or Lord]; 6 and there are varieties of working, but it is the same God who inspires them all in everyone. 7 To each is given the manifestation of the Spirit for the common good. 8 To one is given through the Spirit the utterance of wisdom, and to another the utterance of knowledge according to the same Spirit, 9 to

another faith by the same Spirit, to another gifts of healing by the one Spirit, [10] to another the working of miracles, to another prophecy, to another the ability to distinguish between spirits, to another various kinds of tongues, to another the interpretation of tongues. [11] All these are inspired by one and the same Spirit, who apportions to each one individually as the Spirit wills.

[12] For just as the body is one and has many members, and all the members of the body, though many, are one body, so it is with Christ. [13] For by one Spirit we were all baptized into one body—Jews or Greeks, slaves or free—and all were made to drink of one Spirit.

Gospel ~ John 20:19-23

Jesus breathes the Spirit upon the disciples.

[19] On the evening of that day, the first day of the week, the doors being shut where the disciples were, for fear of the religious authorities,[∇] Jesus came and stood among them and said to them, "Peace be with you." [20] Having said this, Jesus showed them Jesus' hands and side. Then the disciples were glad when they saw the Sovereign [[or Lord]]. [21] Jesus said to them again, "Peace be with you. As [God] the Father [and Mother*] has sent me, even so I send you." [22] Having said this, Jesus breathed on them, and said to them, "Receive the Holy Spirit. [23] If you forgive the sins of any, they are forgiven; if you retain the sins of any, they are retained."

Gospel (alternate) ~ John 7:37-39

Jesus gives the living water which is the Spirit.

[37] On the last day of the feast, the great day, Jesus stood up and proclaimed, "Let anyone who thirsts come to me and drink. [38] Whoever believes in me, as the scripture has said, 'Out of that one's heart shall flow rivers of living water.'" [39] Now this he said about the Spirit, which those who believed in him were to receive; for as yet the Spirit had not been given, because Jesus was not yet glorified.

∇RSV *the Jews.* See Appendix.
*RSV *the Father.* See "Metaphor" and "God the Father and Mother" in the Appendix.

TRINITY

Lesson 1 ~ Deuteronomy 4:32-40

Moses recalls God's wondrous deeds and reminds the people to keep God's commandments.

32 For ask now of the days that are past, which were before you, since the day that God created humankind upon the earth, and ask from one end of heaven to the other, whether such a great thing as this has ever happened or was ever heard of. 33 Did any people ever hear the voice of a god speaking out of the midst of the fire, as you have heard, and still live? 34 Or has any god ever attempted to go and take a nation from the midst of another nation, by trials, by signs, by wonders, and by war, by a mighty hand and an outstretched arm, and by great terrors, according to all that the SOVEREIGN [or LORD] your God did for you in Egypt before your eyes? 35 To you it was shown, that you might know that the SOVEREIGN [or LORD] is God; there is no other. 36 Out of heaven God spoke to you in order to discipline you; and on earth you saw God's great fire, and you heard God's words out of the midst of the fire. 37 And because God loved your ancestors and chose their descendants after them, and brought you out of Egypt with God's own presence and great power, 38 driving out before you nations greater and mightier than yourselves, to bring you in, to give you their land for an inheritance, as at this day; 39 know therefore this day, and lay it to your heart, that the SOVEREIGN [or LORD] is God in heaven above and on the earth beneath; there is no other. 40 Therefore you shall keep God's statutes and commandments, which I command you this day, that it may go well with you, and with your children after you, and that you may prolong your days in the land which the SOVEREIGN [or LORD] your God gives you forever.

[1] Rejoice in GOD [[*or* the LORD]], O you righteous!
    Praise befits the upright.
[2] Praise GOD [[*or* the LORD]] with the lyre,
    make melody on the harp of ten strings!
[3] Sing to God a new song,
    play skillfully on the strings, with loud shouts.
[4] For the word of GOD [[*or* the LORD]] is upright;
    and all God's work is done in faithfulness.
[5] God loves righteousness and justice;
    the earth is full of the steadfast love of GOD [[*or* the LORD]].
[6] By the word of GOD [[*or* the LORD]] the heavens were made,
    and all their host by the breath of God's mouth.
[7] God gathered the waters of the sea as in a bottle,
    and put the deeps in storehouses.
[8] Let all the earth fear GOD [[*or* the LORD]],
    let all the inhabitants of the world stand in awe!
[9] For God spoke, and it came to be;
    God commanded, and it stood forth.
[10] GOD [[*or* The LORD]] brings the counsel of the nations to nought,
    and frustrates the plans of the peoples.
[11] The counsel of GOD [[*or* the LORD]] stands forever,
    the thoughts of God's heart to all generations.
[12] Blessed is the nation whose God is the SOVEREIGN [[*or* LORD]],
    the people whom God has chosen as a heritage!

Lesson 2 ～ 2 Corinthians 13:5-14

Paul exhorts the church at Corinth.

⁵ Examine yourselves, to see whether you are holding to your faith. Test yourselves. Do you not realize that Jesus Christ is in you?—unless indeed you fail to meet the test! ⁶ I hope you will find out that we have not failed. ⁷ But we pray God that you may not do wrong—not that we may appear to have met the test, but that you may do what is right, though we may seem to have failed. ⁸ For we cannot do anything against the truth, but only for the truth. ⁹ For we are glad when we are weak and you are strong. What we pray for is your improvement. ¹⁰ I write this while I am away from you, in order that when I come I may not have to be severe in my use of the authority which the Sovereign [[*or* Lord]] has given me for building up and not for tearing down.

¹¹ Finally, my friends, farewell. Mend your ways, heed my appeal, agree with one another, live in peace, and the God of love and peace will be with you. ¹² Greet one another with a holy kiss. ¹³ All the saints greet you.

¹⁴ The grace of the Sovereign [[*or* Lord]] Jesus Christ and the love of God and the communion of the Holy Spirit be with you all.

Gospel ～ Matthew 28:16-20

The disciples are commissioned to make disciples, to baptize, and to teach.

¹⁶ Now the eleven disciples went to Galilee, to the mountain to which Jesus had directed them. ¹⁷ And when they saw Jesus they worshiped Jesus; but some doubted. ¹⁸ And Jesus came and said to them, "All authority in heaven and on earth has been given to me. ¹⁹ Go therefore and make disciples of all nations, baptizing them in the name of [*God*] the Father [*and Mother**], and of Jesus Christ the beloved Child,◇ and of the Holy Spirit, ²⁰ teaching them to observe all that I have commanded you; and I am with you always, to the close of the age."

---

*Addition to the text. See "Metaphor" and "God the Father and Mother" in the Appendix.
◇RSV *and of the Son*. See Appendix.

PENTECOST 2

Lesson 1 ~ Genesis 12:1-9

Abram and Sarai are chosen to play a decisive role in God's purpose for history.

¹ Now GOD [[*or* the LORD]] said to Abram, "Go from your country and your kindred and your family's house to the land that I will show you. ² And I will make of you a great nation, and I will bless you, and make your name great, so that you will be a blessing. ³ I will bless those who bless you, and the one who curses you I will curse; and by you all the families of the earth shall bless themselves."

⁴ So Abram went, as GOD [[*or* the LORD]] had told him; and Lot went with him. Abram was seventy-five years old when he departed from Haran. ⁵ And Abram took Sarai his wife, and Lot his nephew, and all their possessions which they had gathered, and the persons that they had gotten in Haran; and they set forth to go to the land of Canaan. When they had come to the land of Canaan, ⁶ Abram passed through the land to the place at Shechem, to the oak of Moreh. At that time the Canaanites were in the land. ⁷ Then GOD [[*or* the LORD]] appeared to Abram, and said, "To your descendants I will give this land." So Abram built there an altar to GOD [[*or* the LORD]], who had appeared to him. ⁸ Then Abram went to the mountain on the east of Bethel, and pitched a tent, with Bethel on the west and Ai on the east; and there Abram built an altar to GOD [[*or* the LORD]] and called on the name of the SOVEREIGN [[*or* LORD]]. ⁹ And Abram journeyed on, still going toward the Negeb.

¹² Blessed is the nation whose God is the SOVEREIGN [*or* LORD],
  the people whom God has chosen as a heritage!
¹³ GOD [*or* The LORD] looks down from heaven,
  and sees all humankind;
¹⁴ from where God sits enthroned God looks forth
  on all the inhabitants of the earth,
¹⁵ God who fashions the hearts of them all,
  and observes all their deeds.
¹⁶ A ruler⸋ is not saved by a great army;
  a warrior is not delivered by great strength.
¹⁷ The war horse is a vain hope for victory,
  and by its great might it cannot save.
¹⁸ The eye of the SOVEREIGN [*or* LORD] is on those who fear God,
  on those who hope in God's steadfast love,
¹⁹ that God may deliver their soul from death,
  and keep them alive in famine.
²⁰ Our soul waits for the SOVEREIGN [*or* LORD],
  who is our help and shield.
²¹ Indeed, our heart is glad in God,
  because we trust in God's holy name.
²² Let your steadfast love, O SOVEREIGN [*or* LORD], be upon us,
  even as we hope in you.

⸋RSV *king*. See Appendix.

Lesson 2 ～ Romans 3:21-28

Righteousness is based on faith, not on works.

21 But now the righteousness of God has been manifested apart from law, although the law and the prophets bear witness to it, 22 the righteousness of God through faith in Jesus Christ for all who believe. For there is no distinction; 23 since all have sinned and fall short of the glory of God, 24 they are justified by God's grace as a gift, through the redemption which is in Christ Jesus, 25 whom God put forward as a blood expiation, to be received by faith. This was to show God's righteousness, because in divine forbearance God had passed over former sins; 26 it was to prove at the present time that God is indeed righteous and justifies one who has faith in Jesus. 27 Then what becomes of our boasting? It is excluded. On what principle? On the principle of works? No, but on the principle of faith. 28 For we hold that one is justified by faith apart from works of law.

Gospel ～ Matthew 7:21-29

Jesus tells the parable of a house built on the rock and a house built on the sand.

21 "Not everyone who says to me, 'Sovereign, Sovereign [[*or* Lord, Lord]],' shall enter the realm☆ of heaven, but those who do the will of [*God*] my Father [*and Mother**] who is in heaven. 22 On that day many will say to me, 'Sovereign, Sovereign [[*or* Lord, Lord]], did we not prophesy in your name, and cast out demons in your name, and do many mighty works in your name?' 23 And then will I declare to them, 'I never knew you; depart from me, you evildoers.'

24 "Everyone then who hears these words of mine and does them will be like someone wise enough to build a house upon the rock; 25 and the rain fell, and the floods came, and the winds blew and beat upon that house, but it did not fall, because it had been founded on the rock. 26 And everyone who hears these words of mine and does not do them will be like the fool who built a house upon the sand; 27 and the rain fell, and the floods came, and the winds blew and beat against that house, and it fell; and great was the fall of it."

28 And when Jesus finished these sayings, the crowds were astonished at his teaching, 29 for he taught them as one who had authority, and not as their scribes.

☆RSV *kingdom.* See Appendix.
*Addition to the text. See "Metaphor" and "God the Father and Mother" in the Appendix.

PENTECOST 3

Lesson 1 ~ Genesis 22:1-18

God puts Abraham to the test.

¹ After these things God tested Abraham, and said to him, "Abraham!" And he said, "Here am I." ² "Take your son, your only son Isaac, whom you love, and go to the land of Moriah, and offer him there as a burnt offering upon one of the mountains of which I shall tell you." ³ So Abraham rose early in the morning, saddled his donkey, and took two of his young men with him, and his son Isaac; and he cut the wood for the burnt offering, and arose and went to the place of which God had told him. ⁴ On the third day Abraham lifted up his eyes and saw the place afar off. ⁵ Then Abraham said to the young men, "Stay here with the donkey; I and the lad will go yonder and worship, and come again to you." ⁶ And Abraham took the wood of the burnt offering, and laid it on Isaac his son; and he took in his hand the fire and the knife. So they went both of them together. ⁷ And Isaac said to his father Abraham, "My father!" And Abraham said, "Here am I, my son." Isaac said, "Here is the fire and the wood; but where is the lamb for a burnt offering?" ⁸ Abraham said, "God will provide the lamb for a burnt offering, my son." So they went both of them together.

⁹ When they came to the place of which God had told him, Abraham built an altar there, and laid the wood in order, and bound Isaac his son, and laid him on the altar, upon the wood. ¹⁰ Then Abraham put forth his hand, and took the knife to slay his son. ¹¹ But the angel of GOD [or the LORD] called to him from heaven, and said, "Abraham, Abraham!" And he said, "Here am I." ¹² The angel said, "Do not lay your hand on the lad or do anything to him; for now I know that you fear God, seeing you have not withheld your son, your only son, from me." ¹³ And Abraham lifted up his eyes and looked, and there, behind him was a ram, caught in a thicket by his horns; and Abraham went and took the ram, and offered it up as a burnt offering instead of his son. ¹⁴ So Abraham called the name of that place "GOD [or The LORD] will provide"; as it is said to this day, "On the mount of GOD [or the LORD] it shall be provided."

¹⁵ And the angel of GOD [or the LORD] called to Abraham a second time from heaven, ¹⁶ and said, "By myself I have sworn, says GOD [or the LORD], because you have done this, and have not withheld your son, your only son, ¹⁷ I will indeed bless you, and I will multiply your descendants as the stars of heaven and as the sand which is on the seashore. And your descendants shall possess the gate of their enemies, ¹⁸ and by your descendants shall all the nations of the earth bless themselves, because you have obeyed my voice."

Psalm 13

¹ How long, O GOD ⟦*or* LORD⟧? Will you forget me forever?
  How long will you hide your face from me?
² How long must I bear pain in my soul,
    and have sorrow in my heart all the day?
  How long shall my enemy be exalted over me?
³ Consider and answer me, O SOVEREIGN ⟦*or* LORD⟧ my God;
    lighten my eyes, lest I sleep the sleep of death;
⁴ lest my enemy say, "I have prevailed over you";
    lest my foes rejoice because I am shaken.
⁵ But I have trusted in your steadfast love;
    my heart shall rejoice in your salvation.
⁶ I will sing to GOD ⟦*or* the LORD⟧,
    because God has dealt bountifully with me.

Lesson 2 ~ Romans 4:13-18

Paul writes that nothing depends upon what one does but that everything depends on faith and the grace of God.

¹³ The promise to Abraham and to the descendants of Abraham [*and Sarah**], that they should inherit the world, did not come through the law but through the righteousness of faith. ¹⁴ If it is the adherents of the law who are to be the heirs, faith is null and the promise is void. ¹⁵ For the law brings wrath, but where there is no law there is no transgression.

¹⁶ That is why it depends on faith, in order that the promise may rest on grace and be guaranteed to all their descendants—not only to the adherents of the law but also to those who share the faith of Abraham, who [*with Sarah**] is the ancestor of us all; ¹⁷ as it is written, "I have made you the ancestor of many nations"—in the presence of the God in whom Abraham believed, who gives life to the dead and calls into existence the things that do not exist. ¹⁸ In hope Abraham believed against hope, in order to become the ancestor of many nations; as he had been told, "So shall your descendants be."

---

*Addition to the text. See "Addition of Women's Names to the Text" in the Appendix.

Jesus calls a tax collector as a disciple, and announces that he goes not to those who are well but to those who are sick.

⁹ Passing on from there, Jesus saw someone called Matthew sitting at the tax office; and Jesus said to him, "Follow me." And Matthew rose and followed Jesus.

¹⁰ And as Jesus sat at table in the house, many tax collectors and sinners came and sat down with him and the disciples. ¹¹ And when the Pharisees saw this, they said to the disciples, "Why does your teacher eat with tax collectors and sinners?" ¹² But hearing this, Jesus said, "Those who are well have no need of a physician, but those who are sick. ¹³ Go and learn what this means, 'I desire mercy, and not sacrifice.' For I came not to call the righteous, but sinners."

PENTECOST 4

Lesson 1 ~ Genesis 25:19-34

Jacob tricks Isaac and steals Esau's birthright.

19 These are the descendants of Isaac, Abraham's son: Abraham was the father of Isaac, 20 and Isaac was forty years old when he married Rebekah, the daughter of Bethuel the Aramean of Paddanaram, the sister of Laban the Aramean. 21 And Isaac prayed to GOD [[*or* the LORD]] for his wife, because she was barren; and GOD [[*or* the LORD]] granted his prayer, and Rebekah his wife conceived. 22 The children struggled together within her; and she said, "If it is thus, why do I live?" So she went to inquire of GOD [[*or* the LORD]]. 23 And GOD [[*or* the LORD]] said to her,

"Two nations are in your womb,
  and two peoples, born of you, shall be divided;
the one shall be stronger than the other,
  the elder shall serve the younger."

24 When her days to be delivered were fulfilled, there were twins in her womb. 25 The first came forth red, all his body like a hairy mantle; so they called his name Esau. 26 Afterward his brother came forth, and his hand had taken hold of Esau's heel; so his name was called Jacob. Isaac was sixty years old when Rebekah bore them.

27 When the boys grew up, Esau was a skillful hunter, a man of the field, while Jacob was a quiet man, dwelling in tents. 28 Isaac loved Esau, because he ate of Esau's game; but Rebekah loved Jacob.

29 Once when Jacob was boiling stew, Esau came in from the field, and he was famished. 30 And Esau said to Jacob, "Let me eat some of that red stew, for I am famished!" (Therefore his name was called Edom.) 31 Jacob said, "First sell me your birthright." 32 Esau said, "I am about to die; of what use is a birthright to me?" 33 Jacob said, "Swear to me first." So Esau swore to him, and sold his birthright to Jacob. 34 Then Jacob gave Esau bread and lentil stew, and Esau ate and drank, and rose and went his way. Thus Esau despised his birthright.

¹ God is our refuge and strength,
a very present help in trouble.
² Therefore we will not fear though the earth should change,
though the mountains shake in the heart of the sea;
³ though its waters roar and foam,
though the mountains tremble with its tumult.
⁴ There is a river whose streams make glad the city of God,
the holy habitation of the Most High.
⁵ God is in the midst of it and it shall not be moved;
God will help it right early.
⁶ The nations rage, the kingdoms totter;
God speaks, the earth melts.
⁷ The GOD [or LORD] of hosts is with us;
the God of Jacob is our refuge.
⁸ Come, behold the works of GOD [or the LORD],
who has wrought desolations in the earth,
⁹ making wars cease to the end of the earth,
breaking the bow, shattering the spear,
and burning the chariots with fire!
¹⁰ "Be still, and know that I am God.
I am exalted among the nations,
I am exalted in the earth!"
¹¹ The GOD [or LORD] of hosts is with us;
the God of Jacob is our refuge.

Lesson 2 ~ Romans 5:6-11

Paul reflects on the significance of Christ's death.

⁶ While we were still weak, at the right time Christ died for the ungodly. ⁷ Why, one will hardly die for a righteous person—though perhaps for a good person one will dare even to die. ⁸ But God shows love for us in that while we were yet sinners, Christ died for us. ⁹ Since, therefore, we are now justified by the blood of Christ, much more shall we be saved by Christ from the wrath of God. ¹⁰ For if while we were enemies we were reconciled to God by the death of God's Child,◇ much more, now that we are reconciled, shall we be saved by the life of Christ. ¹¹ Not only so, but we also rejoice in God through our Sovereign [or Lord] Jesus Christ, through whom we have now received our reconciliation.

◇RSV *of his Son.* See Appendix.

Matthew narrates Jesus' calling of the twelve disciples and his charge to them when they are sent out.

35 And Jesus went about all the cities and villages, teaching in their synagogues and preaching the gospel of the realm of heaven, ✩ and healing every disease and every infirmity. 36 Seeing the crowds, Jesus had compassion for them, because they were harassed and helpless, like sheep without a shepherd. 37 Then Jesus said to the disciples, "The harvest is plentiful, but the laborers are few; 38 pray therefore to the Sovereign [[or Lord]] of the harvest, to send out laborers into the harvest."

10:1 And Jesus summoned the twelve disciples and gave them authority over unclean spirits, to cast them out, and to heal every disease and every infirmity. 2 The names of the twelve apostles are these: first, Simon, who is called Peter, and Andrew his brother; James the son of Zebedee, and John his brother; 3 Philip and Bartholomew; Thomas and Matthew the tax collector; James the son of Alphaeus, and Thaddaeus; 4 Simon the Cananaean, and Judas Iscariot, who betrayed Jesus.

5 These twelve Jesus sent out, charging them, "Go nowhere among the Gentiles, and enter no town of the Samaritans, 6 but go rather to the lost sheep of the house of Israel. 7 And preach as you go, saying, 'The realm✩ of heaven is at hand.' 8 Heal those who are sick, raise the dead, cleanse those who have leprosy, cast out demons. You received without paying, give without pay."

✩RSV 9:35 *gospel of the kingdom*; 10:7 *kingdom*. See Appendix.

PENTECOST 5

Lesson 1 ~ Genesis 28:10-17

God's promise to Abraham is renewed to Jacob in a dream.

10 Jacob left Beersheba, and went toward Haran. 11 And he came to a certain place, and stayed there that night, because the sun had set. Taking one of the stones of the place, he put it under his head and lay down in that place to sleep. 12 And he dreamed that there was a ladder set up on the earth, and the top of it reached to heaven; and the angels of God were ascending and descending on it! 13 And GOD [or the LORD] stood above it and said, "I am the SOVEREIGN [or LORD], the God of Abraham, your ancestor, and the God of Isaac; the land on which you lie I will give to you and to your descendants; 14 and your descendants shall be like the dust of the earth, and you shall spread abroad to the west and to the east and to the north and to the south; and by you and your descendants shall all the families of the earth bless themselves. 15 I am with you and will keep you wherever you go, and will bring you back to this land; for I will not leave you until I have done that of which I have spoken to you." 16 Then Jacob awoke from sleep and said, "Surely GOD [or the LORD] is in this place; and I did not know it." 17 And he was afraid, and said, "How awesome is this place! This is none other than the house of God, and this is the gate of heaven."

Psalm 91:1-10

1 Whoever dwells in the shelter of the Most High,
　　who abides in the shadow of the Almighty,
2 will say to GOD [or the LORD], "My refuge and my fortress;
　　my God, in whom I trust."
3 For God will deliver you from the snare of the fowler
　　and from the deadly pestilence;
4 God will cover you with God's pinions,
　　and under God's wings you will find refuge;
　　God's faithfulness is a shield and buckler.
5 You will not fear the terror of the night,
　　nor the arrow that flies by day,
6 nor the pestilence that stalks at midnight,
　　nor the destruction that wastes at noonday.
7 A thousand may fall at your side,
　　ten thousand at your right hand;
　　but it will not come near you.

⁸ You will only look with your eyes
    and see the recompense of the wicked.
⁹ Because you have made GOD [[*or* the LORD]] your refuge,
    the Most High your habitation,
¹⁰ no evil shall befall you,
    no scourge come near your tent.

Lesson 2 ∼ Romans 5:12-19

Paul writes of the trespass of Adam and of the grace of Jesus Christ.

¹² Therefore as sin came into the world through one human being and death through sin, and so death spread to all humankind because all sinned—¹³ sin indeed was in the world before the law was given, but sin is not counted where there is no law. ¹⁴ Yet death reigned from Adam to Moses, even over those whose sins were not like the transgression of Adam, who was a type of the one who was to come.

¹⁵ But the free gift is not like the trespass. For if many died through the trespass of one, much more have the grace of God and the free gift in the grace of that one person Jesus Christ abounded for many. ¹⁶ And the free gift is not like the effect of that one person's sin. For the judgment following one trespass brought condemnation, but the free gift following many trespasses brings justification. ¹⁷ If, because of the trespass of one, death reigned through that one, much more will those who receive the abundance of grace and the free gift of righteousness reign in life through the one person Jesus Christ.

¹⁸ Then as the trespass of one led to condemnation for all, so the act of righteousness of one leads to acquittal and life for all. ¹⁹ For as by the disobedience of one many were made sinners, so by the obedience of one many will be made righteous.

Jesus tells the disciples that they will be treated shamefully by the world, but that they should have nothing to fear.

24 A disciple is not above the teacher, nor a servant above the one who is served; 25 it is enough for the disciple to be like the teacher, and the servant like the one who is served. If they have called the householder Beelzebul, how much more will they malign those of that household?

26 So have no fear of them; for nothing is covered that will not be revealed, or hidden that will not be known. 27 What I tell you in the dark, utter in the light; and what you hear whispered, proclaim upon the housetops. 28 And do not fear those who kill the body but cannot kill the soul; rather fear the one who can destroy both soul and body in hell. 29 Are not two sparrows sold for a penny? And not one of them will fall to the ground without the will of God.⊗ 30 But even the hairs of your head are all numbered. 31 Fear not, therefore; you are of more value than many sparrows. 32 So everyone who acknowledges me before others, I also will acknowledge before [God] my [Mother and*] Father who is in heaven; 33 but whoever denies me before others, I also will deny before God⊗ who is in heaven.

⊗RSV v. 29 *your Father's will*; v. 33 *my Father*. See Appendix.
*Addition to the text. See "Metaphor" and "God the Father and Mother" in the Appendix.

PENTECOST 6

During the night, Jacob wrestles with a stranger and is given the name Israel.

22 The same night Jacob arose and took his two wives, his two maids, and his eleven children, and crossed the ford of the Jabbok. 23 He took them and sent them across the stream, and likewise everything that he had. 24 And Jacob was left alone; and a stranger wrestled with him until the breaking of the day. 25 Seeing that he did not prevail against Jacob, the stranger touched the hollow of Jacob's thigh; and Jacob's thigh was put out of joint as they wrestled with each other. 26 Then the stranger said, "Let me go, for the day is breaking." But Jacob said, "I will not let you go, unless you bless me." 27 And he said to Jacob, "What is your name?" And he replied, "Jacob." 28 Then the stranger said, "Your name shall no more be called Jacob, but Israel, for you have striven with God and with human beings, and have prevailed." 29 Then Jacob asked, "Tell me, I pray, your name." But the stranger said, "Why is it that you ask my name?" And there the stranger blessed him. 30 So Jacob called the name of the place Peniel, saying, "For I have seen God face to face, and yet my life is preserved." 31 The sun rose upon Jacob as he passed Penuel, limping because of his thigh. 32 Therefore to this day the Israelites do not eat the sinew of the hip which is upon the hollow of the thigh, because the stranger touched the hollow of Jacob's thigh on the sinew of the hip.

Psalm 17:1-7, 15

1 Hear a just cause, O GOD [[or LORD]]; attend to my cry!
Give ear to my prayer from lips free of deceit!
2 From you, let my vindication come!
Let your eyes see the right!
3 If you try my heart, if you visit me by night,
if you test me, you will find no wickedness in me;
my mouth does not transgress.
4 With regard to human works, by the word of your lips
I have avoided the ways of the violent.
5 My steps have held fast to your paths,
my feet have not slipped.
6 I call upon you, for you will answer me, O God;
incline your ear to me, hear my words.
7 Wondrously show your steadfast love,
O savior of those who seek refuge
from their adversaries at your right hand.
15 As for me, I shall behold your face in righteousness;
when I awake, I shall be satisfied with beholding your form.

Lesson 2 ~ Romans 6:3-11

Having written that where sin increases, grace abounds, Paul continues to speak of one's life with Christ.

3 Do you not know that all of us who have been baptized into Christ Jesus were baptized into Christ's death? 4 We were buried therefore with Christ by baptism into death, so that as Christ was raised from the dead by the glory of [God] the Father [and Mother*], we too might walk in newness of life.

5 For if we have been united with Christ in a death like that of Christ, we shall certainly be united with Christ in a resurrection like that of Christ. 6 We know that our old self was crucified with Christ so that the sinful body might be destroyed, and we might no longer be enslaved to sin. 7 For anyone who has died is freed from sin. 8 But if we have died with Christ, we believe that we shall also live with Christ. 9 For we know that Christ, being raised from the dead, will never die again; death no longer has dominion over Christ. 10 The death Christ died, Christ died to sin, once for all; but the life Christ lives, Christ lives to God. 11 So you also must consider yourselves dead to sin and alive to God in Christ Jesus.

---

*Addition to the text. See "Metaphor" and "God the Father and Mother" in the Appendix.

Jesus' coming into the world divides people from each other: some take up the cross, and some do not.

34 Do not think that I have come to bring peace on earth; I have not come to bring peace, but a sword. 35 For I have come to set a man against his father, and a daughter against her mother, and a daughter-in-law against her mother-in-law; 36 and one's foes will be those of one's own household. 37 Whoever loves father or mother more than me is not worthy of me; and whoever loves son or daughter more than me is not worthy of me; 38 and those who do not take their own cross and follow me are not worthy of me. 39 Those who find their life will lose it, and those who lose their life for my sake will find it.

40 Anyone who receives you receives me, and anyone who receives me receives the one who sent me. 41 Anyone who receives a prophet because that one is a prophet shall receive the reward of a prophet, and anyone who receives the righteous because they are righteous shall receive the reward of the righteous. 42 And whoever gives to one of these little ones even a cup of cold water because that little one is a disciple, truly, I say to you, the giver shall not go unrewarded.

PENTECOST 7

Lesson 1 ~ Exodus 1:6–2:10⁺

During the oppression of Israel by Egypt, women rescue from death the male babies of the Israelites.

⁶ Then Joseph died, and all his brothers, and all that generation. ⁷But the descendants of Israel were fruitful and increased greatly; they multiplied and grew exceedingly strong; so that the land was filled with them. ⁸ Now there arose a new king over Egypt, who did not know Joseph. ⁹And the king said to his people, "Behold, the people of Israel are too many and too mighty for us. ¹⁰Come, let us deal shrewdly with them, lest they multiply, and, if war befall us, they join our enemies and fight against us and escape from the land." ¹¹Therefore they set taskmasters over the Israelites to afflict them with heavy burdens; and they built for Pharaoh store-cities, Pithom and Raamses. ¹²But the more they were oppressed, the more the Israelites multiplied and the more they spread abroad. And the Egyptians were in dread of the people of Israel. ¹³So they made the people of Israel serve with rigor, ¹⁴and made their lives bitter with hard service, in mortar and brick, and in all kinds of work in the field; in all their work they made them serve with rigor.

¹⁵ Then the king of Egypt said to the Hebrew midwives, one of whom was named Shiphrah and the other Puah, ¹⁶"When you serve as midwife to the Hebrew women, and see them upon the birthstool, if it is a son, you shall kill him; but if it is a daughter, she shall live." ¹⁷But the midwives feared God, and did not do as the king of Egypt commanded them, but let the male children live. ¹⁸So the king of Egypt called the midwives, and said to them, "Why have you done this, and let the male children live?" ¹⁹The midwives said to Pharaoh, "Because the Hebrew women are not like the Egyptian women; for they are vigorous and are delivered before the midwife comes to them." ²⁰So God dealt well with the midwives; and the people multiplied and grew very strong. ²¹And because the midwives feared God, God gave them families. ²²Then Pharaoh commanded all his people, "Every son that is born to the Hebrews you shall cast into the Nile, but you shall let every daughter live."

²:¹ Now a man from the house of Levi went and took to wife a daughter of Levi. ²The woman conceived and bore a son; and when she saw that he was a goodly child, she hid him three months. ³And when she could hide him no longer she took for him a basket made of bulrushes, and daubed it with bitumen and pitch; and she put the child in it and placed it among

---

⁺NACCL reads Exodus 1:6-14, 22–2:10. See Appendix, p. 277.

the reeds at the river's brink. ⁴And his sister stood at a distance, to know what would be done to him. ⁵Now the daughter of Pharaoh came down to bathe at the river, and her young women walked beside the river; she saw the basket among the reeds and sent her servant to fetch it. ⁶When she opened it she saw the baby, and he was crying. She took pity on him and said, "This is one of the Hebrews' children." ⁷Then his sister said to Pharaoh's daughter, "Shall I go and call you a nurse from the Hebrew women to nurse the child for you?" ⁸And Pharaoh's daughter said to her, "Go." So the girl went and called the child's mother. ⁹And Pharaoh's daughter said to her, "Take this child away, and nurse him for me, and I will give you your wages." So the woman took the child and nursed him. ¹⁰And the child grew, and she brought him to Pharaoh's daughter, and he became her son; and she named him Moses, for she said, "Because I drew him out of the water."

Psalm 124

¹ If it had not been GOD [[or the LORD]] who was on our side,
    let Israel now say—
² if it had not been GOD [[or the LORD]] who was on our side,
    when people rose up against us,
³ then they would have swallowed us up alive,
    when their anger was kindled against us;
⁴ then the flood would have swept us away,
    the torrent would have gone over us;
⁵ then over us would have gone
    the raging waters.
⁶ Blessed be GOD [[or the LORD]],
    who has not given us
    as prey to their teeth!
⁷ We have escaped as a bird
    from the snare of the fowlers;
  the snare is broken,
    and we have escaped!
⁸ Our help is in the name of GOD [[or the LORD]],
    who made heaven and earth.

Lesson 2 ~ Romans 7:14-25a

Paul speaks of sin and the law, and of freedom from condemnation in Christ Jesus.

14 We know that the law is spiritual; but I am carnal, sold under sin. 15 I do not understand my own actions. For I do not do what I want, but I do the very thing I hate. 16 Now if I do what I do not want, I agree that the law is good. 17 So then it is no longer I that do it, but sin which dwells within me. 18 For I know that nothing good dwells within me, that is, in my flesh. I can will what is right, but I cannot do it. 19 For I do not do the good I want, but the evil I do not want is what I do. 20 Now if I do what I do not want, it is no longer I that do it, but sin which dwells within me. 21 So I find it to be a law that when I want to do right, evil lies close at hand. 22 For I delight in the law of God, in my inmost self, 23 but I see in my members another law at war with the law of my mind and making me captive to the law of sin which dwells in my members. 24 How wretched I am! Who will deliver me from this body of death? 25 Thanks be to God through Jesus Christ our Sovereign [[or Lord]]!

Gospel ~ Matthew 11:25-30

Jesus speaks of the relationship of the Child of God to God the Father and Mother.

25 At that time Jesus declared, "I thank you, [God, my Mother and*] Father, Sovereign [[or Lord]] of heaven and earth, that you have hidden these things from the wise and understanding and have revealed them to children; 26 for such, O God,⊗ was your gracious will. 27 All things have been delivered to me by [God] my Father [and Mother*]; and no one knows the Child◇ except God,⊗ and no one knows God⊗ except the Child◇ and anyone to whom the Child◇ chooses to reveal God. 28 Come to me, all who labor and are heavy laden, and I will give you rest. 29 Take my yoke upon you, and learn from me; for I am gentle and lowly in heart, and you will find rest for your souls. 30 For my yoke is easy, and my burden is light."

---

*Addition to the text. See "Metaphor" and "God the Father and Mother" in the Appendix.
⊗RSV v. 26 *Father;* v. 27 *the Father.* See Appendix.
◇RSV *Son.* See Appendix.

PENTECOST 8

Lesson 1 ~ Exodus 2:11-22

Moses kills an Egyptian and flees to Midian.

¹¹ One day, when Moses had grown up, he went out to his people and looked on their burdens; and he saw an Egyptian beating a Hebrew, one of his people. ¹² Moses looked this way and that, and seeing no one, he killed the Egyptian and hid the body in the sand. ¹³When he went out the next day, two Hebrews were struggling together; and Moses said to the one that did the wrong, "Why do you strike your neighbor?" ¹⁴ He answered, "Who made you a prince and a judge over us? Do you mean to kill me as you killed the Egyptian?" Then Moses was afraid, and thought, "Surely the thing is known." ¹⁵ When Pharaoh heard of it, he sought to kill Moses.

But Moses fled from Pharaoh, and stayed in the land of Midian; and he sat down by a well. ¹⁶ Now the priest of Midian had seven daughters; and they came and drew water, and filled the troughs to water their father's flock. ¹⁷ The shepherds came and drove them away; but Moses stood up and helped them, and watered their flock. ¹⁸ When they came to their father Reuel, he said, "How is it that you have come so soon today?" ¹⁹They said, "An Egyptian delivered us out of the hand of the shepherds, and even drew water for us and watered the flock." ²⁰ Reuel said to his daughters, "And where is he? Why have you left the man? Call him, that he may eat bread." ²¹ And Moses was content to dwell with the man, and he gave Moses his daughter Zipporah. ²² She bore a son, and Moses called his name Gershom, saying, "I have been a resident alien in a foreign land."

Psalm 69:6-15

⁶ Let not those who hope in you be put to shame through me,
  O Sovereign [*or* Lord] GOD of hosts;
 let not those who seek you be brought to dishonor through me,
  O God of Israel.
⁷ For it is for your sake that I have borne reproach,
  that shame has covered my face.
⁸ I have become a stranger to my family,
  an alien to my mother's children.
⁹ For zeal for your house has consumed me,
  and the insults of those who insult you have fallen on me.

¹⁰ When I humbled my soul with fasting,
    it became my reproach.
¹¹ When I made sackcloth my clothing,
    I became a byword to them.
¹² I am the talk of those who sit in the gate,
    and the drunkards make songs about me.
¹³ But as for me, my prayer is to you, O GOD [or LORD].
    At an acceptable time, O God,
    in the abundance of your steadfast love answer me.
With your faithful help ¹⁴ rescue me
    from sinking in the mire;
let me be delivered from my enemies
    and from the deep waters.
¹⁵ Let not the flood sweep over me,
    or the deep swallow me up,
    or the pit close its mouth over me.

Lesson 2 ~ Romans 8:9-17

Paul exhorts the Romans to live in the Spirit.

⁹ But you are not in the flesh, you are in the Spirit, if in fact the Spirit of God dwells in you. Anyone who does not have the Spirit of Christ does not belong to Christ. ¹⁰ But if Christ is in you, although your bodies are dead because of sin, your spirits are alive because of righteousness. ¹¹ If the Spirit of the one who raised Jesus from the dead dwells in you, the one who raised Christ Jesus from the dead will give life to your mortal bodies also through that same Spirit which dwells in you.

¹² So then, brothers and sisters, we are debtors, not to the flesh, to live according to the flesh— ¹³ for if you live according to the flesh you will die, but if by the Spirit you put to death the deeds of the body you will live. ¹⁴ For all who are led by the Spirit of God are daughters and sons of God. ¹⁵ For you did not receive the spirit of slavery to fall back into fear, but you have received the spirit of adoption as children of God. When we cry, "[*God! my Mother and**] Father!" ¹⁶ it is the Spirit bearing witness with our spirit that we are children of God, ¹⁷ and if children, then heirs, heirs of God and joint heirs with Christ, provided we suffer with Christ in order that we may also be glorified with Christ.

---

*Addition to the text. RSV *"Abba!"* See "Metaphor" and "God the Father and Mother" in the Appendix.

Jesus tells the parable of the sower.

¹ That same day Jesus went out of the house and sat beside the sea. ² And great crowds gathered around, so that Jesus got into a boat and sat there; and the whole crowd stood on the beach. ³ And Jesus told them many things in parables, saying: "A sower went out to sow. ⁴ And as the seeds were being scattered, some seeds fell along the path, and the birds came and devoured them. ⁵ Other seeds fell on rocky ground, where they had not much soil, and immediately they sprang up, since they had no depth of soil, ⁶ but when the sun rose they were scorched; and since they had no root they withered away. ⁷ Other seeds fell upon thorns, and the thorns grew up and choked them. ⁸ Other seeds fell on good soil and brought forth grain, some a hundredfold, some sixty, some thirty. ⁹ Those who have ears, let them hear."

¹⁸ "Hear then the parable of the sower. ¹⁹ When any hear the word of the realm☆ of heaven and do not understand it, the evil one comes and snatches away what is sown in the heart; this is what was sown along the path. ²⁰ As for what was sown on rocky ground, this is the one who hears the word and immediately receives it with joy; ²¹ yet having no root within, this one endures for a while, and when tribulation or persecution arises on account of the word, immediately falls away. ²² As for what was sown among thorns, this is the one who hears the word, but the cares of the world and the delight in riches choke the word, and it proves unfruitful. ²³ As for what was sown on good soil, this is the one who hears the word and understands it, who indeed bears fruit, and yields, in one case a hundredfold, in another sixty, and in another thirty."

☆RSV *kingdom*. See Appendix.

PENTECOST 9

Lesson 1 ~ Exodus 3:1-12

From a flaming bush, God calls Moses to deliver Israel.

¹ Now Moses was keeping the flock of his father-in-law, Jethro, the priest of Midian; and he led his flock to the west side of the wilderness, and came to Horeb, the mountain of God. ² And the angel of GOD [or the LORD] appeared to him in a flame of fire out of the midst of a bush; and Moses looked, and lo, the bush was burning, yet it was not consumed. ³ And Moses said, "I will turn aside and see this great sight, why the bush is not burnt." ⁴ When GOD [or the LORD] saw that he turned aside to see, God called to him out of the bush, "Moses, Moses!" And he said, "Here am I." ⁵ Then God said, "Do not come near; put off your shoes from your feet, for the place on which you are standing is holy ground." ⁶ And God said, "I am the God of your ancestor, the God of Abraham [and Sarah*], the God of Isaac [and Rebekah*], and the God of Jacob [and Rachel and Leah*]." And Moses hid his face, for he was afraid to look at God.

⁷ Then GOD [or the LORD] said, "I have seen the affliction of my people who are in Egypt, and have heard their cry because of their taskmasters; I know their sufferings, ⁸ and I have come down to deliver them out of the hand of the Egyptians, and to bring them up out of that land to a good and broad land, a land flowing with milk and honey, to the place of the Canaanites, the Hittites, the Amorites, the Perizzites, the Hivites, and the Jebusites. ⁹ And now the cry of the people of Israel has come to me, and I have seen the oppression with which the Egyptians oppress them. ¹⁰ Come, I will send you to Pharaoh that you may bring forth my people, the children of Israel, out of Egypt." ¹¹ But Moses said to God, "Who am I that I should go to Pharaoh, and bring the children of Israel out of Egypt?" ¹² God said, "But I will be with you; and this shall be the sign for you, that I have sent you: when you have brought forth the people out of Egypt, you shall serve God upon this mountain."

Psalm 103:1-13

¹ Bless GOD [or the LORD], O my soul;
    and all that is within me, bless God's holy name!
² Bless GOD [or the LORD], O my soul,
    and forget not all God's benefits,
³ who forgives all your iniquity,
    who heals all your diseases,

---

*Addition to the text. See "Addition of Women's Names to the Text" in the Appendix.

⁴ who redeems your life from the Pit,
    who crowns you with steadfast love and mercy,
⁵ who satisfies you with good as long as you live
    so that your youth is renewed like the eagle's.
⁶ GOD [or The LORD] works vindication
    and justice for all who are oppressed.
⁷ God made known God's ways to Moses,
    God's acts to the people of Israel.
⁸ GOD [or The LORD] is merciful and gracious,
    slow to anger and abounding in steadfast love,
⁹ not always chiding,
    and not remaining angry forever.
¹⁰ God does not deal with us according to our sins,
    nor repay us according to our iniquities.
¹¹ For as the heavens are high above the earth,
    so great is God's steadfast love toward those who fear God;
¹² as far as the east is from the west,
    so far does God remove our transgressions from us.
¹³ As parents pity their children,
    so GOD [or the LORD] pities those who fear God.

Lesson 2 ~ Romans 8:18-25

Along with the children of God, the whole creation groans as it waits for redemption.

¹⁸ I consider that the sufferings of this present time are not worth comparing with the glory that is to be revealed to us. ¹⁹ For the creation waits with eager longing for the revealing of the children of God; ²⁰ for the creation was subjected to futility, not of its own will but by the will of the one who subjected it in hope; ²¹ because the creation itself will be set free from its bondage to decay and obtain the glorious liberty of the children of God. ²² We know that the whole creation has been groaning in travail together until now; ²³ and not only the creation, but we ourselves, who have the firstfruits of the Spirit, groan inwardly as we wait for adoption as children of God, the redemption of our bodies. ²⁴ For in this hope we were saved. Now hope that is seen is not hope. For who hopes for what is already seen? ²⁵ But if we hope for what we do not see, we wait for it with patience.

Jesus tells three parables.

24 Jesus put a parable before them, saying, "The realm✩ of heaven may be compared to someone who sowed good seed in a field; 25 but while everyone was sleeping, an enemy came and sowed weeds among the wheat, and went away. 26 So when the plants came up and bore grain, then the weeds appeared also. 27 And the servants of the householder came and asked, 'Did you not sow good seed in your field? How then has it weeds?' 28 The householder said to them, 'An enemy has done this.' The servants replied, 'Then do you want us to go and gather them?' 29 But the householder said, 'No; lest in gathering the weeds you root up the wheat along with them. 30 Let both grow together until the harvest; and at harvest time I will tell the reapers, Gather the weeds first and bind them in bundles to be burned, but gather the wheat into my barn.' "

31 Another parable he put before them, saying, "The realm✩ of heaven is like a grain of mustard seed which a man took and sowed in his field; 32 it is the smallest of all seeds, but when it has grown it is the greatest of shrubs and becomes a tree, so that the birds of the air come and make nests in its branches."

33 He told them another parable. "The realm✩of heaven is like leaven which a woman took and hid in three measures of meal, till it was all leavened."

34 All this Jesus said to the crowds in parables; indeed he said nothing to them without a parable. 35 This was to fulfill what was spoken by the prophet:

"I will open my mouth in parables,
I will utter what has been hidden since the foundation of the
     world."

36 Then Jesus left the crowds and went into the house. And the disciples came to him, saying, "Explain to us the parable of the weeds of the field." 37 Jesus answered, "The one who sows the good seed is the Human One;○ 38 the field is the world, and the good seed means the children of the heavenly realm;✩ the weeds are the children of the evil one, 39 and the enemy who sowed them is the devil; the harvest is the close of the age,

---

+NAACL reads Matthew 13:24-30, 36-43. See Appendix, p. 277.
✩RSV *kingdom.* See Appendix.
○RSV *Son of man.* See Appendix.
✩RSV v. 38 *the sons of the kingdom;* v. 43 *kingdom.*

and the reapers are angels. [40] Just as the weeds are gathered and burned with fire, so will it be at the close of the age. [41] The Human One° will send angels, and they will gather out of the world all causes of sin and all evildoers, [42] and throw them into the furnace of fire, where there shall be weeping and gnashing of teeth. [43] Then the righteous will shine like the sun in the realm☆ of their God.⊗ Those who have ears, let them hear."

⊗RSV *Father.* See Appendix.

PENTECOST 10

Lesson 1 ~ Exodus 3:13-20

God's name is revealed to Moses.

[13] Then Moses said to God, "If I come to the people of Israel and say to them, 'The God of your ancestors has sent me to you,' and they ask me, 'What is the name of that God?' what shall I say to them?" [14] God said to Moses, "I AM WHO I AM." And God said, "Say this to the people of Israel, 'I AM has sent me to you.'" [15] God also said to Moses, "Say this to the people of Israel, 'The SOVEREIGN [or LORD], the God of your ancestors, the God of Abraham [and Sarah*], the God of Isaac [and Rebekah*], and the God of Jacob [and Rachel and Leah*], has sent me to you': this is my name forever, and thus I am to be remembered throughout all generations. [16] Go and gather the elders of Israel together, and say to them, 'The SOVEREIGN [or LORD], the God of your ancestors, the God of Abraham [and Sarah*], of Isaac [and Rebekah*], and of Jacob [and Rachel and Leah*], has appeared to me, saying, "I have observed you and what has been done to you in Egypt; [17] and I promise that I will bring you up out of the affliction of Egypt, to the land of the Canaanites, the Hittites, the Amorites, the Perizzites, the Hivites, and the Jebusites, a land flowing with milk and honey."' [18] And they will hearken to your voice; and you and the elders of Israel shall go to the king of Egypt and shall say to him, 'The SOVEREIGN [or LORD], the God of the Hebrews, has met with us; and now, we pray you, let us go a three days' journey into the wilderness, that we may sacrifice to the SOVEREIGN [or LORD] our God.' [19] I know that the king of Egypt will not let you go unless compelled by a mighty hand. [20] So I will stretch out my hand and smite Egypt with all the wonders which I will do in it; after that he will let you go."

---

*Addition to the text. See "Addition of Women's Names to the Text" in the Appendix.

¹ O give thanks to GOD ⟦*or* the LORD⟧, call on God's name,
    make known God's deeds among the nations!
² Sing to God, sing praises to God,
    tell of all God's wonderful works!
³ Glory in God's holy name;
    let the hearts of those who seek GOD ⟦*or* the LORD⟧ rejoice!
⁴ Seek GOD ⟦*or* the LORD⟧ and God's strength,
    seek God's presence continually!
⁵ Remember the wonderful works that God has done,
    the miracles, and the judgments God uttered,
⁶ O offspring of Abraham [*and Sarah,**] God's servants,
    children of Jacob, [*Rachel, and Leah,**] God's chosen ones!
⁷ This is the SOVEREIGN ⟦*or* LORD⟧ our God,
    whose judgments are in all the earth.
⁸ God is mindful of the covenant forever,
    of the word commanded for a thousand generations,
⁹ the covenant which God made with Abraham,
    God's sworn promise to Isaac,
¹⁰ confirmed to Jacob as a statute,
    to Israel as an everlasting covenant,
¹¹ saying, "To you I will give the land of Canaan
    as your portion for an inheritance."

---

*Addition to the text. See "Addition of Women's Names to the Text" in the Appendix.

Lesson 2 ~ Romans 8:26-30

Paul asserts that God works for good with those who love God.

26 The Spirit helps us in our weakness; for we do not know how to pray as we ought, but that very Spirit intercedes for us with sighs too deep for words. 27 And the one who searches human hearts knows what is the mind of the Spirit, because the Spirit intercedes for the saints according to the will of God.

28 We know that in everything God works for good with those who love God, who are called according to God's purpose. 29 For those whom God foreknew were also predestined to be conformed to the image of God's Child,◇ in order that Christ might be the firstborn among many believers. 30 And those whom God predestined, God also called; and those whom God called, God also justified; and those whom God justified, God also glorified.

Gospel ~ Matthew 13:44-52

Jesus speaks in three different ways about the realm of heaven.

44 "The realm✫ of heaven is like treasure hidden in a field, which someone found and covered up; then in great joy the finder goes and sells everything and buys that field.

45 "Again, the realm✫ of heaven is like a merchant in search of fine pearls, 46 who, on finding one pearl of great value, went and sold everything and bought it.

47 "Again, the realm✫ of heaven is like a net which was thrown into the sea and gathered fish of every kind; 48 when the net was full, it was drawn ashore and people sat down and sorted the good into vessels but threw away the bad. 49 So it will be at the close of the age. The angels will come out and separate the evil from the righteous, 50 and throw them into the furnace of fire, where there will be weeping and gnashing of teeth.

51 "Have you understood all this?" They answered, "Yes." 52 And Jesus said to them, "Therefore every scribe who has been trained for the realm✫ of heaven is like a householder who brings out of the treasury what is new and what is old."

◇RSV *his Son*. See Appendix.
✫RSV *kingdom*. See Appendix.

PENTECOST 11

Lesson 1 ~ Exodus 12:1-14

God instructs Israel about keeping the Passover.

¹ GOD [*or* The LORD] said to Moses and Aaron in the land of Egypt, ² "This month shall be for you the beginning of months; it shall be the first month of the year for you. ³ Tell all the congregation of Israel that on the tenth day of this month each of them shall take a lamb according to their families' houses, a lamb for a household; ⁴ and if the household is too small for a lamb, two households shall take according to the number of persons; according to what each can eat you shall make your count for the lamb. ⁵ Your lamb shall be without blemish, a male a year old; you shall take it from the sheep or from the goats; ⁶ and you shall keep it until the fourteenth day of this month, when the whole assembly of the congregation of Israel shall kill their lambs in the evening. ⁷ Then they shall take some of the blood, and put it on the two doorposts and the lintel of the houses in which they eat them. ⁸ They shall eat the flesh that night, roasted; with unleavened bread and bitter herbs they shall eat it. ⁹ Do not eat any of it raw or boiled with water, but roasted, its head with its legs and its inner parts. ¹⁰ And you shall let none of it remain until the morning, anything that remains until the morning you shall burn. ¹¹ In this manner you shall eat it: your loins girded, your sandals on your feet, and your staff in your hand; and you shall eat it in haste. It is the passover of GOD [*or* the LORD]. ¹² For I will pass through the land of Egypt that night, and I will smite all the firstborn in the land of Egypt, both human and animal; and on all the gods of Egypt I will execute judgments: I am the SOVEREIGN [*or* LORD]. ¹³ The blood shall be a sign for you, upon the houses where you are; and when I see the blood, I will pass over you, and no plague shall fall upon you to destroy you, when I smite the land of Egypt.

¹⁴ "This day shall be for you a memorial day, and you shall keep it as a feast to GOD [*or* the LORD]; throughout your generations you shall observe it as an ordinance forever."

Psalm 143:1-10

¹ Hear my prayer, O GOD [[or LORD]]; give ear to my supplications!
  In your faithfulness answer me, in your righteousness!
² Enter not into judgment with your servant;
  for no one living is righteous before you.
³ For the enemy has pursued me,
  has crushed my life to the ground,
  and has made me sit in darkness like those long dead.
⁴ Therefore my spirit faints within me;
  my heart within me is appalled.
⁵ I remember the days of old,
  I meditate on all that you have done;
  I muse on what your hands have wrought.
⁶ I stretch out my hands to you;
  my soul thirsts for you like a parched land.
⁷ Make haste to answer me, O GOD [[or LORD]]!
  My spirit fails!
 Hide not your face from me,
  lest I be like those who go down to the Pit.
⁸ Let me hear in the morning of your steadfast love,
  for in you I put my trust.
 Teach me the way I should go,
  for to you I lift up my soul.
⁹ Deliver me, O GOD [[or LORD]], from my enemies!
  I have fled to you for refuge!
¹⁰ Teach me to do your will,
  for you are my God!
 Let your good spirit lead me
  on a level path!

Lesson 2 ~ Romans 8:31-39

In a lyrical passage Paul glories in the love of God in Christ Jesus.

31 What then shall we say to this? If God is for us, who is against us?
32 God who did not spare God's own Child◇ but gave up that Child for us
all, will not God also give us all things with Christ? 33 Who shall bring any
charge against God's elect? It is God who justifies; 34 who is to condemn?
Is it Christ Jesus, who died, yes, who was raised from the dead, who is at
the right hand of God, who indeed intercedes for us? 35 Who shall
separate us from the love of Christ? Shall tribulation, or distress, or
persecution, or famine, or nakedness, or peril, or sword? 36 As it is
written,

> "For your sake we are being killed all the day long;
> we are regarded as sheep to be slaughtered."

37 No, in all these things we are more than conquerors through the one
who loved us. 38 For I am sure that neither death, nor life, nor angels, nor
principalities, nor things present, nor things to come, nor powers, 39 nor
height, nor depth, nor anything else in all creation, will be able to
separate us from the love of God in Christ Jesus our Sovereign [or Lord].

Gospel ~ Matthew 14:13-21

Jesus feeds the five thousand.

13 Jesus withdrew in a boat to a lonely place apart. But when the crowds
heard it, they followed on foot from the towns. 14 Going ashore, Jesus saw
a great throng and had compassion on them, and healed their sick.
15 When it was evening, the disciples returned, saying, "This is a lonely
place, and the day is now over; send the crowds away to go into the
villages and buy food for themselves." 16 Jesus said, "They need not go
away; you give them something to eat." 17 They replied, "We have only
five loaves here and two fish." 18 Jesus said, "Bring them here to me."
19 Then he ordered the crowds to sit down on the grass; and taking the five
loaves and the two fish Jesus looked up to heaven, and blessed, and broke
and gave the loaves to the disciples, and the disciples gave them to the
crowds. 20 And they all ate and were satisfied. And they took up twelve
baskets full of the broken pieces left over. 21 And those who ate were about
five thousand men and women and children.

◇RSV *Son*. See Appendix.

PENTECOST 12

Lesson 1 ~ Exodus 14:19-31

God delivers Israel from Pharaoh's army at the Red Sea.

¹⁹ Then the angel of God who went before the host of Israel moved and went behind them; and the pillar of cloud moved from before them and stood behind them, ²⁰ coming between the host of Egypt and the host of Israel. And there was the cloud and the darkness; and the night passed without one coming near the other all night.

²¹ Then Moses stretched out his hand over the sea; and GOD [or the LORD] drove the sea back by a strong east wind all night, and made the sea dry land, and the waters were divided. ²² And the people of Israel went into the midst of the sea on dry ground, the waters being a wall to them on their right hand and on their left. ²³ The Egyptians pursued, and went in after them into the midst of the sea, all Pharaoh's horses, chariots, and drivers. ²⁴ And in the morning watch GOD [or the LORD] in the pillar of fire and of cloud looked down upon the host of the Egyptians, and confounded the host of the Egyptians, ²⁵ clogging their chariot wheels so that they drove heavily; and the Egyptians said, "Let us flee from before Israel; for GOD [or the LORD] fights for them against the Egyptians."

²⁶ Then GOD [or the LORD] said to Moses, "Stretch out your hand over the sea, that the water may come back upon the Egyptians, upon their chariots, and upon their drivers." ²⁷ So Moses stretched forth his hand over the sea, and the sea returned to its normal flow when the morning appeared; and the Egyptians fled into it, and GOD [or the LORD] routed the Egyptians in the midst of the sea. ²⁸ The waters returned and covered the chariots and the drivers and all the host of Pharaoh that had followed them into the sea; not so much as one of them remained. ²⁹ But the people of Israel walked on dry ground through the sea, the waters being a wall to them on their right hand and on their left.

³⁰ Thus GOD [or the LORD] saved Israel that day from the hand of the Egyptians; and Israel saw the Egyptians dead upon the seashore. ³¹ And Israel saw the great work which GOD [or the LORD] did against the Egyptians, and the people feared GOD [or the LORD]; and they believed in GOD [or the LORD] and in God's servant Moses.

⁴ Remember me, O GOD [or LORD], when you show favor to your
people;
help me when you deliver them;
⁵ that I may see the prosperity of your chosen ones,
that I may rejoice in the gladness of your nation,
that I may glory with your heritage.
⁶ Both we and our ancestors have sinned;
we have committed iniquity, we have done wickedly.
⁷ Our ancestors, when they were in Egypt,
did not consider your wonderful works;
they did not remember the abundance of your steadfast love,
but rebelled against the Most High at the Red Sea,
⁸ yet were saved for the sake of God's name,
in order to make known God's mighty power.
⁹ God rebuked the Red Sea, and it became dry,
and God led them through the deep as through a desert.
¹⁰ So God saved them from the hand of the foe,
and delivered them from the power of the enemy.
¹¹ And the waters covered their adversaries;
not one of them was left.
¹² Then they believed God's words;
they sang God's praise.

Lesson 2 ~ Romans 9:1-5

Paul speaks with anguish about his own people.

¹ I am speaking the truth in Christ, I am not lying; my conscience
bears me witness in the Holy Spirit, ² that I have great sorrow and
unceasing anguish in my heart. ³ For I could wish that I myself were
accursed and cut off from Christ for the sake of my own people, my
kinsfolk by race. ⁴ They are Israelites, and to them belong the relationship of children to God, the glory, the covenants, the giving of
the law, the worship, and the promises; ⁵ to them belong the ancestors in
faith, and from them, according to the flesh, is the Christ. God who is
over all be blessed forever. Amen.

Jesus comes to the disciples who are in a boat on the sea.

[22] Jesus made the disciples get into the boat and go on ahead to the other side, while he dismissed the crowds. [23] After dismissing the crowds, he went up on the mountain by himself to pray. When evening came, he was there alone, [24] but the boat by this time was many furlongs distant from the land, beaten by the waves; for the wind was against them. [25] And in the fourth watch of the night Jesus came to the disciples, walking on the sea. [26] But when the disciples saw Jesus walking on the sea, they were terrified, saying, "It is a ghost!" And they cried out in fear. [27] But immediately Jesus spoke to them, saying, "Take heart, it is I; have no fear."

[28] And Peter answered, "Sovereign [[or Lord]], if it is you, bid me come to you on the water." [29] Jesus said, "Come." So Peter got out of the boat and walked on the water and came to Jesus; [30] but seeing the wind, Peter was afraid and, beginning to sink, cried out, "Sovereign [[or Lord]], save me." [31] Jesus immediately reached out and caught Peter, saying, "O you of little faith, why did you doubt?" [32] And when Jesus and Peter got into the boat, the wind ceased. [33] And those in the boat worshiped Jesus, saying, "Truly you are the Child◇ of God."

◇RSV *Son*. See Appendix.

PENTECOST 13

Lesson 1 ~ Exodus 16:2-15

God gives Israel manna to eat.

² And the whole congregation of the people of Israel murmured against Moses and Aaron in the wilderness, ³ and said to them, "Would that we had died by the hand of GOD [[*or* the LORD]] in the land of Egypt, when we sat by the fleshpots and ate bread to the full; for you have brought us out into this wilderness to kill this whole assembly with hunger."

⁴ Then GOD [[*or* the LORD]] said to Moses, "Behold, I will rain bread from heaven for you; and the people shall go out and gather a day's portion every day, that I may prove them, whether they will walk in my law or not. ⁵ On the sixth day, when they prepare what they bring in, it will be twice as much as they gather daily." ⁶ So Moses and Aaron said to all the people of Israel, "At evening you shall know that it was GOD [[*or* the LORD]] who brought you out of the land of Egypt, ⁷ and in the morning you shall see the glory of GOD [[*or* the LORD]], because God has heard your murmurings against GOD [[*or* the LORD]]. For what are we, that you murmur against us?" ⁸ And Moses said, "When GOD [[*or* the LORD]] gives you in the evening flesh to eat and in the morning bread to the full, because GOD [[*or* the LORD]] has heard your murmurings which you murmur against God— what are we? Your murmurings are not against us but against GOD [[*or* the LORD]]."

⁹ And Moses said to Aaron, "Say to the whole congregation of the people of Israel, 'Come near before GOD [[*or* the LORD]], for God has heard your murmurings.'" ¹⁰ And as Aaron spoke to the whole congregation of the people of Israel, they looked toward the wilderness, and behold, the glory of GOD [[*or* the LORD]] appeared in the cloud. ¹¹ And GOD [[*or* the LORD]] said to Moses, ¹² "I have heard the murmurings of the people of Israel; say to them, 'At twilight you shall eat flesh, and in the morning you shall be filled with bread; then you shall know that I am the SOVEREIGN [[*or* LORD]] your God.'"

¹³ In the evening quails came up and covered the camp; and in the morning dew lay round about the camp. ¹⁴ And when the dew had gone up, there was on the face of the wilderness a fine, flake-like thing, fine as hoarfrost on the ground. ¹⁵ When the people of Israel saw it, they said to one another, "What is it?" For they did not know what it was. And Moses said to them, "It is the bread which GOD [[*or* the LORD]] has given you to eat."

Psalm 78:1-3, 10-20

[1] Give ear, O my people, to my teaching;
   incline your ears to the words of my mouth!
[2] I will open my mouth in a parable;
   I will utter obscure sayings from of old,
[3] things that we have heard and known,
   that our ancestors have told us.
[10] They did not keep God's covenant,
   but refused to walk according to God's law.
[11] They forgot what God had done,
   and the miracles that God had shown them.
[12] In the sight of their ancestors God wrought marvels
   in the land of Egypt, in the fields of Zoan.
[13] God divided the sea and let them pass through it,
   and made the waters stand like a heap.
[14] In the daytime God led them with a cloud,
   and all the night with a fiery light.
[15] God cleft rocks in the wilderness,
   and gave them drink abundantly as from the deep.
[16] God made streams come out of the rock,
   and caused waters to flow down like rivers.
[17] Yet they sinned still more against God,
   rebelling against the Most High in the desert.
[18] They tested God in their heart
   by demanding the food they craved.
[19] They spoke against God, saying,
   "Can God spread a table in the wilderness?
[20] God smote the rock so that water gushed out
   and streams overflowed.
   Can God also give bread,
   or provide meat for God's people?"

Lesson 2 ~ Romans 11:13-16, 29-32

Paul speaks of his own people, the Jews, and of the irrevocable character of God's call to them.

13 Now I am speaking to you Gentiles. Inasmuch then as I am an apostle to the Gentiles, I magnify my ministry 14 in order to make my own people jealous, and thus save some of them. 15 For if their rejection means the reconciliation of the world, what will their acceptance mean but life from the dead? 16 If the dough offered as firstfruits is holy, so is the whole lump; and if the root is holy, so are the branches.

29 For the gifts and call of God are irrevocable. 30 Just as you were once disobedient to God but now have received mercy because of their disobedience, 31 so they have now been disobedient in order that by the mercy shown to you they also may receive mercy. 32 For God has consigned all people to disobedience, that God may have mercy upon all.

Gospel ~ Matthew 15:21-28

Matthew tells the story of Jesus and the Canaanite woman who comes for mercy.

21 And Jesus went away from there and withdrew to the district of Tyre and Sidon. 22 And a Canaanite woman from that region came out and cried, "Have mercy on me, Sovereign [*or* Lord], Son of David, my daughter is severely possessed by a demon." 23 But Jesus did not answer her a word. And the disciples came and begged Jesus, saying, "Send her away, for she is crying after us." 24 Jesus answered, "I was sent only to the lost sheep of the house of Israel." 25 But she came and knelt before Jesus, saying, "Sovereign [*or* Lord], help me." 26 And Jesus answered, "It is not fair to take the children's bread and throw it to the dogs." 27 She said, "Yes, Sovereign [*or* Lord], yet even the dogs eat the crumbs that fall from their owners' table." 28 Then Jesus answered her, "O woman, great is your faith! Be it done for you as you desire." And her daughter was healed instantly.

PENTECOST 14

Lesson 1 ~ Exodus 17:1-7

Moses brings water from a rock at Massah.

¹ All the congregation of the people of Israel moved on from the Wilderness of Sin by stages, according to the commandment of GOD [[*or* the LORD]], and camped at Rephidim; but there was no water for the people to drink. ² Therefore the people found fault with Moses, and said, "Give us water to drink." And Moses said to them, "Why do you find fault with me? Why do you put GOD [[*or* the LORD]] to the proof?" ³ But the people thirsted there for water, and the people murmured against Moses, and said, "Why did you bring us up out of Egypt, to kill us and our children and our cattle with thirst?" ⁴ So Moses cried to GOD [[*or* the LORD]], "What shall I do with this people? They are almost ready to stone me." ⁵ And GOD [[*or* the LORD]] said to Moses, "Pass on before the people, taking with you some of the elders of Israel; and take in your hand the rod with which you struck the Nile, and go. ⁶ I will stand before you there on the rock at Horeb; and you shall strike the rock, and water shall come out of it, that the people may drink." And Moses did so, in the sight of the elders of Israel. ⁷ And he called the name of the place Massah and Meribah, because of the faultfinding of the children of Israel, and because they put GOD [[*or* the LORD]] to the proof by saying, "Is GOD [[*or* the LORD]] among us or not?"

Psalm 95

¹ O come, let us sing to GOD [[*or* the LORD]];
   let us make a joyful noise to the rock of our salvation!
² Let us come into God's presence with thanksgiving;
   let us make a joyful noise to God with songs of praise!
³ For the SOVEREIGN [[*or* LORD]] is a great God,
   and a great Ruler⊡ above all gods.
⁴ The depths of the earth are in the hand of God;
   the heights of the mountains are God's also.
⁵ The sea belongs to God, for God made it;
   for God's hands formed the dry land.
⁶ O come, let us worship and bow down,
   let us kneel before GOD [[*or* the LORD]], our Maker!
⁷ For this is our God,
   and we are the people of God's pasture,
   and the sheep of God's hand,
 O that today you would hearken to the voice of God!
⁸   Harden not your hearts, as at Meribah,
   as on the day at Massah in the wilderness,
⁹ when your ancestors tested me,
   and put me to the proof, though they had seen my work.
¹⁰ For forty years I loathed that generation
   and said, "They are a people who err in heart,
   and they do not regard my ways."
¹¹ Therefore I swore in my anger
   that they should not enter my rest.

Lesson 2 ~ Romans 11:33-36

Paul writes of the mystery and the inscrutability of the ways of God.

³³ O the depth of the riches and wisdom and knowledge of God! How unsearchable are God's judgments and how inscrutable God's ways!

³⁴ "For who has known the mind of the Sovereign [[*or* Lord]],
   or who has been God's counselor?"
³⁵ "Or who has given a gift to God
   in order to be repaid?"

³⁶ For from God and through God and to God are all things. To God be glory forever. Amen.

⊡RSV *King*. See Appendix.

Peter confesses Jesus to be the Christ, and Jesus teaches about the cost of discipleship.

13 Now coming into the district of Caesarea Philippi, Jesus asked the disciples, "Who do people say that the Human One° is?" 14 And they said, "Some say John the Baptist, others say Elijah, and others Jeremiah or one of the prophets." 15 Jesus said to them, "But who do you say that I am?" 16 Simon Peter replied, "You are the Christ, the Child◇ of the living God." 17 And Jesus answered Peter, "Blessed are you, Simon Bar-Jona! For flesh and blood has not revealed this to you, but [*God*] my Father [*and Mother**] who is in heaven. 18 And I tell you, you are Peter, and on this rock I will build my church, and the powers of death shall not prevail against it. 19 I will give you the keys of the realm✶ of heaven, and whatever you bind on earth shall be bound in heaven, and whatever you loose on earth shall be loosed in heaven." 20 Then Jesus strictly charged the disciples to say to no one, "Jesus is the Christ."

°RSV *Son of man*. See Appendix.
◇RSV *Son*. See Appendix.
*Addition to the text. See "Metaphor" and "God the Father and Mother" in the Appendix.
✶RSV *kingdom*. See Appendix.

PENTECOST 15

Lesson 1 ~ Exodus 19:1-9

Israel becomes God's covenant people.

¹ On the third new moon after the people of Israel had gone forth out of the land of Egypt, on that day they came into the wilderness of Sinai. ² And when they set out from Rephidim and came into the wilderness of Sinai, they encamped in the wilderness; and there Israel encamped before the mountain. ³ And Moses went up to God, and GOD [[*or* the LORD]] called to him out of the mountain, saying, "Thus you shall say to the house of Jacob, and tell the people of Israel: ⁴ You have seen what I did to the Egyptians, and how I bore you on eagles' wings and brought you to myself. ⁵ Now therefore, if you will obey my voice and keep my covenant, you shall be my own possession among all peoples; for all the earth is mine, ⁶ and you shall be to me a priestly people and a holy nation. These are the words which you shall speak to the children of Israel."

⁷ So Moses came and called the elders of the people, and set before them all these words which GOD [[*or* the LORD]] had commanded him. ⁸ And all the people answered together and said, "All that GOD [[*or* the LORD]] has spoken we will do." And Moses reported the words of the people to GOD [[*or* the LORD]]. ⁹ And GOD [[*or* the LORD]] said to Moses, "I am coming to you in a thick cloud, that the people may hear when I speak with you, and may also believe you forever."

Then Moses told the words of the people to GOD [[*or* the LORD]].

Psalm 114

¹ When Israel went forth from Egypt,
    the house of Jacob from a people of strange language,
² Judah became their sanctuary,
    Israel their dominion.
³ The sea looked and fled,
    Jordan turned back.
⁴ The mountains skipped like rams,
    the hills like lambs.
⁵ What ails you, O sea, that you flee?
    O Jordan, that you turn back?

⁶ O mountains, that you skip like rams?
    O hills, like lambs?
⁷ Tremble, O earth, at the presence of GOD [[*or* the LORD]],
    at the presence of the God of Jacob,
⁸ who turns the rock into a pool of water,
    the flint into a spring of water.

Lesson 2 ~ Romans 12:1-13

Paul writes to the Christians at Rome that they, with their diverse gifts, are one body in Christ.

¹ I appeal to you therefore, sisters and brothers, by the mercies of God, to present your bodies as a living sacrifice, holy and acceptable to God, which is your spiritual worship. ² Do not be conformed to this world but be transformed by the renewal of your mind, that you may prove what is the will of God, what is good and acceptable and perfect.

³ For by the grace given to me I bid everyone among you not to think of yourself more highly than you ought to think, but to think with sober judgment, each according to the measure of faith which God has assigned you. ⁴ For as in one body we have many members, and all the members do not have the same function, ⁵ so we, though many, are one body in Christ, and individually members one of another. ⁶ Having gifts that differ according to the grace given to us, let us use them: if prophecy, in proportion to our faith; ⁷ if service, in our serving; the one who teaches, in teaching; ⁸ the one who exhorts, in exhortation; the one who contributes, in liberality; the one who gives aid, with zeal; the one who does acts of mercy, with cheerfulness.

⁹ Let love be genuine; hate what is evil, hold fast to what is good; ¹⁰ be affectionately devoted to one another; outdo one another in showing honor. ¹¹ Never flag in zeal, be aglow with the Spirit, serve the Sovereign [[*or* Lord]]. ¹² Rejoice in your hope, be patient in tribulation, be constant in prayer. ¹³ Contribute to the needs of the saints, practice hospitality.

Gospel ~ Matthew 16:21-28

Jesus tells the disciples about what the future will hold for them.

²¹ From that time Jesus began to show the disciples that he must go to Jerusalem and suffer many things from the elders and chief priests and scribes, and be killed, and on the third day be raised. ²² And Peter took Jesus and spoke in rebuke, "God forbid! This shall never happen to you." ²³ But Jesus turned and said to Peter, "Get behind me, Satan! You are a hindrance to me; for you are not siding with God, but with humankind."

²⁴ Then Jesus told the disciples, "If any would come after me, let them deny themselves and take up their cross and follow me. ²⁵ For those who would save their life will lose it, and those who lose their life for my sake will find it. ²⁶ For what advantage will it be to gain the whole world and forfeit one's life? Or what shall one give in return for one's life? ²⁷ For the Human One° is to come with the angels in the heavenly glory of God, and will then repay everyone for their actions. ²⁸ Truly, I say to you, there are some standing here who will not taste death before they see the Human One° coming in power and glory."

°RSV *Son of man.* See Appendix.

PENTECOST 16

Lesson 1 ~ Exodus 19:16-24

Moses and Aaron represent Israel to God on Mt. Sinai.

16 On the morning of the third day there were thunders and lightnings, and a thick cloud upon the mountain, and a very loud trumpet blast, so that all the people who were in the camp trembled. 17 Then Moses brought the people out of the camp to meet God; and they took their stand at the foot of the mountain. 18 And Mount Sinai was wrapped in smoke, because GOD [[or the LORD]] descended upon it in fire; and the smoke of it went up like the smoke of a kiln, and the whole mountain quaked greatly. 19 And as the sound of the trumpet grew louder and louder, Moses spoke, and God answered him in thunder. 20 And GOD [[or the LORD]] came down upon Mount Sinai, to the top of the mountain; and GOD [[or the LORD]] called Moses to the top of the mountain, and Moses went up. 21 And GOD [[or the LORD]] said to Moses, "Go down and warn the people, lest they break through to GOD [[or the LORD]] to gaze and many of them perish. 22 And also let the priests who come near to GOD [[or the LORD]] consecrate themselves, lest GOD [[or the LORD]] break out upon them." 23 And Moses said to GOD [[or the LORD]], "The people cannot come up to Mount Sinai; for you yourself charged us, saying, 'Set bounds about the mountain, and consecrate it.'" 24 And GOD [[or the LORD]] said to him, "Go down, and come up bringing Aaron with you; but do not let the priests and the people break through to come up to GOD [[or the LORD]], lest God break out against them."

Psalm 115:1-11

1 Not to us, O GOD [[or LORD]], not to us, but to your name give glory,
   for the sake of your steadfast love and your faithfulness!
2 Why should the nations say,
   "Where is their God?"
3 Our God is in the heavens,
   and does whatever God pleases.
4 Their idols are silver and gold,
   the work of human hands.
5 They have mouths, but do not speak;
   eyes, but do not see.
6 They have ears, but do not hear;
   noses, but do not smell.

^{7} They have hands, but do not feel;
    feet, but do not walk;
    and they do not make a sound in their throat.
^{8} Those who make them are like them;
    so are all who trust in them.
^{9} O Israel, trust in GOD [[or the LORD]],
    who is their help and their shield!
^{10} O house of Aaron, put your trust in GOD [[or the LORD]],
    who is their help and their shield!
^{11} You who fear GOD [[or the LORD]], trust in GOD [[or the LORD]],
    who is their help and their shield!

Lesson 2 ~ Romans 13:1-10

Paul exhorts believers and speaks about their relationships to authorities.

^{1} Let every person be subject to the governing authorities. For there is no authority except from God, and those that exist have been instituted by God. ^{2} Therefore whoever resists the authorities resists what God has appointed, and those who resist will incur judgment. ^{3} For rulers are not a terror to good conduct, but to bad. Would you have no fear of authority? Then do what is good, and you will receive approval, ^{4} for the one in authority is God's servant for your good. But if you do wrong, be afraid, for the one in authority does not bear the sword in vain, but is the servant of God to execute God's wrath on the wrongdoer. ^{5} Therefore one must be subject, not only to avoid God's wrath but also for the sake of conscience. ^{6} For the same reason you also pay taxes, for the authorities are ministers of God, attending to this very thing. ^{7} Pay all of them their dues, taxes to whom taxes are due, revenue to whom revenue is due, respect to whom respect is due, honor to whom honor is due.

^{8} Owe no one anything, except to love one another, for whoever loves one's neighbor has fulfilled the law. ^{9} The commandments, "You shall not commit adultery, You shall not kill, You shall not steal, You shall not covet," and any other commandment, are summed up in this sentence, "You shall love your neighbor as yourself." ^{10} Love does no wrong to a neighbor; therefore love is the fulfilling of the law.

Gospel ~ Matthew 18:15-20

Jesus responds to a question from the disciples, stating the practice the church is to follow if our neighbor sins against us.

¹⁵ If your neighbor in the church sins against you, go and point out the fault between the two of you alone. If your neighbor listens to you, you have gained your neighbor. ¹⁶ But if your neighbor does not listen, take one or two others along with you, that every word may be confirmed by the evidence of two or three witnesses. ¹⁷ If your neighbor refuses to listen to them, tell it to the church; and if your neighbor refuses to listen even to the church, let that neighbor be to you as a Gentile and a tax collector. ¹⁸ Truly, I say to you, whatever you bind on earth shall be bound in heaven, and whatever you loose on earth shall be loosed in heaven. ¹⁹ Again I say to you, if two of you agree on earth about anything they ask, it will be done for them by [God] my [Mother and*] Father in heaven. ²⁰ For where two or three are gathered in my name, there am I in the midst of them.

---

*Addition to the text. See "Metaphor" and "God the Father and Mother" in the Appendix.

PENTECOST 17

Lesson 1 ~ Exodus 20:1-20

God gives the Ten Commandments to Moses.

¹ And God spoke all these words, saying,

² "I am the SOVEREIGN [*or* LORD] your God, who brought you out of the land of Egypt, out of the house of bondage.

³ "You shall have no other gods before me.

⁴ "You shall not make for yourself a graven image, or any likeness of anything that is in heaven above, or that is in the earth beneath, or that is in the water under the earth; ⁵you shall not bow down to them or serve them; for I the SOVEREIGN [*or* LORD] your God am a jealous God, visiting the iniquity of the parents upon the children to the third and the fourth generation of those who hate me, ⁶but showing steadfast love to thousands of those who love me and keep my commandments.

⁷ "You shall not take the name of the SOVEREIGN [*or* LORD] your God in vain; for GOD [*or* the LORD] will not hold anyone guiltless who takes God's name in vain.

⁸ "Remember the sabbath day, to keep it holy. ⁹Six days you shall labor, and do all your work; ¹⁰but the seventh day is a sabbath to the SOVEREIGN [*or* LORD] your God; in it you shall not do any work, you, or your son, or your daughter, or your manservant, or your womanservant, or your cattle, or the resident alien who is within your gates; ¹¹for in six days GOD [*or* the LORD] made heaven and earth, the sea, and all that is in them, and rested the seventh day; therefore GOD [*or* the LORD] blessed the sabbath day and hallowed it.

¹² "Honor your father and your mother, that your days may be long in the land which the SOVEREIGN [*or* LORD] your God gives you.

¹³ "You shall not kill.

¹⁴ "You shall not commit adultery.

¹⁵ "You shall not steal.

¹⁶ "You shall not bear false witness against your neighbor.

¹⁷ "You shall not covet your neighbor's house; you shall not covet your neighbor's wife, [*or husband,**] or manservant, or womanservant, or ox, or donkey, or anything that is your neighbor's."

¹⁸ Now when all the people perceived the thunderings and the lightnings and the sound of the trumpet and the mountain smoking, the people were afraid and trembled; and they stood afar off, ¹⁹and said to

---

*Addition to the text.

Moses, "You speak to us, and we will hear; but let not God speak to us, lest we die." [20] And Moses said to the people, "Do not fear; for God has come to prove you, and that the fear of God may be before your eyes, that you may not sin."

Psalm 19:7-14

[7] The law of GOD [[*or* the LORD]] is perfect,
    reviving the soul;
  the testimony of GOD [[*or* the LORD]] is sure,
    making wise the simple;
[8] the precepts of GOD [[*or* the LORD]] are right,
    rejoicing the heart;
  the commandment of GOD [[*or* the LORD]] is pure,
    enlightening the eyes;
[9] the fear of GOD [[*or* the LORD]] is clean,
    enduring forever;
  the ordinances of GOD [[*or* the LORD]] are true,
    and righteous altogether.
[10] More to be desired are they than gold,
    even much fine gold;
  sweeter also than honey
    and drippings of the honeycomb.
[11] Moreover by them is your servant warned;
    in keeping them there is great reward.
[12] But who can discern one's errors?
    Clear me from hidden faults.
[13] Keep back your servant also from presumptuous sins;
    let them not have dominion over me!
  Then I shall be blameless,
    and innocent of great transgression.
[14] Let the words of my mouth and the meditation of my heart
    be acceptable in your sight,
    O GOD [[*or* LORD]], my rock and my redeemer.

Paul admonishes the Christians at Rome not to pass judgment on each other, for they are all judged by God.

⁵ Some people esteem one day as better than another, while others esteem all days alike. Let all be fully convinced in their own mind. ⁶ Those who observe the day, observe it in honor of the Sovereign ⟦*or* Lord⟧. Those also who eat, eat in honor of Christ, since they give thanks to God; while those who abstain, abstain in honor of Christ and give thanks to God. ⁷ None of us live to ourselves, and none of us die to ourselves. ⁸ If we live, we live to Christ, and if we die, we die to Christ; so then, whether we live or whether we die, we are Christ's. ⁹ For to this end, Christ died and lived again, to be Sovereign ⟦*or* Lord⟧ both of the dead and of the living.

¹⁰ Why do you pass judgment on your brother or sister? Or you, why do you despise your sister or brother? For we shall all stand before the judgment seat of God; ¹¹ for it is written,

> "As I live, says the Sovereign ⟦*or* Lord⟧, every knee shall bow to me, and every tongue shall give praise to God."

¹² So each of us shall give account of ourselves to God.

Jesus compares the realm of heaven to a king who wishes to settle accounts with his servants.

²¹ Then Peter came up and said to Jesus, "Sovereign [or Lord], how often shall my brother or sister sin against me, and I forgive them? As many as seven times?" ²² Jesus answered, "I do not say to you seven times, but seventy times seven.

²³ "Therefore the realm✩ of heaven may be compared to a king who wished to settle accounts with his servants. ²⁴ When the king began the reckoning, one servant was brought in owing ten thousand talents; ²⁵ and as the servant could not pay, the king ordered the servant to be sold, with spouse and children and all possessions, and payment to be made. ²⁶ So the servant fell down and implored, 'Have patience with me, and I will pay you everything.' ²⁷ And out of pity the king released the servant and forgave the debt. ²⁸ But that same servant went out, and came upon a co-worker who owed the first servant a hundred denarii, and seizing the debtor by the throat said, 'Pay what you owe.' ²⁹ So the co-worker fell down, pleading, 'Have patience with me, and I will pay you.' ³⁰ But the first servant refused and went and put the debtor in prison till the debt should be paid. ³¹ When the other servants saw what had taken place, they were greatly distressed, and they went and reported to their king all that had taken place. ³² Then the king summoned the first servant and said, 'You wicked servant! I forgave you all that debt because you pleaded with me; ³³ and should not you have had mercy on your co-worker, as I had mercy on you?' ³⁴ And in anger the king delivered that servant to the jailers, till the debt should be paid in full. ³⁵ So also my God who is in heaven⊗ will do to every one of you, if you do not forgive your sister or brother from your heart."

✩RSV *kingdom*. See Appendix.
⊗RSV *my heavenly Father*. See Appendix.

PENTECOST 18

Lesson 1 ~ Exodus 32:1-14

Moses pleads for God's mercy for the people of Israel, who are worshiping the golden calf.

¹ When the people saw that Moses delayed to come down from the mountain, the people gathered themselves together to Aaron, and said to him, "Arise, make us gods, who shall go before us; as for this Moses, the man who brought us up out of the land of Egypt, we do not know what has become of him." ² And Aaron said to them, "Take off the rings of gold which are in the ears of your wives, your sons, and your daughters, and bring them to me." ³ So all the people took off the rings of gold which were in their ears, and brought them to Aaron. ⁴ And he received the gold at their hand, and fashioned it with a graving tool, and made a molten calf; and they said, "These are your gods, O Israel, who brought you up out of the land of Egypt!" ⁵ When Aaron saw this, he built an altar before it; and Aaron made proclamation and said, "Tomorrow shall be a feast to GOD [*or* the LORD]." ⁶ And they rose up early on the morrow, and offered burnt offerings and brought peace offerings; and the people sat down to eat and drink, and rose up to play.

⁷ And GOD [*or* the LORD] said to Moses, "Go down, for your people, whom you brought up out of the land of Egypt, have corrupted themselves; ⁸ they have turned aside quickly out of the way which I commanded them; they have made for themselves a molten calf, and have worshiped it and sacrificed to it, and said, 'These are your gods, O Israel, who brought you up out of the land of Egypt!'" ⁹ And GOD [*or* the LORD] said to Moses, "I have seen this people, and it is a stiff-necked people; ¹⁰ now therefore let me alone, that my wrath may burn hot against them and I may consume them; but of you I will make a great nation."

¹¹ But Moses besought the SOVEREIGN [*or* LORD] his God, and said, "O GOD [*or* LORD], why does your wrath burn hot against your people, whom you have brought forth out of the land of Egypt with great power and with a mighty hand? ¹² Why should the Egyptians say, 'With evil intent did God bring them forth, to slay them in the mountains, and to consume them from the face of the earth'? Turn from your fierce wrath, and repent of this evil against your people. ¹³ Remember Abraham, Isaac, and Israel, your servants, to whom you swore by your own self, and said to them, 'I will multiply your descendants as the stars of heaven, and all this land that I have promised I will give to your descendants, and they shall inherit it forever.'" ¹⁴ And GOD [*or* the LORD] repented of the evil which God thought to do to this people.

Psalm 106:7-8, 19-23

7 Our ancestors, when they were in Egypt,
   did not consider your wonderful works;
  they did not remember the abundance of your steadfast love,
   but rebelled against the Most High at the Red Sea,
8 yet were saved for the sake of God's name,
   in order to make known God's mighty power.
19 They made a calf in Horeb
   and worshiped a molten image.
20 They exchanged the glory of God
   for the image of an ox that eats grass.
21 They forgot God, their Savior,
   who had done great things in Egypt,
22 wondrous works in the land of Ham,
   and terrible things by the Red Sea.
23 Therefore God vowed to destroy them—
   had not Moses, God's chosen one,
  stood in the breach before God,
   to turn away God's wrath from destroying them.

Lesson 2 ~ Philippians 1:21-27

Paul gives thanks to the Philippians for their partnership in the gospel, expressing belief that his life belongs to Christ.

21 For to me to live is Christ, and to die is gain. 22 If it is to be life in the flesh, that means fruitful labor for me. Yet which I shall choose I cannot tell. 23 I am hard pressed between the two. My desire is to depart and be with Christ, for that is far better. 24 But to remain in the flesh is more necessary on your account. 25 Convinced of this, I know that I shall remain and continue with you all, for your progress and joy in the faith, 26 so that in me you may have ample cause to glory in Christ Jesus, because of my coming to you again.

27 Only let your manner of life be worthy of the gospel of Christ, so that whether I come and see you or am absent, I may hear of you that you stand firm in one spirit, with one mind striving side by side for the faith of the gospel.

Jesus tells the parable of the laborers in the vineyard.

¹ For the realm☆ of heaven is like a householder who went out early in the morning to hire laborers for the vineyard. ² After agreeing with the laborers for a denarius a day, the householder sent them into the vineyard. ³ And going out about the third hour the householder saw others standing idle in the marketplace, ⁴ and said to them, "You go into the vineyard too, and whatever is right I will give you." So they went. ⁵ Going out again about the sixth hour and the ninth hour, the householder did the same. ⁶ And about the eleventh hour the householder went out and found others standing, and said to them, "Why do you stand here idle all day?" ⁷ They replied, "Because no one has hired us." The householder said to them, "You go into the vineyard too." ⁸ And when evening came, the owner of the vineyard said to the steward, "Call the laborers and pay them their wages, beginning with the last, up to the first." ⁹ And when those hired about the eleventh hour came, each of them received a denarius. ¹⁰ Now when the first came, they thought they would receive more; but each of them also received a denarius. ¹¹ And on receiving it they grumbled at the householder, ¹² saying, "These last worked only one hour, and you have made them equal to us who have borne the burden of the day and the scorching heat." ¹³ But the householder replied to one of them, "Friend, I am doing you no wrong; did you not agree with me for a denarius? ¹⁴ Take what belongs to you, and go; I choose to give to this last as I give to you. ¹⁵ Am I not allowed to do what I choose with what belongs to me? Or do you begrudge my generosity?" ¹⁶ So the last will be first, and the first last.

☆RSV *kingdom*. See Appendix.

PENTECOST 19

Lesson 1 ~ Exodus 33:12-23

Moses is given a glimpse of God's glory.

¹² Moses said to GOD [[*or* the LORD]], "See, you say to me, 'Bring up this people'; but you have not let me know whom you will send with me. Yet you have said, 'I know you by name, and you have also found favor in my sight.' ¹³ Now therefore, I beseech you, if I have found favor in your sight, show me now your ways, that I may know you and find favor in your sight. Consider too that this nation is your people." ¹⁴ And God said, "My presence will go with you, and I will give you rest." ¹⁵ And Moses said to God, "If your presence will not go with me, do not carry us up from here. ¹⁶ For how shall it be known that I have found favor in your sight, I and your people? Is it not in your going with us, so that we are distinct, I and your people, from all other people that are upon the face of the earth?"

¹⁷ And GOD [[*or* the LORD]] said to Moses, "This very thing that you have spoken I will do; for you have found favor in my sight, and I know you by name." ¹⁸ Moses said, "I beseech you, show me your glory." ¹⁹ And God said, "I will make all my goodness pass before you, and will proclaim before you my name 'The SOVEREIGN [[*or* The LORD]]'; and I will be gracious to whom I will be gracious, and will show mercy on whom I will show mercy. ²⁰ But," God said, "you cannot see my face; for a human being shall not see me and live." ²¹ And GOD [[*or* the LORD]] said, "There is a place by me where you shall stand upon the rock; ²² and while my glory passes by I will put you in a cleft of the rock, and I will cover you with my hand until I have passed by; ²³ then I will take away my hand, and you shall see my back; but my face shall not be seen."

¹ God [[*or* The LORD]] reigns; let all people tremble!
  God sits enthroned upon the cherubim; let the earth quake!
² GOD [[*or* The LORD]] is great in Zion,
  and is exalted over all the nations.
³ Let them praise your great and terrible name!
  Holy is God!
⁴ Mighty Ruler,⊡ lover of justice,
  you have established equity;
 you have executed justice
  and righteousness in Jacob.
⁵ Extol the SOVEREIGN [[*or* LORD]] our God;
  worship at God's footstool!
  Holy is God!
⁶ Moses and Aaron were among the priests of God,
  Samuel also was among those who called on God's name.
  They cried to GOD [[*or* the LORD]] who answered them,
⁷ and spoke to them in the pillar of cloud.
  They kept God's testimonies,
  and the statutes that God gave them.
⁸ O SOVEREIGN [[*or* LORD]] our God, you answered them;
  you were a forgiving God to them,
  but an avenger of their wrongdoings.
⁹ Extol the SOVEREIGN [[*or* LORD]] our God,
  and worship at God's holy mountain;
  for the SOVEREIGN [[*or* LORD]] our God is holy!

⊡RSV *King*. See Appendix.

Lesson 2 ~ Philippians 2:1-13

Paul reminds us of Christ's example of humility and obedience.

¹ So if there is any encouragement in Christ, any incentive of love, any participation in the Spirit, any affection and sympathy, ²complete my joy by being of the same mind, having the same love, being in full accord and of one mind. ³ Do nothing from selfishness or conceit, but in humility count others better than yourselves. ⁴ Let each of you look not only to your own interests but also to the interests of others. ⁵ Have this mind among yourselves, which is yours in Christ Jesus ⁶who, though being in the form of God, did not count equality with God a thing to be grasped, ⁷but emptied Christ's self, taking the form of a servant, being born in the likeness of human beings. ⁸And being found in human form, Christ humbled Christ's self and became obedient unto death, even death on a cross. ⁹Therefore God has highly exalted Jesus and bestowed on Jesus the name which is above every name, ¹⁰that at the name of Jesus every knee should bow, in heaven and on earth and under the earth, ¹¹and every tongue confess that Jesus Christ is Sovereign [[or Lord]], to the glory of God the Father [and Mother*].

¹² Therefore, my beloved, as you have always obeyed, so now, not only as in my presence but much more in my absence, work out your own salvation with fear and trembling; ¹³for God is at work in you, both to will and to work for God's good pleasure.

---

*Addition to the text. See "Metaphor" and "God the Father and Mother" in the Appendix.

Having spoken to the disciples about the source of his authority, Jesus told them another parable.

[28] "What do you think? Someone who owned a vineyard had two children, and went to the first and said, 'My child, go and work in the vineyard today.' [29] And the child answered, 'I will not'; but afterward repented and went. [30] And the owner of the vineyard went to the second child and said the same; and that child answered, 'I will go,' but did not go. [31] Which of the two did the will of the parent?" They said, "The first." Jesus said to them, "Truly, I say to you, the tax collectors and the harlots go into the realm✩ of God before you. [32] For John came to you in the way of righteousness, and you did not believe him, but the tax collectors and the harlots did believe him; and even when you saw it, you did not afterward repent and believe John."

✩RSV *kingdom*. See Appendix.

PENTECOST 20

Lesson ~ Numbers 27:12-23

Joshua is invested with the authority of Moses.

¹² GOD [*or* The LORD] said to Moses, "Go up into this mountain of Abarim, and see the land which I have given to the people of Israel. ¹³ And when you have seen it, you also shall be gathered to your people, as your brother Aaron was gathered, ¹⁴ because you rebelled against my word in the wilderness of Zin during the strife of the congregation, to sanctify me at the waters before their eyes." (These are the waters of Meribah of Kadesh in the wilderness of Zin.) ¹⁵ Moses said to GOD [*or* the LORD], ¹⁶ "Let the SOVEREIGN [*or* LORD], the God of the spirits of all flesh, appoint a man over the congregation, ¹⁷ who shall go out before them and come in before them, and who shall lead them out and bring them in; that the congregation of GOD [*or* the LORD] may not be as sheep which have no shepherd." ¹⁸ And GOD [*or* the LORD] said to Moses, "Take Joshua the son of Nun, a man in whom is the spirit, and lay your hand upon him; ¹⁹ cause him to stand before Eleazar the priest and all the congregation, and you shall commission Joshua in their sight. ²⁰ You shall invest him with some of your authority, that all the congregation of the people of Israel may obey. ²¹ And he shall stand before Eleazar the priest, who shall inquire for Joshua by the judgment of the Urim before GOD [*or* the LORD]; at the word of Joshua they shall go out, and at the word of Joshua they shall come in, both Joshua and all the people of Israel with him, the whole congregation." ²² And Moses did as GOD [*or* the LORD] commanded him; he took Joshua and caused him to stand before Eleazar the priest and the whole congregation, ²³ and Moses laid his hands upon Joshua, and commissioned him as GOD [*or* the LORD] directed through Moses.

Psalm 81:1-10

¹ Sing aloud to God our strength;
    shout for joy to the God of Jacob!
² Raise a song, sound the timbrel,
    the sweet lyre with the harp.
³ Blow the trumpet at the new moon,
    at the full moon, on our feast day.
⁴ For it is a statute for Israel,
    an ordinance of the God of Jacob.

⁵ God made it a decree in Joseph,
   when God went out over the land of Egypt.
I hear a voice I had not known:
⁶ "I relieved your shoulder of the burden;
   your hands were freed from the basket.
⁷ In distress you called, and I delivered you;
   I answered you in the secret place of thunder;
   I tested you at the waters of Meribah.
⁸ Hear, O my people, while I admonish you!
   O Israel, if you would but listen to me!
⁹ There shall be no strange god among you;
   you shall not bow down to a foreign god.
¹⁰ I am the SOVEREIGN [[or LORD]] your God,
   who brought you up out of the land of Egypt.
   Open your mouth wide, and I will fill it."

Lesson 2 ～ Philippians 3:12-21

Paul, taken hold of by Christ Jesus, exhorts his friends at Philippi.

¹² Not that I have already obtained the goal or am already perfect; but I press on to make it my own, because I have been taken hold of by Christ Jesus. ¹³ Sisters and brothers, I do not consider that I have made it my own; but one thing I do, forgetting what lies behind and straining forward to what lies ahead, ¹⁴ I press on toward the goal for the prize of the upward call of God in Christ Jesus. ¹⁵ Let those of us who are mature be thus minded; and if in anything you are otherwise minded, God will reveal that also to you. ¹⁶ Only let us hold true to what we have attained.

¹⁷ Brothers and sisters, join in imitating me, and mark those who so live as you have an example in us. ¹⁸ For many, of whom I have often told you and now tell you even with tears, live as enemies of the cross of Christ. ¹⁹ Their end is destruction, their god is the belly, and they glory in their shame, with minds set on earthly things. ²⁰ But our commonwealth is in heaven, and from it we await a Savior, the Sovereign [[or Lord]] Jesus Christ, ²¹ who will change our lowly body to be like Christ's glorious body, by the power which enables Christ even to subject all things to Christ's self.

Hear another parable about the realm of God.

33 There was a householder who planted a vineyard, and set a hedge around it, and dug a wine press in it, and built a tower, and let it out to tenants, and went into another country. 34 When the season of fruit drew near, the householder sent servants to the tenants, to get the fruit; 35 and the tenants took the servants and beat one, killed another, and stoned another. 36 Again the householder sent other servants, more than the first; and they did the same to them. 37 Afterward the householder sent the heir to them, the one who would inherit the vineyard, saying, "They will respect my heir, my very own child." 38 But when the tenants saw the owner's child, they said to themselves, "This is the heir; come, let us kill this one too and have the inheritance." 39 And they took and cast the heir out of the vineyard, and killed the heir. 40 When therefore the owner of the vineyard comes, what will be done to those tenants? 41 Those hearing the parable said to Jesus, "The owner will put those wretches to a miserable death, and let out the vineyard to other tenants who will give the owner the fruits in their seasons."

42 Jesus said to them, "Have you never read in the scriptures:

'The very stone which the builders rejected
has become the head of the corner;
this was the Sovereign's [[*or* Lord's]] doing,
and it is marvelous in our eyes'?

43 Therefore I tell you, the realm☆ of God will be taken away from you and given to a nation producing the fruits of it."

☆RSV *kingdom*. See Appendix.

PENTECOST 21

Lesson 1 ∼ Deuteronomy 34:1-12

Moses the great prophet dies after seeing the land Israel will inherit.

¹ And Moses went up from the plains of Moab to Mount Nebo, to the top of Pisgah, which is opposite Jericho. And GOD [[or the LORD]] showed him all the land, Gilead as far as Dan, ²all Naphtali, the land of Ephraim and Manasseh, all the land of Judah as far as the Western Sea, ³the Negeb, and the Plain, that is, the valley of Jericho the city of palm trees, as far as Zoar. ⁴And GOD [[or the LORD]] said to Moses, "This is the land of which I swore to Abraham, to Isaac, and to Jacob, 'I will give it to your descendants.' I have let you see it with your eyes, but you shall not go over there." ⁵So Moses the servant of GOD [[or the LORD]] died there in the land of Moab, according to the word of GOD [[or the LORD]], ⁶and God buried Moses in the valley in the land of Moab opposite Beth-peor; but no one knows the place of Moses' burial to this day. ⁷Moses was a hundred and twenty years old when he died; his eye was not dim, nor his natural force abated. ⁸And the people of Israel wept for Moses in the plains of Moab thirty days; then the days of weeping and mourning for Moses were ended.

⁹ And Joshua the son of Nun was full of the spirit of wisdom, for Moses had laid his hands upon him; so the people of Israel obeyed Joshua, and did as GOD [[or the LORD]] had commanded Moses. ¹⁰And since then, there has not arisen a prophet in Israel like Moses, whom GOD [[or the LORD]] knew face to face, ¹¹none like Moses for all the signs and the wonders which GOD [[or the LORD]] sent him to do in the land of Egypt, to Pharaoh and to all his servants and to all his land, ¹²and for all the mighty power and all the great and terrible deeds which Moses wrought in the sight of all Israel.

Psalm 135:1-14

¹ Praise GOD [[or the LORD]].
  Praise the name of GOD [[or the LORD]],
    give praise, O servants of GOD [[or the LORD]],
² you that stand in the house of GOD [[or the LORD]],
    in the courts of the house of our God!
³ Praise GOD [[or the LORD]], for GOD [[or the LORD]] is good;
    sing to God's name, for God is gracious!
⁴ For GOD [[or the LORD]] has chosen Jacob for Godself,
    Israel as God's own possession.

⁵ For I know that GOD ⟦*or* the LORD⟧ is great,
  and that our God ⟦*or* Lord⟧ is above all gods.
⁶ Whatever GOD ⟦*or* the LORD⟧ pleases God does,
  in heaven and on earth,
  in the seas and all deeps.
⁷ God it is who makes the clouds rise at the end of the earth,
  who makes lightnings for the rain
  and brings forth the wind from God's storehouses.
⁸ God it was who smote the firstborn of Egypt,
  both human and animal;
⁹ who in your midst, O Egypt,
  sent signs and wonders
  against Pharaoh and all his servants;
¹⁰ who smote many nations
  and slew mighty kings,
¹¹ Sihon, king of the Amorites,
  and Og, king of Bashan,
  and all the kingdoms of Canaan,
¹² and gave their land as a heritage,
  a heritage to God's people Israel.
¹³ Your name, O GOD ⟦*or* LORD⟧, endures forever,
  your renown, O GOD ⟦*or* LORD⟧, throughout all ages.
¹⁴ For GOD ⟦*or* the LORD⟧ will vindicate God's people,
  and have compassion on God's servants.

Lesson 2 ~ Philippians 4:1-9

Paul gives thanks to the sisters and brothers in Philippi for their kindness to him.

¹ Therefore, my sisters and brothers, whom I love and long for, my joy and crown, stand firm thus in the Sovereign ⟦*or* Lord⟧, my beloved.
² I entreat Euodia and I entreat Syntyche to agree in the Sovereign ⟦*or* Lord⟧. ³ And I ask you also, true companion, help these women, for they have labored side by side with me in the gospel together with Clement and the rest of my co-workers, whose names are in the book of life.
⁴ Rejoice in the Sovereign ⟦*or* Lord⟧ always; again I will say, Rejoice.
⁵ Let everyone know your forbearance. The Sovereign ⟦*or* Lord⟧ is at hand.
⁶ Have no anxiety about anything, but in everything, by prayer and supplication with thanksgiving, let your requests be made known to God.
⁷ And the peace of God, which passes all understanding, will keep your hearts and your minds in Christ Jesus.

⁸ Finally, my friends, whatever is true, whatever is honorable, whatever is just, whatever is pure, whatever is lovely, whatever is gracious, if there is any excellence, if there is anything worthy of praise, think about these things. ⁹ What you have learned and received and heard and seen in me, do; and the God of peace will be with you.

Gospel ~ Matthew 22:1-14

Jesus tells the parable of the marriage feast.

¹ And again Jesus spoke to them in parables, saying, ² "The realm☆ of heaven may be compared to a king who gave a marriage feast for his son, ³ and sent servants to call those who were invited to the marriage feast; but they would not come. ⁴ Again the king sent other servants, saying, 'Tell those who are invited, I have made ready my dinner, my oxen and my fat calves are killed, and everything is ready; come to the marriage feast.' ⁵ But those who were invited made light of it and went off, one to a farm, another to a business, ⁶ while the rest seized the king's servants, treated them shamefully, and killed them. ⁷ The king was angry, and sent his troops and destroyed those murderers and burned their city. ⁸ Then the king said to the servants, 'The wedding is ready, but those invited were not worthy. ⁹ Go therefore to the thoroughfares, and invite to the marriage feast as many as you find.' ¹⁰ And those servants went out into the streets and gathered all whom they found, both bad and good; so the wedding hall was filled with guests.

¹¹ "But when the king came in to look at the guests, he saw someone who had no wedding garment; ¹² and the king said, 'Friend, how did you get in here without a wedding garment?' And the guest was speechless. ¹³ Then the king said to the attendants, 'Let the guest be bound hand and foot and cast into the night, where there will be weeping and gnashing of teeth.' ¹⁴ For many are called, but few are chosen."

☆RSV *kingdom*. See Appendix.

PENTECOST 22

Lesson 1 ~ Ruth 1:1-19a

Ruth the Moabite vows lifelong faithfulness to her mother-in-law, Naomi.

¹ In the days when the judges ruled there was a famine in the land, and a certain man of Bethlehem in Judah went to sojourn in the country of Moab, he and his wife and his two sons. ²The name of the man was Elimelech and the name of his wife Naomi, and the names of his two sons were Mahlon and Chilion; they were Ephrathites from Bethlehem in Judah. They went into the country of Moab and remained there. ³But Elimelech, the husband of Naomi, died, and she was left with her two sons. ⁴These took Moabite wives; the name of the one was Orpah and the name of the other Ruth. They lived there about ten years; ⁵and both Mahlon and Chilion died, so that the woman was bereft of her two sons and her husband.

⁶ Then she started with her daughters-in-law to return from the country of Moab, for she had heard in the country of Moab that GOD [or the LORD] had visited God's people and given them food. ⁷So she set out from the place where she was, with her two daughters-in-law, and they went on the way to return to the land of Judah. ⁸But Naomi said to her two daughters-in-law, "Go, return each of you to her mother's house. May GOD [or the LORD] deal kindly with you, as you have dealt with the dead and with me. ⁹GOD [or The LORD] grant that you may find a home, each of you in the house of her husband!" Then she kissed them, and they lifted up their voices and wept. ¹⁰And they said to her, "No, we will return with you to your people." ¹¹But Naomi said, "Turn back, my daughters, why will you go with me? Have I yet sons in my womb that they may become your husbands? ¹²Turn back, my daughters, go your way, for I am too old to have a husband. If I should say I have hope, even if I should have a husband this night and should bear sons, ¹³would you therefore wait till they were grown? Would you therefore refrain from marrying? No, my daughters, for it is exceedingly bitter to me for your sake that the hand of GOD [or the LORD] has gone forth against me." ¹⁴Then they lifted up their voices and wept again; and Orpah kissed her mother-in-law, but Ruth clung to her.

¹⁵ And Naomi said, "See, your sister-in-law has gone back to her people and to her gods; return after your sister-in-law." ¹⁶But Ruth said, "Entreat me not to leave you or to return from following you; for where you go I will go, and where you lodge I will lodge; your people shall be my people, and your God my God; ¹⁷where you die I will die, and there will I be buried.

May GOD [[*or* the LORD]] do so to me and more also if even death parts me from you." ¹⁸ And when Naomi saw that she was determined to go with her, she said no more.

¹⁹ So the two of them went on until they came to Bethlehem.

Psalm 146

¹ Praise GOD [[*or* the LORD]]!
  Praise GOD [[*or* the LORD]], O my soul!
² I will praise GOD [[*or* the LORD]] as long as I live;
  I will sing praises to my God while I have being.
³ Put not your trust in rulers,
  in mortals, in whom there is no help.
⁴ When their breath departs they return to their earth;
  on that very day their plans perish.
⁵ Happy is the one whose help is the God of Jacob,
  whose hope is in God, the SOVEREIGN [[*or* LORD]],
⁶ who made heaven and earth,
  the sea, and all that is in them;
 who keeps faith forever;
⁷   who executes justice for the oppressed;
  who gives food to the hungry.
 GOD [[*or* The LORD]] sets the prisoners free;
⁸   GOD [[*or* the LORD]] opens the eyes of those who are blind.
 GOD [[*or* The LORD]] lifts up those who are bowed down;
  GOD [[*or* the LORD]] loves the righteous.
⁹ GOD [[*or* The LORD]] watches over the sojourners,
  and upholds the widow and the orphan,
  but brings the way of the wicked to ruin.
¹⁰ GOD [[*or* The LORD]] will reign forever,
  your God, O Zion, to all generations.
  Praise GOD [[*or* the LORD]]!

Lesson 2 ~ 1 Thessalonians 1:1-10

Paul writes to the Christians at Thessalonica, giving thanks for them.

¹ Paul, Silvanus, and Timothy,
To the church of the Thessalonians in God the [*Mother and**] Father and in the Sovereign [[*or* Lord]] Jesus Christ:
    Grace to you and peace.

² We give thanks to God always for you all, constantly mentioning you in our prayers, ³ remembering before God our Father [*and Mother**] your work of faith and labor of love and steadfastness of hope in our Sovereign [[*or* Lord]] Jesus Christ. ⁴ For we know, friends beloved by God, that God has chosen you; ⁵ for our gospel came to you not only in word, but also in power and in the Holy Spirit and with full conviction. You know what kind of people we proved to be among you for your sake. ⁶ And you became imitators of us and of the Sovereign [[*or* Lord]], for you received the word in much affliction, with joy inspired by the Holy Spirit; ⁷ so that you became an example to all the believers in Macedonia and in Achaia. ⁸ For not only has the word of the Sovereign [[*or* Lord]] sounded forth from you in Macedonia and Achaia, but your faith in God has gone forth everywhere, so that we need not say anything. ⁹ For they themselves report concerning us what a welcome we had among you, and how you turned to God from idols, to serve a living and true God, ¹⁰ and to wait for God's Child◊ from heaven, whom God raised from the dead, Jesus who delivers us from the wrath to come.

---

*Addition to the text. RSV v. 1 *God the Father;* v. 3 *our God and Father.* See "Metaphor" and "God the Father and Mother" in the Appendix.
◊RSV *his Son.* See Appendix.

Jesus responds to the Pharisees' question about paying taxes to Caesar.

15 Then the Pharisees went and took counsel how to entangle Jesus in his talk. 16 And they sent their disciples to Jesus, along with the Herodians, saying, "Teacher, we know that you are true, and teach the way of God truthfully, and court no one's favor; for you do not regard a person's status. 17 Tell us, then, what you think. Is it lawful to pay taxes to Caesar, or not?" 18 But Jesus, aware of their malice, said, "Why put me to the test, you hypocrites? 19 Show me the money for the tax." And they brought him a coin. 20 And Jesus said to them, "Whose likeness and inscription is this?" 21 They said, "Caesar's." Then Jesus said to them, "Render therefore to Caesar the things that are Caesar's, and to God the things that are God's." 22 When they heard it, they marveled; and they left him and went away.

PENTECOST 23

Lesson 1 ~ Ruth 2:1-13

Ruth the Moabite wins the favor of Boaz.

¹ Now Naomi had a relative of her husband's, a man of wealth, of the family of Elimelech, whose name was Boaz. ² And Ruth the Moabite said to Naomi, "Let me go to the field, and glean among the stalks of grain after him in whose sight I shall find favor." And Naomi answered her, "Go, my daughter." ³ So Ruth set forth and went and gleaned in the field after the reapers; and she happened to come to the part of the field belonging to Boaz, who was of the family of Elimelech. ⁴ And Boaz came from Bethlehem; and he said to the reapers, "GOD [[*or* The LORD]] be with you!" And they answered, "GOD [[*or* The LORD]] bless you." ⁵ Then Boaz said to his servant who was in charge of the reapers, "Whose young woman is this?" ⁶ And the servant who was in charge of the reapers answered, "It is the Moabite woman, who came back with Naomi from the country of Moab. ⁷ She said, 'Please, let me glean and gather among the sheaves after the reapers.' So she came, and she has continued from early morning until now, without resting even for a moment."

⁸ Then Boaz said to Ruth, "Now, listen, my daughter, do not go to glean in another field or leave this one, but keep close to my young women. ⁹ Let your eyes be upon the field which they are reaping, and go after them. Have I not charged the young men not to molest you? And when you are thirsty, go to the vessels and drink what the young men have drawn." ¹⁰ Then she fell on her face, bowing to the ground, and said to him, "Why have I found favor in your eyes, that you should take notice of me, when I am a foreigner?" ¹¹ But Boaz answered her, "All that you have done for your mother-in-law since the death of your husband has been fully told me, and how you left your father and mother and your native land and came to a people that you did not know before. ¹² GOD [[*or* The LORD]] recompense you for what you have done, and a full reward be given you by the SOVEREIGN [[*or* LORD]], the God of Israel, under whose wings you have come to take refuge!" ¹³ Then Ruth said, "You are most gracious to me, my lord, for you have comforted me and spoken kindly to your servant, though I am not one of your servants."

Psalm 128

1 Blessed is everyone who fears GOD [[*or* the LORD]],
   who walks in God's ways!
2 You shall eat the fruit of the labor of your hands;
   you shall be happy, and it shall be well with you.
3 Your beloved will be like a fruitful vine
   within your house;
  your children will be like olive shoots
   around your table.
4 Thus shall the one be blessed
   who fears GOD [[*or* the LORD]].
5 GOD [[*or* The LORD]] bless you from Zion!
   May you see the prosperity of Jerusalem
   all the days of your life!
6 May you see your children's children!
   Peace be upon Israel!

Lesson 2 ~ 1 Thessalonians 2:1-8

Paul replies to opponents of the gospel, who accused him of heresy, immorality, trickery, and greed.

1 For you yourselves know, my friends, that our visit to you was not in vain; 2 but though we had already suffered and been shamefully treated at Philippi, as you know, we had courage in our God to declare to you the gospel of God in the face of great opposition. 3 For our appeal does not spring from error or uncleanness, nor is it made with guile; 4 but just as we have been approved by God to be entrusted with the gospel, so we speak, not to please human beings, but to please God who tests our hearts. 5 For we never used either words of flattery, as you know, or a cloak for greed, as God is witness; 6 nor did we seek glory from anyone, whether from you or from others, though we might have made demands as apostles of Christ. 7 But we were gentle among you, like a nurse taking care of children. 8 So, being affectionately desirous of you, we were ready to share with you not only the gospel of God but also our own selves, because you had become very dear to us.

Jesus answers the lawyer, stating the two great commandments.

34 But when the Pharisees heard that Jesus had silenced the Sadducees, they came together. 35 And one of them, a lawyer, asked Jesus a question, as a test. 36 "Teacher, which is the great commandment in the law?" 37 And Jesus said to him, "You shall love the Sovereign [or Lord] your God with all your heart, and with all your soul, and with all your mind. 38 This is the great and first commandment. 39 And a second is like it, You shall love your neighbor as yourself. 40 On these two commandments depend all the law and the prophets."

41 Now while the Pharisees were gathered together, Jesus asked them a question, 42 saying, "What do you think of the Christ? Whose offspring is the Christ?" They said to Jesus, "The offspring of David." 43 Jesus said to them, "How is it then that David, inspired by the Spirit, calls the Christ, Sovereign [or Lord], saying,

44 'God said to my Sovereign [or Lord],
Sit at my right hand,
till I put your enemies under your feet'?

45 If David thus calls the Christ, Sovereign [or Lord], how is the Christ David's offspring?" 46 And no one was able to answer Jesus a word, nor from that day did anyone dare to ask Jesus any more questions.

PENTECOST 24

Ruth, the wife of Boaz, bears a son, Obed, who was an ancestor of David.

⁷ Now this was the custom in former times in Israel concerning redeeming and exchanging: to confirm a transaction, the one drew off his sandal and gave it to the other, and this was the manner of attesting in Israel. ⁸ So when the next of kin said to Boaz, "Buy it for yourself," he drew off his sandal. ⁹ Then Boaz said to the elders and all the people, "You are witnesses this day that I have bought from the hand of Naomi all that belonged to Elimelech and all that belonged to Chilion and to Mahlon. ¹⁰ Also Ruth the Moabite, the widow of Mahlon, I have bought to be my wife, to perpetuate the name of Mahlon in his inheritance, that the name of Mahlon may not be cut off from among his family and from the gate of his native place; you are witnesses this day." ¹¹ Then all the people who were at the gate, and the elders, said, "We are witnesses. May GOD [or the LORD] make the woman, who is coming into your house, like Rachel and Leah, who together built up the house of Israel. May you prosper in Ephrathah and be renowned in Bethlehem; ¹² and may your house be like the house of Perez, whom Tamar bore to Judah, because of the children that GOD [or the LORD] will give you by this young woman."

¹³ So Boaz took Ruth and she became his wife; and he went in to her, and GOD [or the LORD] gave her conception, and she bore a son. ¹⁴ Then the women said to Naomi, "Blessed be GOD [or the LORD], who has not left you this day without next of kin; and may the name of this child be renowned in Israel! ¹⁵ He shall be to you a restorer of life and a nourisher of your old age; for your daughter-in-law who loves you, who is more to you than seven sons, has borne him." ¹⁶ Then Naomi took the child and laid him in her bosom, and became his nurse. ¹⁷ And the women of the neighborhood gave the child a name, saying, "A son has been born to Naomi." They named the child Obed; he was the father of Jesse, the father of David.

Psalm 127

¹ Unless GOD [or the LORD] builds the house,
    those who build it labor in vain.
Unless GOD [or the LORD] watches over the city,
    the watcher stays awake in vain.

² It is in vain that you rise up early
  and go late to rest,
 eating the bread of anxious toil;
  for God gives sleep to God's beloved.
³ Children are a heritage from GOD [[*or* the LORD]],
  the fruit of the womb a reward.
⁴ Like arrows in the hand of a warrior
  are the children of one's youth.
⁵ Happy is the one who has
  a quiver full of them!
 That one shall not be put to shame
  when speaking with enemies in the gate.

Lesson 2 ~ 1 Thessalonians 2:9-13, 17-20

Paul reminds the church that he worked at a trade so as not to be a burden while among them.

⁹ For you remember our labor and toil, my friends; we worked night and day, that we might not burden any of you, while we preached to you the gospel of God. ¹⁰ You are witnesses, and God also, how holy and righteous and blameless was our behavior to you believers; ¹¹ for you know how, like a parent with a child, we exhorted each one of you and encouraged you and charged you ¹² to lead a life worthy of God, who calls you into God's own realm✩ and glory.

¹³ And we also thank God constantly for this, that when you received the word of God which you heard from us, you accepted it not as a human word but as what it really is, the word of God, which is at work in you believers.

¹⁷ But since for a short time, brothers and sisters, we were bereft of you, in person not in heart, we endeavored the more eagerly and with great desire to see you face to face, ¹⁸ because we wanted to come to you—I, Paul, again and again—but Satan hindered us. ¹⁹ For what is our hope or joy or crown of boasting before our Sovereign [[*or* Lord]] Jesus at the expected return? Is it not you? ²⁰ For you are our glory and joy.

✩RSV *kingdom*. See Appendix.

Jesus teaches about discipleship.

¹ Then Jesus said to the crowds and to the disciples, ² "The scribes and the Pharisees sit on Moses' seat; ³ so practice and observe whatever they tell you, but not what they do; for they preach, but do not practice. ⁴ They bind heavy burdens, hard to bear, and lay them on people's shoulders; but they themselves will not move them with their finger. ⁵ They do all their deeds to be seen by others; for they make their phylacteries broad and their fringes long, ⁶ and they love the place of honor at feasts and the best seats in the synagogues, ⁷ and salutations in the marketplaces, and hearing people call them rabbi. ⁸ But you are not to be called rabbi, for you have one teacher, and you are all brothers and sisters. ⁹ And call no one on earth by the title 'father,' for you have only one who deserves such a title, [*God, your heavenly*] Father [*and Mother**]. ¹⁰ Neither be called teachers, for you have one teacher, the Christ. ¹¹ The one who is greatest among you shall be your servant; ¹² all who exalt themselves will be humbled, and all who humble themselves will be exalted."

---

*Addition to the text. RSV *for you have one Father, who is in heaven*. See "Metaphor" and "God the Father and Mother" in the Appendix.

PENTECOST 25

Lesson 1 ~ Amos 5:18-24

The day of God will be a day of judgment.

¹⁸ Woe to you who desire the day of GOD ⟦*or* the LORD⟧!
   Why would you have the day of GOD ⟦*or* the LORD⟧?
  It is deepest shadow, and not light;
¹⁹   as if one fled from a lion,
      and was met by a bear;
  and went into the house and leaned a hand against the wall,
      and was bitten by a serpent.
²⁰ Is not the day of GOD ⟦*or* the LORD⟧ deepest shadow, and not light,
      and gloom with no brightness in it?
²¹ "I hate, I despise your feasts,
      and I take no delight in your solemn assemblies.
²² Even though you offer me your burnt offerings and cereal offerings,
      I will not accept them,
   and the peace offerings of your fatted beasts
      I will not look upon.
²³ Take away from me the noise of your songs;
      to the melody of your harps I will not listen.
²⁴ But let justice roll down like waters,
      and righteousness like an ever-flowing stream."

Lesson 1 (alternate) ~ Wisdom of Solomon 6:12-16

Wisdom seeks out those who desire to know her and gives them understanding.

¹² Wisdom is radiant and unfading,
      easily discerned by those who love her
      and found by those who seek her.
¹³ Wisdom hastens to make herself known to those who desire her.
¹⁴ The one who rises early to seek wisdom will have no difficulty,
      and will find wisdom sitting at the gates.
¹⁵ To fix one's thought on wisdom is perfect understanding,
      and the one who is vigilant on account of wisdom will soon be free
         from care,
¹⁶ because wisdom goes about seeking those worthy of her,
      graciously appears to them in their paths,
      and meets them in every thought.

⁷ Hear, O my people, and I will speak
 O Israel, I will testify against you.
 I am God, your God.
⁸ I do not reprove you for your sacrifices;
 your burnt offerings are continually before me.
⁹ I will accept no bull from your house,
 nor he-goat from your folds.
¹⁰ For every beast of the forest is mine,
 the cattle on a thousand hills.
¹¹ I know all the birds of the air,
 and all that moves in the field is mine.
¹² If I were hungry, I would not tell you;
 for the world and all that is in it is mine.
¹³ Do I eat the flesh of bulls,
 or drink the blood of goats?
¹⁴ Offer to God a sacrifice of thanksgiving,
 and pay your vows to the Most High;
¹⁵ and call upon me in the day of trouble;
 I will deliver you, and you shall glorify me.

Lesson 2 ~ 1 Thessalonians 4:13-18

Paul believes that at Christ's coming, the dead will be raised first, and then those who are alive.

¹³ But we would not have you ignorant, sisters and brothers, concerning those who are asleep, that you may not grieve as others do who have no hope. ¹⁴ For since we believe that Jesus died and rose again, even so, through Jesus, God will bring with Jesus those who have fallen asleep. ¹⁵ For this we declare to you by the word of the Sovereign [[or Lord]], that we who are alive, who are left until the coming of the Sovereign [[or Lord]], shall not precede those who have fallen asleep. ¹⁶ For the Sovereign [[or Lord]], indeed, will descend from heaven with a cry of command, with the archangel's call, and with the sound of the trumpet of God. And the dead in Christ will rise first; ¹⁷ then we who are alive, who are left, shall be caught up together with them in the clouds to meet the Sovereign [[or Lord]] in the air; and so we shall always be with the Sovereign [[or Lord]]. ¹⁸ Therefore comfort one another with these words.

Jesus, sitting on the Mount of Olives, tells the parable of the wise and foolish young women.

¹ Then the realm☆ of heaven shall be compared to ten young women who took their lamps and went to meet the bridegroom. ² Five of them were foolish, and five were wise. ³ For when the foolish took their lamps, they took no oil with them; ⁴ but the wise took flasks of oil with their lamps. ⁵ As the bridegroom was delayed, they all slumbered and slept. ⁶ But at midnight there was a cry, "Behold, the bridegroom! Come out to meet him." ⁷ Then all the women rose and trimmed their lamps. ⁸ And the foolish said to the wise, "Give us some of your oil, for our lamps are going out." ⁹ But the wise replied, "Perhaps there will not be enough for us and for you; go rather to the dealers and buy for yourselves." ¹⁰ And while they went to buy, the bridegroom came, and those who were ready went in with him to the marriage feast; and the door was shut. ¹¹ Afterward the other young women came also, saying, "Sovereign, Sovereign [[or Lord, Lord]], open to us." ¹² But the bridegroom replied, "Truly, I say to you, I do not know you." ¹³ Watch therefore, for you know neither the day nor the hour.

☆RSV *kingdom*. See Appendix.

PENTECOST 26

Lesson 1 ~ Zephaniah 1:7, 12-18

Zephaniah proclaims that the day of God will be disaster and will not be salvation for the people.

⁷ Be silent before the Sovereign [*or* Lord] GOD!
   For the day of GOD [*or* the LORD] is at hand;
   GOD [*or* the LORD] has prepared a sacrifice
   and consecrated the guests.
¹² At that time I will search Jerusalem with lamps,
   and I will punish the people
who are stupefied with wine,
   those who say in their hearts,
   "GOD [*or* The LORD] will not do good,
   nor will God do ill."
¹³ Their goods shall be plundered,
   and their houses laid waste.
Though they build houses,
   they shall not inhabit them;
though they plant vineyards,
   they shall not drink wine from them.
¹⁴ The great day of GOD [*or* the LORD] is near,
   near and hastening fast;
   the sound of the day of GOD [*or* the LORD] is bitter,
   the mighty warrior cries aloud there.
¹⁵ A day of wrath is that day,
   a day of distress and anguish,
a day of ruin and devastation,
   a day of shadow and gloom,
a day of clouds and deepest shadows,
¹⁶   a day of trumpet blast and battle cry
against the fortified cities
   and against the lofty battlements.
¹⁷ I will bring distress on the people,
   so that they shall walk like those who are blind,
   because they have sinned against GOD [*or* the LORD];
their blood shall be poured out like dust,
   and their flesh like dung.
¹⁸ Neither their silver nor their gold
   shall be able to deliver them
   on the day of the wrath of GOD [*or* the LORD].

In the fire of God's jealous wrath,
    all the earth shall be consumed;
for a full, sudden end
    God will make of all the inhabitants of the earth.

Lesson 1 (alternate) ~ Proverbs 31:10-13, 19-20, 30-31

A good wife has a status of honor, according to the author of Proverbs.

10 A good wife who can find?
    She is far more precious than jewels.
11 The heart of her husband trusts in her,
    and he will have no lack of gain.
12 She does him good, and not harm,
    all the days of her life.
13 She seeks wool and flax,
    and works with willing hands.
19 She puts her hands to the distaff,
    and her hands hold the spindle.
20 She opens her hand to the poor,
    and reaches out her hands to the needy.
30 Charm is deceitful, and beauty is vain,
    but a woman who fears GOD [[*or* the LORD]] is to be praised.
31 Give her of the fruit of her hands,
    and let her works praise her in the gates.

Psalm 76

1 In Judah God is known,
    God's name is great in Israel.
2 God's abode has been established in Salem,
    God's dwelling place in Zion.
3 There God broke the flashing arrows,
    the shield, the sword, and the weapons of war.
4 Glorious are you, more majestic
    than the everlasting mountains.
5 The stouthearted were stripped of their spoil;
    they sank into sleep;
all the warriors
    were unable to use their hands.
6 At your rebuke, O God of Jacob,
    both rider and horse lay stunned.

⁷ But you, terrible are you!
  Who can stand before you
  when once your anger is roused?
⁸ From the heavens you did utter judgment;
  the earth feared and was still,
⁹ when God arose to establish judgment
  to save all the oppressed of the earth.
¹⁰ Surely the wrath of humans shall praise you;
  the residue of wrath you will gird upon you.
¹¹ Make your vows to the SOVEREIGN [[*or* LORD]] your God, and perform
    them;
  let all around God bring gifts
  to God who is to be feared,
¹² who cuts off the spirit of princes,
  who is terrible to the kings of the earth.

Lesson 2 ~ 1 Thessalonians 5:1-11

Paul expresses belief that we are children of the light and of the day and will obtain salvation through Jesus Christ.

¹ But as to the times and the seasons, brothers and sisters, you have no need to have anything written to you. ² For you yourselves know well that the day of the Sovereign [[*or* Lord]] will come like a thief in the night. ³ When people say, "There is peace and security," then sudden destruction will come upon them as travail comes upon a woman with child, and there will be no escape. ⁴ But you are not in the night, sisters and brothers, for that day to surprise you like a thief. ⁵ For you are all children of light and children of the day; we are not of the night. ⁶ So then let us not sleep, as others do, but let us keep awake and be sober. ⁷ For those who sleep, sleep at night, and those who get drunk are drunk at night. ⁸ But, since we belong to the day, let us be sober, and put on the breastplate of faith and love, and for a helmet the hope of salvation. ⁹ For God has not destined us for wrath, but to obtain salvation through our Sovereign [[*or* Lord]] Jesus Christ, ¹⁰ who died for us so that whether we wake or sleep we might live with Christ. ¹¹ Therefore encourage one another and build one another up, just as you are doing.

Jesus tells the parable of the talents.

14 For it will be as when someone going on a journey called in servants and entrusted to them some money, 15 giving to one five talents, to another two, to another one, to each according to their ability, and then went away. 16 The one who had received the five talents went at once and traded with the money, and made five talents more. 17 So also, the one who had the two talents made two talents more. 18 But the one who had received the one talent went and dug in the ground and hid the money. 19 Now after a long time the sovereign⌐ of those servants returned and settled accounts with them. 20 And the servant who had received the five talents came forward, bringing five talents more, saying, "Sovereign,⌐ you delivered to me five talents; here I have made five talents more." 21 The sovereign⌐ said, "Well done, good and faithful servant; you have been faithful over a little, I will set you over much; enter into the joy of your sovereign.⌐"22 And the one also who had the two talents came forward, saying, "Sovereign,⌐ you delivered to me two talents; here I have made two talents more." 23 The reply came, "Well done, good and faithful servant; you have been faithful over a little, I will set you over much; enter into the joy of your sovereign.⌐"24 The one who had received the one talent came forward, saying, "Sovereign,⌐ I knew you to be a demanding person, reaping where you did not sow, and gathering where you did not winnow; 25 so I was afraid, and I went and hid your talent in the ground. Here you have what is yours." 26 But the sovereign⌐ answered, "You wicked and slothful servant! You knew that I reap where I have not sowed, and gather where I have not winnowed? 27 Then you ought to have invested my money with the bankers, and at my coming I should have received what was my own with interest. 28 So take back the talent, and give it to the one who has the ten talents. 29 For to everyone who has will more be given, and they will have abundance; but from everyone who has not, even what they have will be taken away. 30 And cast the worthless servant into the outer regions, where there will be weeping and gnashing of teeth."

⌐RSV vs. 19, 21b, 23 *master;* vs. 20, 22, 24 *Master;* vs. 21a, 26 *his master.* See "Sovereign" in the Appendix.

PENTECOST 27

Lesson 1 ~ Ezekiel 34:11-16, 20-24

God is the good shepherd who will gather the dispersed and injured flock, and place God's servant, one like David, over the people.

¹¹ For thus says the Sovereign [*or* Lord] GOD: I, I myself will search for my sheep, and will seek them out. ¹² As a shepherd seeks out the flock when some of the sheep have been scattered abroad, so will I seek out my sheep; and I will rescue them from all places where they have been scattered on a day of cloud and thick shadow. ¹³ And I will bring them out from the peoples, and gather them from the countries, and will bring them into their own land; and I will feed them on the mountains of Israel, by the fountains, and in all the inhabited places of the country. ¹⁴ I will feed them with good pasture, and upon the mountain heights of Israel shall be their pasture; there they shall lie down in good grazing land, and on fat pasture they shall feed on the mountains of Israel. ¹⁵ I myself will be the shepherd of my sheep, and I will make them lie down, says the Sovereign [*or* Lord] GOD. ¹⁶ I will seek the lost, and I will bring back the strayed, and I will bind up those who are crippled, and I will strengthen those who are weak, and the fat and the strong I will watch over; I will feed them in justice.

²⁰ Therefore, thus says the Sovereign [*or* Lord] GOD to them: I, I myself will judge between the fat sheep and the lean sheep. ²¹ Because you push with side and shoulder, and thrust at all the weak with your horns, till you have scattered them abroad, ²² I will save my flock, they shall no longer be a prey; and I will judge between sheep and sheep. ²³ And I will set up over them one shepherd, my servant David, who shall feed them: David shall feed them and be their shepherd. ²⁴ And I, the SOVEREIGN [*or* LORD], will be their God, and my servant David shall be prince among them; I, the SOVEREIGN [*or* LORD], have spoken.

Psalm 23

¹ GOD [[or The LORD]] is my shepherd, I shall not want;
²   God makes me lie down in green pastures,
   and leads me beside still waters;
³   God restores my soul.
   God leads me in paths of righteousness
     for God's name's sake.
⁴ Even though I walk through the valley of the shadow of death,
   I fear no evil;
for you are with me;
   your rod and your staff,
   they comfort me.
⁵ You prepare a table before me
   in the presence of my enemies;
you anoint my head with oil,
   my cup overflows.
⁶ Surely goodness and mercy shall follow me
   all the days of my life;
and I shall dwell in the house of GOD [[or the LORD]]
forever.

Lesson 2 ~ 1 Corinthians 15:20-28

Paul writes of the resurrection of Christ and the subjection of all things to Christ and then to God.

²⁰ But in fact Christ has been raised from the dead, the firstfruits of those who have fallen asleep. ²¹ For as by a human being came death, by a human being has come also the resurrection of the dead. ²² For as in Adam all die, so also in Christ shall all be made alive. ²³ But each in the proper order: Christ the firstfruits, then at Christ's coming those who belong to Christ. ²⁴ Then comes the end, when Christ delivers the sovereignty☆ to God the Father [*and Mother**] after destroying every rule and every authority and power. ²⁵ For Christ must reign until all enemies are put under Christ's feet. ²⁶ The last enemy to be destroyed is death. ²⁷ "For God has put all things in subjection under Christ's feet." But when it says, "All things are put in subjection," it is clear that the one who put all things under Christ is not included. ²⁸ When all things are subjected to Christ, then Christ also will be subjected to God who put all things under Christ, that God may be everything to everyone.

☆RSV *kingdom*. See Appendix.
*Addition to the text. See "Metaphor" and "God the Father and Mother" in the Appendix.

Jesus tells the parable of the last judgment.

31 When the Human One° comes in glory, with all the angels, then that one will sit on a glorious throne. 32 All the nations will be gathered before the Human One,° who will separate them one from another as a shepherd separates the sheep from the goats, 33 placing the sheep on the right, but the goats on the left. 34 Then the Ruler⊡ will say to those on the right, "Come, O blessed of [*God*] my Father [*and Mother**], inherit the realm☆ prepared for you from the foundation of the world; 35 for I was hungry and you gave me food, I was thirsty and you gave me drink, I was a stranger and you welcomed me, 36 I was naked and you clothed me, I was sick and you visited me, I was in prison and you came to me." 37 Then the righteous will answer, "Sovereign ⟦*or* Lord⟧, when did we see you hungry and feed you, or thirsty and give you drink? 38 And when did we see you a stranger and welcome you, or naked and clothe you? 39 And when did we see you sick or in prison and visit you?" 40 And the Ruler⊡ will answer them, "Truly, I say to you, as you did it to one of the least of these my sisters and brothers, you did it to me." 41 Then the Ruler⊡ will say to those on the left, "Depart from me, you cursed, into the eternal fire prepared for the devil and the devil's angels; 42 for I was hungry and you gave me no food, I was thirsty and you gave me no drink, 43 I was a stranger and you did not welcome me, naked and you did not clothe me, sick and in prison and you did not visit me." 44 Then they also will answer, "Sovereign ⟦*or* Lord⟧, when did we see you hungry or thirsty or a stranger or naked or sick or in prison, and did not minister to you?" 45 Then the Ruler will answer them, "Truly, I say to you, as you did it not to one of the least of these, you did it not to me." 46 And they will go away into eternal punishment, but the righteous into eternal life.

°RSV *Son of man*. See Appendix.
⊡RSV *King*. See Appendix.
*Addition to the text. See "Metaphor" and "God the Father and Mother" in the Appendix.
☆RSV *kingdom*. See Appendix.

PRESENTATION—FEBRUARY 2

Lesson 1 ~ Malachi 3:1-4

The messenger goes before God to bring judgment to the people.

¹ I am sending my messenger to prepare the way before me, and God ⟦*or* the Lord⟧ whom you seek will suddenly come to the temple; the messenger of the covenant in whom you delight—that one is coming, says the GOD ⟦*or* LORD⟧ of hosts. ² But who can endure the day of that coming, and who can stand when the messenger appears?

For my messenger is like a refiner's fire and like launderers' bleach, ³ who will sit as a refiner and purifier of silver, and will purify the tribe of Levi and refine them like gold and silver, till they present right offerings to GOD ⟦*or* the LORD⟧. ⁴ Then the offering of Judah and Jerusalem will be pleasing to GOD ⟦*or* the LORD⟧ as in the days of old and as in former years.

Psalm 84

¹ How lovely is your dwelling place,
   O GOD ⟦*or* LORD⟧ of hosts!
² My soul longs, even faints
   for the courts of GOD ⟦*or* the LORD⟧;
my heart and flesh sing for joy
   to the living God.
³ Even the sparrow finds a home,
   and the swallow a nest for herself,
   where she may lay her young,
at your altars, O GOD ⟦*or* LORD⟧ of hosts,
   my Ruler▱ and my God.
⁴ Blessed are those who dwell in your house,
   ever singing your praise!
⁵ Blessed are those whose strength is in you,
   in whose heart are the highways to Zion.
⁶ As they go through the valley of Baca
   they make it a place of springs;
   the early rain also covers it with pools.
⁷ They go from strength to strength;
   the God of gods will be seen in Zion.
⁸ O SOVEREIGN ⟦*or* LORD⟧ God of hosts, hear my prayer;
   give ear, O God of Jacob!

▱RSV *King*. See Appendix.

⁹ Behold our shield, O God;
    look upon the face of your anointed!
¹⁰ For a day in your courts is better than a thousand elsewhere.
    I would rather be a doorkeeper in the house of my God
      than dwell in the tents of wickedness.
¹¹ For the SOVEREIGN [[*or* LORD]] God is a sun and shield,
    who bestows favor and honor.
  No good thing does GOD [[*or* the LORD]] withhold
    from those who walk uprightly.
¹² O GOD [[*or* LORD]] of hosts,
    blessed is the one who trusts in you!

Psalm 24:7-10 (alternate)

⁷ Lift up your heads, O gates!
    and be lifted up, O ancient doors!
    that the Ruler□ of glory may come in.
⁸ Who is the Ruler□ of glory?
    GOD [[*or* The LORD]], strong and mighty,
    GOD [[*or* the LORD]], mighty in battle!
⁹ Lift up your heads, O gates!
    and be lifted up, O ancient doors!
    that the Ruler□ of glory may come in.
¹⁰ Who is this Ruler□ of glory?
    The GOD [[*or* LORD]] of hosts,
    that one is the Ruler□ of glory!

□RSV *King*. See Appendix.

Lesson 2 ~ Hebrews 2:14-18

Jesus, by becoming a human being, delivers the people by making expiation for their sins.

14 Since therefore the children share in flesh and blood, Jesus likewise partook of the same nature in order to destroy through death the one who has the power of death, that is, the devil, 15 and to deliver all those who through fear of death were subject to lifelong bondage. 16 For surely it is not with angels that Jesus is concerned but with the descendants of Abraham [and Sarah*]. 17 Therefore Jesus had to be made like human beings in every respect, in order to become a merciful and faithful high priest in the service of God, to make expiation for the sins of the people. 18 For because Jesus also has suffered and been tempted, Jesus is able to help those who are tempted.

Gospel ~ Luke 2:22-40

Mary and Joseph take the infant Jesus to the temple in Jerusalem, and the child is met there by Simeon and Anna.

22 And when the time came for their purification according to the law of Moses, they brought the child Jesus up to Jerusalem to be presented to God [or the Lord] 23 (as it is written in the law of God [or the Lord], "Every male that opens the womb shall be called holy to God [or the Lord]"), 24 and to offer a sacrifice according to what is said in the law of God [or the Lord], "a pair of turtledoves, or two young pigeons." 25 Now there was a man in Jerusalem, whose name was Simeon, who was righteous and devout, looking for the consolation of Israel, and the Holy Spirit was upon him. 26 And it had been revealed to Simeon by the Holy Spirit that he should not see death before he had seen the Christ of God [or the Lord]. 27 And inspired by the Spirit, Simeon came into the temple; and when the parents brought in the child Jesus, to do for him according to the custom of the law, 28 Simeon took the child in his arms and blessed God and said,

29 "Sovereign [or Lord], now let your servant depart in peace,
   according to your word;
30 for my eyes have seen your salvation
31 which you have prepared in the presence of all people,
32 a light for revelation to the Gentiles,
   and for glory to your people Israel."

---

*Addition to the text. See "Addition of Women's Names to the Text" in the Appendix.

³³ And the father and mother of Jesus marveled at what was said about their child; ³⁴ and Simeon blessed them and said to Mary, Jesus' mother,

"This child is set for the fall and rising of many in Israel,
and for a sign that is spoken against
³⁵ (and a sword will pierce through your own soul also),
that thoughts out of many hearts may be revealed."

³⁶ And there was a prophet, Anna, the daughter of Phanuel, of the tribe of Asher; she was of a great age, having lived with her husband seven years, ³⁷ and as a widow till she was eighty-four. She did not depart from the temple, worshiping with fasting and prayer night and day. ³⁸ And coming up at that very hour she gave thanks to God, and spoke about the child to all who were looking for the redemption of Jerusalem.

³⁹ And when Mary and Joseph had performed everything according to the law of God [[or the Lord]], they returned into Galilee, to their own city, Nazareth. ⁴⁰ And the child grew and became strong, filled with wisdom; and the favor of God was upon the child.

ANNUNCIATION—MARCH 25

Lesson 1 ~ Isaiah 7:10-14

Isaiah brings a word of assurance from God to Ahaz, ruler of Judah, in the face of a threat from the rulers of Syria.

¹⁰ Again GOD [[*or* the LORD]] spoke to Ahaz, ¹¹ "Ask a sign of the SOVEREIGN [[*or* LORD]] your God; let it be deep as Sheol or high as heaven." ¹² But Ahaz said, "I will not ask, and I will not put GOD [[*or* the LORD]] to the test." ¹³ And Isaiah said, "Hear then, O house of David! Is it too little for you to weary human beings, that you weary my God also? ¹⁴ Therefore God [[*or* the Lord]] will give you a sign: a young woman shall conceive and bear a child, whom she shall call Immanuel."

Psalm 40:6–10⁺

⁶ Sacrifice and offering you do not desire;
    but you have given me an open ear.
Burnt offering and sin offering
    you have not required.
⁷ Then I said, "I am coming;
    in the scroll of the book it is written of me;
⁸ I delight to do your will, O my God;
    your law is within my heart."
⁹ I have told the glad news of deliverance
    in the great congregation;
I have not restrained my lips,
    as you know, O GOD [[*or* LORD]].
¹⁰ I have not hid your saving help within my heart,
    I have spoken of your faithfulness and your salvation;
I have not concealed your steadfast love and your faithfulness
    from the great congregation.

Lesson 2 ~ Hebrews 10:4-10

Jesus Christ, the high priest, is the single sacrifice for sins.

⁴ For it is impossible that the blood of bulls and goats should take away sins.
⁵ Consequently, Christ, having come into the world, said,

"Sacrifices and offerings you have not desired,
    but a body you have prepared for me;

⁺ Alternate Psalm 45 not included. See Appendix, p. 277.

⁶ in burnt offerings and sin offerings you have taken no pleasure.
⁷ Then I said, 'I have come to do your will, O God,'
as it is written of me in the scroll of the book."

⁸ When Christ said above, "You have neither desired nor taken pleasure in sacrifices and offerings and burnt offerings and sin offerings" (these are offered according to the law), ⁹ then Christ added, "I have come to do your will." Christ abolishes the first in order to establish the second. ¹⁰ And by that will we have been sanctified through the offering of the body of Jesus Christ once for all.

Gospel ~ Luke 1:26-38

The angel Gabriel announces to Mary that she will bear the child of God.

²⁶ In the sixth month the angel Gabriel was sent from God to a city of Galilee named Nazareth, ²⁷ to a virgin betrothed to a man whose name was Joseph, of the house of David; and her name was Mary. ²⁸ And the angel came to her and said, "Hail, O favored one, God ⟦or the Lord⟧ is with you!" ²⁹ But she was greatly troubled at the saying, and considered in her mind what sort of greeting this might be. ³⁰ And the angel said to her, "Do not be afraid, Mary, for you have found favor with God. ³¹ You will conceive in your womb and bear a child, whose name you shall call Jesus.

³² This one will be great, and will be called the Child◇ of the Most
    High;
and the Sovereign ⟦or Lord⟧ God will give to that Child the throne of
    David, the ancestor of the Child,
³³ to reign over the house of Jacob forever;
and of that reign☆ there will be no end."

³⁴ And Mary said to the angel, "How shall this be, since I have no husband?" ³⁵ And the angel said to her,

"The Holy Spirit will come upon you,
and the power of the Most High will overshadow you;
therefore the child to be born will be called holy,
the Child◇ of God.

³⁶ And your kinswoman Elizabeth in her old age has also conceived a child; and this is the sixth month with her who was called barren. ³⁷ For with God nothing will be impossible." ³⁸ And Mary said, "I am the servant of God ⟦or the Lord⟧; let it be to me according to your word." And the angel departed from her.

◇RSV *Son*. See Appendix.
☆RSV *his kingdom*. See Appendix.

Lesson 1 ~ 1 Samuel 2:1-10

Hannah offers a prayer to God.

¹ Hannah also prayed and said,

"My heart exults in GOD [[*or* the LORD]];
my strength is exalted in GOD [[*or* the LORD]].
My mouth derides my enemies,
because I rejoice in your salvation.
² There is none holy like GOD [[*or* the LORD]],
there is none besides you;
there is no rock like our God.
³ Talk no more so very proudly,
let not arrogance come from your mouth;
for GOD [[*or* the LORD]] is a God of knowledge,
by whom actions are weighed.
⁴ The bows of the mighty are broken,
but the feeble gird on strength.
⁵ Those who were full have hired themselves out for bread,
but those who were hungry have ceased to hunger.
The barren has borne seven,
but she who has many children is forlorn.
⁶ It is GOD [[*or* the LORD]] who kills and brings to life,
who brings down to Sheol and raises up,
⁷ who makes poor and makes rich,
who brings low and also exalts.
⁸ It is God who raises up the poor from the dust,
and lifts the needy from the ash heap,
to make them sit with nobles
and inherit a seat of honor.
For the pillars of the earth belong to GOD [[*or* the LORD]],
and on them God has set the world.
⁹ God will guard the feet of the faithful ones;
but the wicked shall be removed from sight;
for not by might shall anyone prevail.
¹⁰ The adversaries of GOD [[*or* the LORD]] shall be broken to pieces;
against them God will thunder in heaven.
GOD [[*or* The LORD]] will judge the ends of the earth,
giving strength to God's ruler, ▢
and exalting the power of the anointed one."

▢RSV *his king*. See Appendix.

Psalm 113

¹ Praise GOD [[*or* the LORD]]!
  Praise, O servants of GOD [[*or* the LORD]],
    praise the name of the SOVEREIGN [[*or* LORD]]!
² Blessed be the name of the SOVEREIGN [[*or* LORD]]
    from this time forth and forevermore!
³ From the rising of the sun to its setting
    the name of the SOVEREIGN [[*or* LORD]] is to be praised!
⁴ GOD [[*or* The LORD]] is high above all nations,
    and God's glory above the heavens!
⁵ Who is like the SOVEREIGN [[*or* LORD]] our God,
    who is seated on high,
⁶ who looks far down
    upon the heavens and the earth?
⁷ God raises the poor from the dust,
    and lifts the needy from the ash heap,
⁸ to make them sit with nobles,
    with the nobles of God's people.
⁹ God gives the barren woman a home,
    making her the joyous mother of children.
  Praise GOD [[*or* the LORD]]!

Lesson 2 ~ Romans 12:9-16b

Paul writes to the Christians at Rome about their relationships with one another.

⁹ Let love be genuine; hate what is evil, hold fast to what is good; ¹⁰ be affectionately devoted to one another; outdo one another in showing honor. ¹¹ Never flag in zeal, be aglow with the Spirit, serve the Sovereign [[*or* Lord]]. ¹² Rejoice in your hope, be patient in tribulation, be constant in prayer. ¹³ Contribute to the needs of the saints, practice hospitality.

¹⁴ Bless those who persecute you; bless and do not curse them. ¹⁵ Rejoice with those who rejoice, weep with those who weep. ¹⁶ Live in harmony with one another; do not be haughty, but associate with the lowly.

Mary greets Elizabeth and sings a song of praise to God.

39 In those days Mary arose and went with haste into the hill country, to a city of Judah, 40and she entered the house of Zechariah and greeted Elizabeth. 41 And when Elizabeth heard the greeting of Mary, the baby leaped in her womb; and Elizabeth was filled with the Holy Spirit 42 and she exclaimed with a loud cry, "Blessed are you among women, and blessed is the fruit of your womb! 43 And why is this granted me, that the mother of my Sovereign [[or Lord]] should come to me? 44 For when the voice of your greeting came to my ears, the baby in my womb leaped for joy. 45 And blessed is she who believed that there would be a fulfillment of what was spoken to her from God [[or the Lord]]." 46 And Mary said,

"My soul magnifies the Sovereign [[or Lord]],
47 and my spirit rejoices in God my Savior,
48 who has regarded the low estate of God's servant.
For henceforth all generations will call me blessed;
49 for the one who is mighty has done great things for me,
and holy is God's name.
50 And God's mercy is on those who fear God
from generation to generation.
51 God has shown strength with God's arm,
and has scattered the proud in the imagination of their hearts,
52 God has put down the mighty from their thrones,
and exalted those of low degree;
53 God has filled the hungry with good things,
and has sent the rich empty away.
54 God has helped God's servant Israel,
in remembrance of God's mercy,
55 as God spoke to our ancestors,
to Abraham [*and Sarah**] and to their posterity forever."

56 And Mary remained with Elizabeth about three months, and returned to her home.
57 Now the time came for Elizabeth to be delivered, and she gave birth to a son.

---

*Addition to the text. RSV *to Abraham and to his posterity.* See "Addition of Women's Names to the Text" in the Appendix.

HOLY CROSS—SEPTEMBER 14

Lesson 1 ~ Numbers 21:4b-9

Moses makes a bronze serpent to heal victims of the plague of fiery serpents.

⁴ The people became impatient on the way, ⁵ and they spoke against God and against Moses, "Why have you brought us up out of Egypt to die in the wilderness? For there is no food and no water, and we loathe this worthless food." ⁶ Then GOD [[*or* the LORD]] sent fiery serpents among the people, and they bit the people, so that many people of Israel died. ⁷ And the people came to Moses, and said, "We have sinned, for we have spoken against GOD [[*or* the LORD]] and against you; pray to GOD [[*or* the LORD]] to take away the serpents from us." So Moses prayed for the people. ⁸ And GOD [[*or* the LORD]] said to Moses, "Make a fiery serpent, and set it on a pole; and all who are bitten, when they see it, shall live." ⁹ So Moses made a bronze serpent, and set it on a pole; and anyone whom a serpent bit would look at the bronze serpent and live.

Psalm 98:1-5

¹ O sing a new song to GOD [[*or* the LORD]],
  who has done marvelous things,
 whose right hand and holy arm
  have gained the victory!
² GOD [[*or* The LORD]] has made known the victory,
  and has revealed God's vindication in the sight of the nations.
³ God has remembered God's steadfast love and faithfulness
  to the house of Israel.
 All the ends of the earth have seen
  the victory of our God.
⁴ Make a joyful noise to GOD [[*or* the LORD]], all the earth;
  break forth into joyous song and sing praises!
⁵ Sing praises to GOD [[*or* the LORD]] with the lyre,
  with the lyre and the sound of melody!

Psalm 78:1-2, 34-38 (alternate)

1 Give ear, O my people, to my teaching;
　　incline your ears to the words of my mouth!
2 I will open my mouth in a parable;
　　I will utter obscure sayings from of old.
34 When God slew them, they sought for God;
　　they repented and sought God earnestly.
35 They remembered that God was their rock,
　　the Most High God their redeemer.
36 But they flattered God with their mouths;
　　they lied to God with their tongues.
37 Their heart was not steadfast toward God;
　　they were not true to God's covenant.
38 Yet God, being compassionate,
　　forgave their iniquity,
　　and did not destroy them,
　　restraining God's anger often,
　　and not arousing all God's wrath.

Lesson 2 ~ 1 Corinthians 1:18-24

Paul writes to the Christians at Corinth about the wisdom of God.

18 For the word of the cross is folly to those who are perishing, but to us who are being saved it is the power of God. 19 For it is written,

　　"I will destroy the wisdom of the wise,
　　and the cleverness of the clever I will thwart."

20 Where is the wise one? Where is the scribe? Where is the debater of this age? Has not God made foolish the wisdom of the world? 21 For since, in the wisdom of God, the world did not know God through wisdom, it pleased God through the folly of what we preach to save those who believe. 22 For Jews demand signs and Greeks seek wisdom, 23 but we preach Christ crucified, a stumbling block to Jews and folly to Gentiles, 24 but to those who are called, both Jews and Greeks, Christ the power of God and the wisdom of God.

Those who believe in the Child of God will have eternal life.

[13] "No one has ascended into heaven but the one who descended from heaven, the Human One.° [14] And as Moses lifted up the serpent in the wilderness, so must the Human One° be lifted up, [15] that whoever believes in that one may have eternal life."

[16] For God so loved the world that God gave God's only Child,◇ that whoever believes in that Child should not perish but have eternal life. [17] For God sent that Child◇ into the world, not to condemn the world, but that through that Child the world might be saved.

°RSV *Son of man*. See Appendix.
◇RSV v. 16 *his only Son;* v. 17 *the Son*. See Appendix.

ALL SAINTS—NOVEMBER 1

(Or the first Sunday in November)

Lesson 1 ~ Revelation 7:9-17

Survivors of great suffering praise God and the Lamb.

⁹ After this I looked, and there was a great multitude which no one could number, from every nation, from all tribes and peoples and tongues, standing before the throne and before the Lamb, clothed in white robes, with palm branches in their hands, ¹⁰ and crying out with a loud voice, "Salvation belongs to our God who sits upon the throne, and to the Lamb!" ¹¹ And all the angels stood round the throne and round the elders and the four living creatures, and they fell on their faces before the throne and worshiped God, ¹² saying, "Amen! Blessing and glory and wisdom and thanksgiving and honor and power and might be to our God forever and ever! Amen."

¹³ Then one of the elders addressed me, saying, "Who are these, clothed in white robes, and from where have they come?" ¹⁴ I answered, "Sir, you know." And he said to me, "These are they who have come out of the great tribulation; they have washed their robes and made them pure in the blood of the Lamb.

¹⁵ Therefore they are before the throne of God,
     and serve God day and night within the temple;
     and the one who sits upon the throne will dwell with them.
¹⁶ They shall hunger no more, neither thirst anymore;
     the sun shall not strike them, nor any scorching heat.
¹⁷ For the Lamb in the midst of the throne will be their shepherd,
     and will guide them to springs of living water;
   and God will wipe away every tear from their eyes."

¹ I will bless GOD [[*or* the LORD]] at all times;
  God's praise shall continually be in my mouth.
² My soul makes its boast in GOD [[*or* the LORD]];
  let those who are afflicted hear and be glad.
³ O magnify GOD [[*or* the LORD]] with me
  and let us exalt God's name together!
⁴ I sought GOD [[*or* the LORD]], who answered me,
  and delivered me from all my fears.
⁵ Look to God, and be radiant;
  so your faces shall never be ashamed.
⁶ This poor one cried, and GOD [[*or* the LORD]] heard me,
  and saved me out of all my troubles.
⁷ The angel of GOD [[*or* the LORD]] encamps
  around those who fear God, and delivers them.
⁸ O taste and see that GOD [[*or* the LORD]] is good!
  Happy is the one who takes refuge in God!
⁹ O fear GOD [[*or* the LORD]], you saints of God,
  for those who fear God have no want!
¹⁰ The young lions suffer want and hunger;
  but those who seek GOD [[*or* the LORD]] lack no good thing.

Lesson 2 ~ 1 John 3:1-3

The love of God calls us to a new life.

¹ See what love [*God*] the Father [*and Mother**] has given us, that we should be called children of God; and so we are. The reason the world does not know us is that it did not know Christ. ² Beloved, we are now God's children; it does not yet appear what we shall be, but we know that when Christ appears we shall be like Christ, for we shall see Christ just as Christ is. ³ And all who thus hope in Christ purify themselves just as Christ is pure.

---

*Addition to the text. See "Metaphor" and "God the Father and Mother" in the Appendix.

Gospel ~ Matthew 5:1-12

In the Sermon on the Mount, Jesus teaches about blessedness.

[1] Seeing the crowds, Jesus went up on the mountain and sat down; and the disciples came to him. [2] And Jesus opened his mouth and taught them, saying:

[3] "Blessed are the poor in spirit, for theirs is the realm☆ of heaven.

[4] "Blessed are those who mourn, for they shall be comforted.

[5] "Blessed are the meek, for they shall inherit the earth.

[6] "Blessed are those who hunger and thirst for righteousness, for they shall be satisfied.

[7] "Blessed are the merciful, for they shall obtain mercy.

[8] "Blessed are the pure in heart, for they shall see God.

[9] "Blessed are the peacemakers, for they shall be called children of God.

[10] "Blessed are those who are persecuted for righteousness' sake, for theirs is the realm☆ of heaven.

[11] "Blessed are you when others revile you and persecute you and utter all kinds of evil against you falsely on my account. [12] Rejoice and be glad, for your reward is great in heaven, for so they persecuted the prophets who were before you."

☆RSV *kingdom*. See Appendix.

THANKSGIVING DAY

Lesson 1 ~ Deuteronomy 8:7-18

The people of Israel are reminded of God's many blessings.

⁷ For the SOVEREIGN [*or* LORD] your God is bringing you into a good land, a land of brooks of water, of fountains and springs, flowing forth in valleys and hills, ⁸ a land of wheat and barley, of vines and fig trees and pomegranates, a land of olive trees and honey, ⁹ a land in which you will eat bread without scarcity, in which you will lack nothing, a land whose stones are iron, and out of whose hills you can dig copper. ¹⁰ And you shall eat and be full, and you shall bless the SOVEREIGN [*or* LORD] your God for the good land God has given you.

¹¹ Take heed lest you forget the SOVEREIGN [*or* LORD] your God, by not keeping God's commandments and ordinances and statutes, which I command you this day: ¹² lest, when you have eaten and are full, and have built goodly houses and live in them, ¹³ and when your herds and flocks multiply, and your silver and gold is multiplied, and all that you have is multiplied, ¹⁴ then your heart be lifted up, and you forget the SOVEREIGN [*or* LORD] your God, who brought you out of the land of Egypt, out of the house of bondage, ¹⁵ who led you through the great and terrible wilderness, with its fiery serpents and scorpions and thirsty ground where there was no water, who brought you water out of the flinty rock, ¹⁶ who fed you in the wilderness with manna which your ancestors did not know, in order to humble you and test you, to do you good in the end. ¹⁷ Beware lest you say in your heart, "My power and the might of my hand have gotten me this wealth." ¹⁸ You shall remember the SOVEREIGN [*or* LORD] your God, for God is the one who gives you power to get wealth, so as to confirm the covenant which God swore to your ancestors, as at this day.

Psalm 65

¹ Praise is due to you,
    O God, in Zion;
  and to you shall vows be performed,
²   O you who hear prayer!
  To you shall all flesh come
³   on account of sins.
  When our transgressions prevail over us,
    you forgive them.

[4] Blessed is the one whom you choose and bring near,
  to dwell in your courts!
We shall be satisfied with the goodness of your house,
  your holy temple!
[5] By dread deeds you answer us with deliverance,
  O God of our salvation,
who are the hope of all the ends of the earth,
  and of the farthest seas;
[6] who by your strength have established the mountains,
  being girded with might;
[7] who still the roaring of the seas,
  the roaring of their waves,
  the tumult of the people;
[8] so that those who dwell at earth's farthest bounds
  are afraid at your signs;
you make the outgoings of the morning and the evening
  to shout for joy.
[9] You visit the earth and water it,
  you greatly enrich it;
the river of God is full of water;
  you provide their grain,
  for thus you have prepared the earth.
[10] You water its furrows abundantly,
  settling its ridges,
softening it with showers,
  and blessing its growth.
[11] You crown the year with your bounty;
  the tracks of your chariot drip with fatness.
[12] The pastures of the wilderness drip,
  the hills gird themselves with joy,
[13] the meadows clothe themselves with flocks,
  the valleys deck themselves with grain,
  they shout and sing together for joy.

Lesson 2 ~ 2 Corinthians 9:6-15

Paul tells the Corinthians that God will enrich them and supply all their needs.

⁶ The point is this: whoever sows sparingly will also reap sparingly, and whoever sows bountifully will also reap bountifully. ⁷ Each must do as they have decided, not reluctantly or under compulsion, for God loves a cheerful giver. ⁸ And God is able to provide you with every blessing in abundance, so that you may always have enough of everything and may provide in abundance for every good work. ⁹ As it is written,

> "God scattered abroad, and gave to the poor;
> God's righteousness endures forever."

¹⁰ The one who supplies seed to the sower and bread for food will supply and multiply your resources and increase the harvest of your righteousness. ¹¹ You will be enriched in every way for great generosity, which through us will produce thanksgiving to God; ¹² for the rendering of this service not only supplies the wants of the saints but also overflows in many thanksgivings to God. ¹³ Under the test of this service, you will glorify God by your obedience in acknowledging the gospel of Christ, and by the generosity of your contribution for them and for all others; ¹⁴ while they long for you and pray for you, because of the surpassing grace of God in you. ¹⁵ Thanks be to God for God's inexpressible gift!

Gospel ~ Luke 17:11-19

Jesus heals the ten people of their leprosy.

¹¹ On the way to Jerusalem Jesus was passing along between Samaria and Galilee. ¹² And entering a village, he was met by ten people with leprosy, who stood at a distance ¹³ and lifted up their voices and said, "Jesus, Teacher,† have mercy on us." ¹⁴ And seeing them, Jesus said, "Go and show yourselves to the priests." And as they went they were cleansed. ¹⁵ Then one of them, seeing that he was healed, turned back, praising God with a loud voice; ¹⁶ and he fell down at Jesus' feet, giving him thanks. Now that one was a Samaritan. ¹⁷ Then said Jesus, "Were not ten cleansed? Where are the nine? ¹⁸ Was no one found to return and give praise to God except this foreigner?" ¹⁹ And Jesus said to him, "Rise and go your way; your faith has made you well."

---

†RSV *Master.* See Appendix.

Appendix

Metaphor

A metaphor is a figure of speech used to extend meaning through comparison of dissimilars. For example, "Life is a dream" is a metaphor. The character of dreams is ascribed to life, and the meaning of "life" is thus extended. "Dream" is used as a screen through which to view "life." Two dissimilars are juxtaposed.

The statement "God is Father" is also a metaphor. Two dissimilars, "Father" and "God," are juxtaposed, and so the meaning of "God" is extended. Although "God the Father" has been a powerful metaphor for communicating the nature of God, like any metaphor it can become worn. It may even be interpreted literally, that is, as describing exactly. The dissimilars become similar. The metaphor becomes a proposition.

Now, if one were to say "God is Mother," the power of the metaphor would be apparent. The image "God the Mother and Father" as a lens through which to view God elicits the response of a true metaphor, just as the statement "God is Father" once did. In this lectionary, "God the Father and Mother" is used as a formal equivalent of "the Father" or "God the Father." "God the Father" is clearly a metaphor, just as "God the Mother" is. God *is* not a father, any more than God *is* a mother, or than life *is* a dream. By reading and hearing "God the Father and Mother" we provide a metaphor for God that balances the more familiar *male* imagery for God with the less familiar *female* imagery.

There are many female images for God in the scriptures. For example, God as mother is found in the Old Testament, "Now I will cry out like a woman in travail" (Isa. 42:14), and "As one whom his mother comforts, so I will comfort you" (Isa. 66:13). In the New Testament, the parable of the woman seeking the lost coin (Luke 15:8-10) functions as a female image for God. Metaphors are figurative and open-ended. Their meanings vary from hearer to hearer, but they are not dispensable, for there is no other way by which to say directly what the metaphor communicates. A metaphor provides a new way of seeing.

269

(*) [God] the Father [and Mother] (RSV the Father; God the Father, God our Father; Abba)

One of the characteristics of the Christian faith is its emphasis on the personal nature of God. While God is also described in impersonal terms (rock, light, love), personal imagery prevails. "Father" is one such personal term. The Gospels record that when Jesus prayed he called God "Abba" ("Father," Mark 14:36), and frequently, especially in the Gospel of John, Jesus refers to God as Father. In the Old Testament, the term "Father" is used infrequently as a designation for God.

For Jesus, "Father" was a sacred word, pointing to the mysterious intimacy Jesus had with God (Matt. 11:27), and pointing to the intimate relationship his disciples also had with God (Matt. 23:9). Jesus' own use of the word "Father" in addressing God supported the church's claim that Jesus was the "Son."

The phrase used in this lectionary, "God the Father and Mother," is offered as a way of expressing the same intimacy, caring, and freedom that is found in Jesus' identification of God as Abba. Jesus' use of this term to refer to God was radically nontraditional. This warrants the use of nontraditional intimate language in contemporary reference to God. Thus the use of the phrase "God the Mother and Father" is a way to affirm the important Christian belief that Jesus is the Child of God. Just as we do not create our children, but give them birth out of our very selves, we believe that God did not create Jesus, but that God "gave birth to" or "begot" Jesus.

It is also the case that Christians rejected as pagan the view that God is father of the world. For Christians, God is Father in relation to the Son. Christians are brought into this relationship of God as "Father" because they are adopted as "sons" or "heirs" (Rom. 8:15, 23; Gal. 4:6; Eph. 1:5).

That Jesus called God "Father" is the basis for the church's thinking about Jesus Christ as one of the persons of the Trinity. The relationship described by the Father/Son imagery of the New Testament opened the way for the church later to identify the Son as of the same substance as the Father. And if God the Son proceeded from God the Father alone, the procession is both a male and a female action, a begetting and a birth. God is the Mother and Father of the Child who comes forth.

The image of God as Father has been misused to support the excessive authority of earthly fathers in a patriarchal social structure. The metaphor "God the Father and Mother" points to the close relationship between language about God and language about the human community. The mutuality and coequality of the persons of the Trinity is a model for human community and especially appropriate, therefore, for readings prepared for worship. Those who worship in the Christian church are struggling to bring about a community where there is "neither male nor female," but where all are "one in Christ Jesus" and "heirs according to promise" (Gal. 3:28-29). (See also Metaphor.)

(⊗) God (RSV my Father, the Father)

In the Gospel of John, and occasionally elsewhere, RSV "Father" is often rendered "God" where "Father" appears frequently in the lection.

Sovereign; God, the SOVEREIGN; etc. (RSV Lord, LORD, etc.)

Sometime in the course of Israel's history the personal name of God, probably pronounced *Yahweh*, ceased to be spoken aloud for fear that it would be profaned, even though it continued to be written in the text of the scriptures. Thus, the practice was already established according to which the faith and piety of the community, shaped by the tradition of scripture itself, takes precedence over the written word in determining what is read for the divine name by the worshiping community. From that time on, the chief word read in place of the divine name was *Adonai*—an honorific title translated "Lord" or "my Lord."

In those places in the RSV where the underlying Hebrew text contains the divine name *(Yahweh)*, and not simply the word *Adonai*, the typography is changed to LORD. Where the divine name is found in the original text, the Lectionary Committee prefers to render it as "GOD" or "the SOVEREIGN." However, because of the deep commitment in the church to the word "Lord" in both Old and New Testaments, and because of a certain ambiguity about the extent to which "Lord" is heard as gender-specific, that term has been included in this lectionary text as an optional or alternative reading, set off in this manner: [[*or* Lord]]; [[*or* LORD]].

In this lectionary the Hebrew word *Elohim* is rendered "God," as in the RSV. The word "God" is also usually used for masculine pronouns referring to the "Sovereign [[*or* Lord]]" or to "God."

Occasionally the divine name, Yahweh, is found in combination with the word for God *(Yahweh Elohim)* or with the word for Lord *(Adonai Yahweh)*. These are rendered in the RSV as "the LORD God" and "the Lord GOD," respectively. In this lectionary the former is rendered as "the SOVEREIGN [[*or* LORD]] God" and the latter as "the Sovereign [[*or* Lord]] GOD. The following chart summarizes these various renderings.

Hebrew Scriptures	RSV	Inclusive-Language Lectionary
Elohim	God	God
Adonai	Lord	God [[*or* the Lord]]; or the Sovereign [[*or* Lord]]
Yahweh	LORD	GOD [[*or* the LORD]]; or the SOVEREIGN [[*or* LORD]]
Yahweh Elohim; or *Elohim Yahweh*	the LORD God	the SOVEREIGN [[*or* LORD]] God
Adonai Yahweh; or *Yahweh Adonai*	the Lord GOD	the Sovereign [[*or* Lord]] GOD

In the Greek New Testament the most frequently used words for God are *Theos* ("God") and *Kyrios* ("Lord"). It is natural that *Kyrios* occurs so often for "God" in the New Testament, because that was the word by which the Greek version of the Old Testament rendered both *Yahweh* and *Adonai;* and it was the Greek version, not the original Hebrew, that was read by the New Testament authors. *Kyrios* was also taken over by the church as a primary way of designating Jesus: "Jesus is Lord."

Kyrios has a wide range of other meanings. It is used for the *owner* of possessions, for the *head* of a family, or for the *master* of a house or of slaves. In the vocative it often means "Sir." *Kyrios* is usually translated into English by "Lord" (in reference to God or Jesus) or "lord" (in reference to a man). In common usage, "lord" means a man with power and authority, such as a titled nobleman.

Because "Lord" is basically a gender-specific word (despite a certain ambiguity in contemporary usage), when used of either God or Christ it connotes, for some, a male being. Since the church believes that God transcends gender and that the risen Christ is one with God, in this lectionary *Kyrios,* occasionally rendered "God" or "Christ," usually has been translated as "Sovereign." (See chart below.) This word, like "Lord," means one supreme in power and authority, but it is inclusive—women as well as men are sovereigns. This translation follows the same principle used in rendering *Yahweh* and *Adonai* as "Sovereign" in the Old Testament lections, and the word "Lord" is included in the text as an alternative reading in the New Testament lections.

Greek New Testament	RSV	Inclusive-Language Lectionary
Kyrios	Lord	Sovereign [or Lord]
		Christ [or the Lord]
		God [or the Lord]

"Sovereign" has another advantage for the translator over "Lord." It is a word in contemporary usage in the political arena, and is not confined to religious usage, as is virtually the case with the word "Lord" in the United States. Not only are there living sovereigns in monarchical societies but nations as well are said to exercise sovereignty. The designation of Jesus Christ as *Kyrios* by the early church carried precisely such a political meaning: Jesus, not Caesar, was *Kyrios*. Christians believed that Jesus Christ is supreme over all earthly authorities. Hence, the status of the authority of the *Sovereign Jesus Christ* in relation to any national sovereignty is expressed in a contemporary idiom which brings to the fore the revolutionary significance of the statement *Kyrios Iēsous* (Jesus is Lord [Sovereign]) for the history of the church.

272

(◇) Child, Child of God (RSV Son, Son of God)

"Son" is used as a designation of Jesus as the Messiah (e.g., Rom. 1:3; 5:10). At Jesus' baptism there was a voice from heaven: "This is my beloved Son" (Matt. 3:17). Jesus also refers to himself as "Son" (Matt. 11:27) though seldom except in the Gospel of John, where the self-designation is common.

A son is male, and of course the historical person, Jesus, was a man. But as the Gospels depict Jesus, his maleness is not said to have any significance for salvation. It is the fact that Jesus was *human* that is crucial, both for Jesus' designation as the Christ and for Jesus' work of salvation.

If the fact that Jesus was a male has no christological significance, then neither has the fact that Jesus was a *son* and not a *daughter.* Therefore, in this lectionary the formal equivalent "Child" or "Child of God" is used for "Son" when the latter has christological significance, and the masculine pronouns that refer to "Child" ("Son") are rendered as "Child." Thus, all hearers of the lectionary readings will be enabled to identify themselves with Jesus' *humanity.*

In traditional language, Jesus as "the Son" makes believers "sons" and therefore heirs. In this lectionary, Jesus as the Child of God makes believers—men and women—"children" of God and therefore heirs. When Jesus is called "Son of God" it is not Jesus' male character that is of primary importance but Jesus' intimate relationship with God (see Matt. 11:25-27). Other connotations of "sonship" are divine authority (see Matt. 28:18-20) and freedom (see Rom. 8:21).

While the word "child" may imply a minor, or childishness, in the New Testament it clearly refers to "adults" in more than half of its occurrences. For example, the word "child" or "children" is used for adult descendants (Acts 13:33; Rom. 9:8); or for adults who are "children" of a teacher or an apostle (1 Cor. 4:14; 2 Cor. 6:13); or for adult Christians (2 John 1, 4); or for adults who are "children of God" (John 11:52; Rom. 8:16). In these and many other passages, "child" or "children" connotes primarily a relationship, and more often of adults than of minors. The canon, therefore, itself provides the church with a substitute for the word "son" that is not gender-specific. The two meanings of the word "child" in the New Testament are also consistent with contemporary usage where the term "child" refers not only to minors but also to a relationship to parents without reference to age.

(○) The Human One (RSV the Son of Man)

The term "the Son of man" is found frequently in the Gospels, and almost nowhere else in the New Testament. Only Jesus uses the term (with a single exception), and the Gospel writers always intended the term to refer to Jesus. How do the Gospel authors interpret its meaning?

Much light would be shed on the meaning of the term if there were clear antecedents to its use in the Gospels, but any such antecedents are impossible to demonstrate. It cannot be shown that Jewish use of the term "Son of man" has influenced its use in the Gospels; in fact, the term does not appear to have functioned as a title prior to its application to Jesus by the church. Furthermore, its meaning varies in different contexts. The term, however, is subject to being misinterpreted as speaking about a male human being, a "son" of a "man." And so, in this lectionary, "the Human One" is used as a formal equivalent for "the Son of man." That formal equivalent is not derived from or dependent on any particular judgment as to the background of "the Son of man" in Judaism, and is not intended to prejudice in any way the ongoing discussion of that question. The Committee believes, however, that the title "the Human One" is open to the same nuances of interpretation allowed by the title "the Son of man." Many of these nuances are derived from the context in which the term is used rather than from the term itself.

In the Old Testament, Ezekiel is often addressed by God as "son of man," which is not a title, and connotes simply a "man." This lectionary renders this expression, "O mortal." In Dan. 7:13, an Aramaic expression is used which is translated "a son of man" in the RSV and "a human one" in this lectionary.

Gender-Specific Pronouns for God and Christ

Because English pronouns are inherently gender-specific, they are not used in this lectionary to refer either to God or to the preexistent or risen Christ.

(✫)Realm of God (RSV Kingdom, Kingdom of God, Kingship)

The Greek word used frequently in the New Testament, and usually translated by the gender-specific word "kingdom," has generally been rendered in this lectionary as "realm," though it has also been translated by other terms as well. The Greek word refers either to the activity of God (i.e., God's "kingship" or "dominion" or "reign" or "rule") or to the state of affairs brought about by God (i.e., God's "kingdom" or "dominion" or "realm"). The Hebrew root usually translated "kingdom" in the RSV is occasionally rendered "kingdom" in this lectionary, but is usually rendered by other terms, primarily "realm."

(□) Ruler, Monarch (RSV King)

The word "king" is used in the Bible both in reference to earthly royal figures and as a metaphor for God. In this lectionary "King" as a metaphor for God is rendered as "Ruler," "Sovereign," or occasionally "Monarch." The word "king" is retained in reference to specific earthly kings, such as David, and in stories and parables about kings.

(†) **Teacher (RSV Master)**

The Greek word used only by Luke in the New Testament and rendered "Master" in the RSV is translated in this lectionary by "Teacher." It had a wide variety of connotations, such as supervisor, administrator, or governor, but no specific religious connotations. It is used by Luke in passages where parallels in Matthew or Mark have "Sovereign," "Teacher," or "Rabbi."

Sisters and Brothers, Friends, Neighbors (RSV Brother, Brethren)

The contemporary use of such phrases as "sisters and brothers in Christ" to address members of the church is helpful in clarifying how the words "brother" and "brethren" are used in the Bible. In Hebrew usage, the same word could refer to a sibling, a more distant relative, a neighbor, or a member of one's community or race. Paul appears to reflect such a broad use of the word "brethren" in a phrase he uses in Rom. 9:3. The RSV renders it *"my brethren,* my kinsmen by race," but in this lectionary the phrase appears as "my own people, my kinsfolk by race." In Greek, "brother" was often used to refer to a friend, or one with whom one shares a common purpose, but not necessarily a blood relative.

In the New Testament, the plural form of the word "brother" appears to have been intended to include both women and men. For example, in Luke 21:16, "brothers" is certainly intended to mean "brothers and sisters"; and when Paul addressed Christians as "brethren" (e.g., Rom. 8:12; 1 Cor. 2:1) he was surely including women as men. In such cases of direct address, "brethren" has been rendered in this lectionary either as "sisters and brothers" ("brothers and sisters") or as "friends." In post-resurrection sayings attributed to Jesus, "brethren" is translated as "followers" (Matt. 28:10) or "friends" (John 20:17) to make clear that the reference is to the nascent church and not to Jesus' siblings.

(*) Addition of Women's Names to the Text

In a few instances, women's names have been added to the text in this lectionary. These names are included where generation or origin of the people is a major concern. The addition of these names is also consistent with the biblical tradition itself, where on occasion Sarah as well as Abraham is explicitly referred to as progenitor (cf. Isa. 51:1-2), or as one who along with Abraham trusted in God and God's promises (cf. Heb. 11:11). Women's names added to the text are placed in brackets and italicized. If the additional words involve a change in the verb form, the RSV rendering is in the footnotes.

(▽) The Jews

The term "the Jews" occurs very frequently in the Gospel of John. Sometimes it refers in a straightforward, historical way to the ethnic people of whom Jesus was one and among whom Jesus lived out his life. Sometimes, however, it is used almost as a code word for religious leaders who misunderstand the true identity of Christ. When "the Jews" is used in the former sense in the lections from the Gospel of John, it remains unchanged in this lectionary. When it is used in the latter sense, it is rendered "the religious authorities" so as to minimize what could be perceived as a warrant for anti-Semitism in the Gospel of John.

Other Excluding Imagery: Darkness

The New Testament imagery of light versus darkness is often used to contrast good with evil. The equation of darkness with evil, or that which is done in secret and out of the light, has unfortunately led some persons and groups to condemn and reject anything that is black or any dark-hued person as evil or somehow condemned by God. This color symbolism has its equally inaccurate and unfortunate correlative in the equation of light with white—with what is true, good, and loved of God—for example, in the verse "Wash me, and I shall be whiter than snow" (Ps. 51:7). In this lectionary the word translated "whiter" in the RSV is rendered "cleaner." While the biblical context may be free from racist intent, the too-easy misconception that dark people are also condemned and to be avoided has led to the use in this lectionary of terminology other than "darkness" and "white" as metaphors for what is either condemned or loved by God.

Use of "They," "Them," "Themselves," "Their" as Singular Pronouns

In some cases, indefinite singular pronouns are rendered in this lectionary by "they," "them," "themselves," or "their." This usage is recognized as appropriate by the National Council of Teachers of English in its *Guidelines for Nonsexist Use of Language in NCTE Publications.* The *Oxford English Dictionary* says that "they" is "often used in reference to a singular noun made universal by *every, any,* or *no,* etc., or is applied to one of either sex (= 'he or she')." Those grammarians who oppose this usage follow common practice established by an 1850 Act of Parliament declaring that "he" is generic and legally includes "she." That declaration in turn was based on a rule invented in 1746 by John Kirby: the male gender is "more comprehensive" than the female. This lectionary follows the precedent of St. John Fisher (1535), who wrote that God "never forsaketh any creature unlesse they before have forsaken themselves," and William Shakespeare, who urged "everyone to rest themselves."

(+) Changes in the Table of Readings and Psalms

The mandate of the Inclusive-Language Lectionary Committee is to recast the language of the RSV in those places where male-biased or otherwise inappropriately exclusive language could be modified to reflect an inclusiveness of all persons. Consistent with the goal of this mandate, the Committee has determined that it is also appropriate to add certain lections about women that have not been included in the listing recommended by the North American Committee on Calendar and Lectionary. These alternate readings are:

In Year A
Easter 5, Lesson 2	Acts 17:1-12
Pentecost 25, Lesson 1	Wisd. of Sol. 6:12-16
Pentecost 26, Lesson 1	Prov. 31:10-13, 19-20, 30-31

In Year B
Epiphany 2, Lesson 2	Rom. 16:1-7
Lent 4, Lesson 1	Judges 4:4-9
Pentecost 12, Lesson 1	2 Sam. 14:4-7
Pentecost 12, Gospel	John 8:2-11

In Year C
Lent 3, Gospel	Luke 13:10-17
Easter 5, Lesson 1	Acts 16:11-15

Furthermore, where consistent with the mandate, the Committee has occasionally added or omitted some verses of a lection or substituted a reading. These alterations are:

In Year A
Pentecost 7, Lesson 1	Ex. 1:15-21
Pentecost 9, Gospel	Matt. 13:31-35
Annunciation	Alternate Ps. 45 not included

In Year B
Epiphany 2, Lesson 2	1 Cor. 6:12-15a, 19-20 (prescribed reading: ch. 6:12-20)
Pentecost 5, Lesson 2	2 Sam. 5:1-5 (prescribed reading: 5:1-12)
Pentecost 14, Lesson 2	Eph. 6:1-4 added
Annunciation	Alternate Ps. 45 not included

In Year C
Pentecost 16, Lesson 2	Heb. 13:8-16, 20-21 (prescribed reading: Philemon 1-20)
Annunciation	Alternate Ps. 45 not included

Index of Readings for Year A

Based on the Lectionary prepared for trial use
by
the North American Committee on
Calendar and Lectionary